The Hole To China

By

Gary Kaschak

First published by AuthorHouse 06/14/04

ISBN: 1-4184-1987-7 (e-book)
ISBN: 1-4184-1986-9 (Paperback)

This book is printed on acid free paper.

DEDICATION

This book is dedicated to all the boys and girls of our great country who have endured persecution and humiliation inflicted by bullies, to those who have survived such arduous memories, and converted them into living sensitive and caring lives. I also dedicate this novel to those boys and girls who have been bullied, but never recovered enough self-esteem to truly realize their place in life. It is my hope that this work of fiction can bring these people to life again, and I would like them to know that sensitive people are on the outside, eagerly waiting to help.

And to Maureen...

For every word I write...

For every page I turn...

For every chapter that ends...

There is great comfort in knowing you are there...

iv

ACKNOWLEDGEMENTS

Thanks are in order to the following people and organizations for their assistance in supplying information critical to the novels integrity:

To Robert Kay, Professor and Director of Undergraduate students, Department of Earth and Atmospheric Sciences, Cornell University, for helping establish a professional estimate of the actual radius of the earth, and to the Broome County Public Library, for providing an accurate census of Binghamton, circa 1966.

To my young manuscript readers, Elyse Emmerling and Marie Fill, and my daughters, Kara and Emily, who make me proud of them every single day. To my dear Aunt Peg for sharing so much more than her opinion of the novel. To my Mother, Irene, an avid reader who still makes me feel like the only writer in the world, and to my Father, John, who, in his own way, has dug many holes to China himself.

Special thanks to my editor, mentor, writing coach, Anton Marco. Your continued positive manner in teaching me so much on the craft of writing, along with your persuasive and skillful methods of pushing me to higher levels, has molded me into a far better writer than I had ever dreamed I could become.

FOREWORD

The idea, that it is humanly possible to dig a hole to China from the other side of the world, has been passed down for generations and is very *American* in its mythology. Though very few references or tales have been written on the subject, the origin seems to point to American writer and Naturalist Henry David Thoreau's accounting of a "Crazy Uncle," who, in 1852, dug his way to China. In the fourth draft of his *Walden or Life In The Woods*, Economy *Chapter*, Thoreau recounts the life of a character known only as "The crazy Uncle." Thoreau writes: "As for your high towers and monuments, there was a crazy fellow in this town once who undertook to dig to China, and he got so far that, he heard the Chinese pots and kettles rattle."

Eight years later, Thoreau's journal updates a discovery at the Eastabrook Farmhouse, in which a local farmer actually stumbles across the hole. He writes, "Farmer says that he found on the 24th, a black snake laying her eggs on the side of the hill between his peach orchard and the ledge in the woods. He showed me the place today…was close by where his Uncle tried to dig through to the other side of the world. Dug more or less for three years. Used to dig nights, as long as one candle lasted."

But could it be possible, considering today's technology, to at least drill through the layers that make up the earth's interior? To penetrate the 25 miles of Continental Crust, the six miles of Oceanic Crust, the 1,505 miles of two crusts forming the Mantle called the Athenospheres and Lithospheres, the 1,165 miles of the Outer Core, and finally the 1,258 miles of the Inner Core? Could it be possible for machinery to withstand temperatures upwards of 5,000 degrees Celsius at the earth's Inner Core?

To answer these questions, it would be prudent to find out how deep we've actually drilled into the earth, how far down man has gone, and how we actually have arrived at knowing the earth is nearly *4,000* miles deep.

The deepest research borehole on record occurred at the Kola Peninsula near Murmansk, Russia. In an effort to break through the Crust and reach the Upper Mantle, a huge purpose built rig managed to penetrate a mere *nine miles*, falling more than 16 miles short of their modest goal. What brings immediate awareness of this seemingly pathetic result to light is the fact that it took over *10 years* to attain. A separate endeavor from the United States', *The Deep Crustal Drilling Program,* attained similarly disappointing results; but the knowledge gained from oceanic sediments and volcanism released through Ophiolite Belts via these shallow holes has contributed to understanding the entire world below us as a result.

But it is the surface of the earth of which understanding and exploration seemed just as impossible only 40 years ago, when communist Russia and the frightening image of an *Iron Curtain* brought fear to young and old alike. And China, though not as imposing as the great Soviet Republic, was just a name on a map thousands of miles from home, only known to most children as *the place you end up in after digging a hole in your yard.*

And there was no better time than the mid 1960's to appreciate and to experience such things. Technology provided the means for these communist countries to blow up the world by simply launching underground missiles with the seemingly menial task of pushing a button on a desk. The Vietnam conflict added more uncertainty to a troubled world, and China, sitting on the sidelines as the struggle ensued, and in total control of all the Asian countries, grew more weary of Russia's relationship with the United States, launching a "Cultural Revolution" in hopes to eliminate any and all Soviet influences in China. Red China accused the Russians of betraying world communism, opting to become secret allies with the United States. The threat escalated into a show of power when China exploded its first Hydrogen bomb in a test in 1967.

The tensions in 1966, the year this story is set, involved a time of great change for the entire world. It was an era when young boys had few distractions, and, as a result, much less knowledge and understanding of the world around them. It was a time of innocence and simplicity, when children played baseball in the streets, when most families were lucky to own *even one* television set, and when information around the world was limited to the nightly news.

Attaining something that appears to be an absolute impossibility requires a great deal of "thinking outside the box." We may never breech the mantle of the earth, and we may never invent machinery or technology to withstand the mighty forces within our earth. But inventive thinking, improvisation and determination will allow us to simply find other alternatives.

So this is the story of a simple 12-year-old boy who finds another way.

PROLOGUE

The young man lifted another shovel full of dirt, walked the few feet to his target, then angled his shovel downward, releasing several pounds of earth into the great hole. He knelt down at the rim, squinting his eyes to note the progress he and his friends had made so far, as the bright light of the full moon behind him allowed him to see exactly how far they'd come.

He shook his head and grinned disgustedly, then glanced at his watch. *Three-Thirty*, he thought. *We should be just about done.* He looked back inside the great hole. He estimated they'd filled in about 10 feet—only a third of his goal of reaching the top. He smirked to himself, wondered how the *fat kid* had been able to dig out such a big hole in such a short time. He'd been so far off in his earlier estimates of needing an hour or two to completely fill in the 30 foot hole, and he'd had no idea it was as wide as eight feet across.

He decided just then that filling in half the hole was better than nothing at all. His adjusted plan was to leave by 4:00 a.m., and to have all the boys back home 15 minutes later, long before any of their parents or neighbors would wake up. If they hurried, maybe they could accomplish another five feet.

"We need to dig faster!" he barked hoarsely to the others, his deep voice barely above a whisper.

"We can't dig any faster!" responded one of the boys, the pitch of his voice a bit louder and stronger than the leader's.

"You're being too loud!" the leader yelled back. "Someone might hear us!"

They stuck to the plan, briskly shoveling for another 30 minutes—30 minutes spent without a break. The leader was relentless, pushing himself and the others until he looked back into the hole, still not satisfied with the results.

"We'll dig another 10 minutes," he said, and as the words escaped his mouth, the first dog began to howl.

The six boys froze in their tracks as the barking across the street at the Johnson's continued on. Moments later, other neighborhood dogs joined in, as if in a barking contest with each other. The leader held up his hand, signaling for total silence. At that very moment, the Johnsons' front porch light blinked on.

The six boys dropped to their knees in unison as old man Johnson emerged from the house, his trusty old German-Shepherd, Spike, pulling him forward on his leash. The old man walked to the curb in front of his house, looked around for any signs or noises, and watched his dog sniff at the air and then tug him towards the house across the street.

Johnson was quickly joined by his younger neighbor, Ned, who'd also been awakened by the baying dogs. The boys watched the men exchange a few words, then cross the street in their direction.

Instinctively, the boys bolted for the broken fence they'd used earlier to trespass onto the property. One by one, they slid their shovels under the hole in the fence, and scaled the few feet to safety on the other side. From there, they scampered across the school playground, crossed Laurel Avenue, and disappeared into the woods on the outskirts of Recreation Park. When they'd finally realized they were safely out of sight, they paused to collectively catch their breaths.

Back at the hole, the two men and the dog had entered the property. They'd been aware that the house's occupants had been away for the evening, and curiously circled the hole. Only a few minutes later, they surmised what had happened here.

As they retreated to call the police, the younger man spotted something on the ground. He crouched down, then picked up a tattered garden glove—a left-handed one – still warm to the touch.

He rose from the ground, displayed the glove to his neighbor, then carefully placed it into his shirt pocket.

CHAPTER 1

"When am I going to cover a *REAL* story?" bellowed second-year reporter Kelly Trapp. The slender brunette folded her arms across her chest, leaned her weight to the left and cocked her head slightly to the right. "I thought I was finally through with those mundane City Hall meetings. I need to start spreading my wings."

Bulletin editor Harry Whiting was accustomed to these tirades. He fidgeted awkwardly, his rather clumsy manner no match against this street-smart girl from Philadelphia. The diminutive and portly middle-aged Whiting thought quickly and nervously, his mind stumbling for the right words that would let him maintain a certain composure before the entire office. Searching for the proper thing to say, he adjusted his bow tie, pulled his collar out as far as he could to create some room for his bulging double-chin, then pulled his suspenders until releasing them back, creating a "slap" against his stocky chest. He clutched the assignment tightly in his sweaty left hand, then waved it in front of Kelly, desperately attempting to distract her from taking her anger any further.

"Now's not the time for any of this," Whiting said, barely above a whisper. "I'll try to get you a story soon, you'll see." He noticed the silence about the newsroom, and swallowed hard. Kelly stamped her right foot, then suddenly moved closer to him.

"A *story—real* soon?" she said calmly. She paused momentarily, reached out to Whiting and adjusted his bow-tie and suspenders, straightened out his thick black glasses, and glanced around the room.

1

She'd also noticed the silence from her co-workers, and instantly seized the opportunity to use it to her advantage. "You told me last week, and the week before that, and the week before that, I'd be doing a *real* story," she said loudly.

"Why, then, am I still the one assigned to city hall?"

She hadn't expected Whiting to respond, as she had willingly placed herself in a vulnerable and compromising position in front of the entire newsroom. She snatched the assignment from Whiting's hand, quickly turned away, tossed back her shoulder-length hair, and briskly walked past her cubicle. Fuming, she grabbed her sweater and stomped out the back door, leaving Whiting alone in his own vulnerable and compromising position.

He glared around him for a couple of seconds. "What are you all staring at?" he shouted. "Get back to work!"

Then, angry as a thwarted child, Whiting stormed out of the newsroom and headed straight for the office of publisher Joel Kincade. He rapped on the door several times, and, although the light in the room was on, he got no response to his incessant knocking.

Joel Kincade was a very busy man who stopped in the newsroom only once or twice per week to gather his mail and go over reports. He had a habit of leaving the light on and the shades drawn in his office, even if he wasn't occupying the room. The reporters figured it was his way of keeping everyone on their toes. In fact, he'd opened the door a few times in the past when it seemed no one was inside. Occasionally he'd step outside and talk to a few of the staff, then retreat back into his office and close the door tightly behind him.

The staff had been convinced that his office had a secret entrance, but one could never be located.

Whiting adjusted his tie once more. *I've been embarrassed by Kelly Trapp once too often,* he thought grudgingly. And she may have gotten away with it once more yet, but vengeance crossed Whiting's mind as he walked towards his own office.

We'll see who gets to do a "REAL" story, he mused. *Nobody treats me like that and gets away with it. I'm the editor around here, what I say goes. She'll be on City Hall duties permanently after I speak to Kincade.*

CHAPTER 2

Mayor Judy Thomas looked as bored to Kelly at this city hall meeting as Kelly felt whenever she had to cover city politics. *This really is one boring place to live*, Kelly thought. Nothing out of the ordinary ever seemed to happen in this town the size of Binghamton. Very few scandals, an occasional murder or two. The weather seemed to be the only thing that held people's interest around here. Kelly had grown up in Philadelphia, and the adjustment to mid-sized town life had been difficult for her. She missed the big city, the Jersey-shore, and all sorts of entertainment all within driving distance. Her dream was to become a reporter for *The Philadelphia Inquirer*. But there would be no chance to realize such a dream covering city hall meetings in Binghamton, New York. There'd be no juicy stories to send with her resume, nothing journalistically tangy to offer. She was stuck with a dull job in a dull town—but hopefully, only for now.

"As most of you know," the mayor began from her seat in the middle of the crescent-shaped council table, "I've been interested for many years establishing some sort of draw to bring people to our city. She shook her head. "I've racked my brain over this issue, and spoken to other civic leaders about this. Personally, I've given it all the thought I can, but sadly, nothing tangible is coming from this mind."

Kelly perked up just then. This topic was certainly out of the ordinary compared with the 18 city hall meetings she'd attended in the past 18 months. All the others had been so similar, so repetitive. She looked towards the mayor for what she'd say next.

Mayor Thomas looked directly at Kelly, seated seven rows back from the front of the room. About 60 of Binghamton's residents were also in attendance, but the mayor's gaze was undoubtedly intended for Kelly.

"We need something to draw people's attention to our city," the mayor continued. "Our civic-center lies empty most of the time—God knows we've tried to fill it. Our hotels' and restaurants' stats are nearly at the same numbers as they were 20 years ago. We need to bring people in year-'round, we need something the people want to see. We need *something* that will bring them to Binghamton, New York."

She sighed, then went on. "Cooperstown has the Baseball Hall of Fame and The Farmers' Museum. New York City has Broadway. Albany has the state capitol building. Even Corning has the Glass Works. My point is, when people think of Binghamton, what do they think of?"

Silence bit at the air. Finally a middle-aged man dressed in dungarees and a flannel shirt cried out, "hunting and fishing!" The mayor peered over her half-eye glasses and scanned the audience, who enjoyed a good laugh.

"That's what I thought," she declared in a deadpan drone. The laughter died down. "And that's why I've decided to empower you, our residents to come up with some creative suggestions in this matter," the mayor said loudly and firmly. "I'd like the word to get around as fast as possible, and I'll be speaking with you, Ms. Trapp, at the conclusion of this meeting." Kelly moved about uneasily in her chair as the locals looked her way.

"Now, I am not interested in fabrications, folklore, myths or legends," the mayor continued. "I want something that's different, unique; something Binghamtonians can be proud of for being theirs. I *especially* do not want anything at all that has to do with *hunting* or *fishing*." As she emphasized "hunting or fishing," the mayor stared directly at the poor soul who'd exercised feeble judgment while looking for a laugh moments earlier. He smiled bravely at the mayor, who obviously did not share in his statement's humor.

A switch went on in Kelly's mind as her heart began to race, a feeling she hadn't experienced since accepting the job at *The Binghamton Bulletin* more than two years ago. Perhaps this was her opportunity to cover her first real story—if one actually could come of the mayor's little speech.

The remaining half-hour of the meeting was the usual boring political wrangling, but Kelly had paid little attention to any of it. Instead, she'd become more interested in what the mayor had said earlier, and found herself for the first time in months looking forward to the post-meeting interview. Her own wheels were spinning, the creative juices had assembled in her veins and flowed like a dam bursting with pent-up pressure lapping its walls. She'd not personally thought of anything in particular separating Binghamton from the rest of New York State, yet fashioned the notion that it would be her— yes, Kelly Trapp—first in line to cover the great story. *It would only be fair*, she thought. She'd suffered enough of these meetings and deserved to be the one to get the nod. That Harry Whiting was such a jerk shouldn't matter to her. This would be her ticket, and hers alone.

"Ms. Trapp, hello, Ms. Trapp!" came the voice from above.

"Oh, excuse me, Mayor Thomas!" Kelly quickly mouthed while jumping to attention.

"So sorry, Mayor Thomas. I—I was just…"

"Never mind, I fully understand" the mayor flippantly said. "I'd be bored to death if I were in your shoes as well. Takes a special person to attend these meetings, let alone report on them."

Kelly felt flushed. "Yes, I've been doing them for…"

"Eighteen months," the mayor said, cutting her off. "I know how long you've been coming down here. When's that dreadful Harry Whiting going to give you something good, anyway?"

Both responses caught Kelly off guard. "You know Harry Whiting?"

"Don't be silly, young lady," the mayor chided. "This city isn't so big, and there's only one paper. Used to work there myself years ago. Covered the same circuit you're doing now. And yes, Harry Whiting was a reporter at the same time. Dreadful scoundrel I must say, but aren't most lawyers?"

"He's an attorney?" asked Kelly, surprised at this bit of news.

5

"Oh, yes, and a darn good one at that. He still consults a few of the firms in town. He's kept his hand in it over the years. Being a single man, he's had the time to maintain his license."

"Why would such a good lawyer be working at a newspaper?" asked Kelly.

"Harry Whiting has multiple degrees, multiple talents," the mayor responded. "He's majored in law, journalism, even sold real estate for a while, has his Realtors license, too. He's a very smart man, despite all his shortcomings."

"Very interesting," noted Kelly. She paused, then said, "I didn't know you were a reporter at *The Bulletin.*"

"Fifteen years," said the mayor.

The next several minutes were spent discussing the old place and its inhabitants. To Kelly, an instant bond had been formed with Mayor Thomas, who willfully and intentionally opened herself up to her with this talk of the past.

"Kelly, what did you think of my idea for a story about our city?" the mayor asked suddenly.

"I think it's wonderful, really, a great idea." Kelly answered enthusiastically.

"Personally, I don't know enough about the area to offer any ideas on the subject, but I'm sure someone will come up with something." She paused. "I'd *love* to be the one writing the story."

"Well, maybe I could put in a good word or two for you down at the paper. I'm pretty close with Joel Kincade, you know."

Joel Kincade, the rock of *The Binghamton Bulletin.* Staunchly conservative, utterly demanding, incredibly well-spoken and equally as handsome and rugged. Kelly had always though of him as John Wayne in a suit. So charismatic, so revered, so magnificent looking, someone to look up to.

She'd had the pleasure of speaking with him at length on those rare occasions when they'd crossed paths in the newsroom or the parking lot. He was always so kind to her, almost like a *father*, she'd thought. She'd often pondered telling him how she felt about her assignments, how Harry Whiting had treated her and a few of the other reporters, but she never did. She'd often wonder why Kincade himself seemed to look the other way on such matters, why he wouldn't seem to take a more active role with his reporters. He seemed to have his hands in on everything else at the *Bulletin*, always on the phone or in some meeting. Kelly had been hearing rumors lately that the circulation of the *Bulletin* was dropping, with a noticeable shift in the reduction of advertising space throughout the paper. According to her way of thinking, the paper needed better stories – the kind she could provide, given half a chance. Something just wasn't quite right here, wasn't adding up. Though she was street smart and outspoken, and she truly hated her city hall duties, she'd figured it would only be a matter of time before a real story came her way, and she wanted no part in jeopardizing her future by basically telling on her boss. She'd bide her time like a good girl, try not to make waves. *But it's so hard*, she thought. Still, she reasoned she'd be better off doing city hall reports than collecting unemployment, since no other newspaper would be willing to take on a young woman with a short fuse and an attitude. For now, she decided against her idea. The right time would come. She was literally stuck between the proverbial rock and a hard place.

Kelly turned her attention again to Mayor Thomas' recollections of her earlier years. "Are you serious?" Kelly said.

"Like I said, fifteen years," the mayor stated. "Plus six years as Mayor. You get to know certain people—even the elusive ones— fairly well. I've lived here my whole life. I know everything about the place—and that's the problem," she sighed.

"Why is that the problem?" asked Kelly.

"Because, young lady, I can't think of one solitary thing about our area that stands out. Oh, we have wonderful people and industry, it's truly a great place to live and to raise a family. But I'm afraid we're a bit too boring. My grandiose way of thinking is a bit unrealistic, a bit skewed, I'm afraid. This isn't Oz, and we're far from any fairy-tale."

"Maybe someone will come up with something," said Kelly enthusiastically, secretly hoping someone would.

8

CHAPTER 3

Horace Mann grade school was literally situated a stone's throw away from the home of sixth-grader Marty Kent, and his parents, Patricia and Don. The crumbling brick edifice resembled a dilapidated old warehouse, only this building was still very much occupied and the windows all intact—at least for the moment. The school was one of the oldest buildings still in use in Binghamton, but after years of patching both the interior and exterior, along with old plumbing, rotting floors and bad heating and ventilation, the ancient "gal" was scheduled for the wrecking ball in the fall.

Along with the demolition of the school, several homes in the area, including the Kents' modest single-family dwelling, would be leveled. These aged houses would be eventually replaced by a larger, more sprawling Horace Mann II. His humble dwelling had been Marty's life for his entire 12 years, part of the only neighborhood he'd ever lived in. Yet he wasn't feeling particularly sad about matters today, the last official day of school before summer vacation. In fact, Marty was looking forward to house-hunting with his parents— anything to escape the daily badgering and bullying by the bully of all bullies: fellow sixth-grader Scott Gardner, who traveled always with his trusty band of mean losers.

"Hey Kent, bet you're sorry school's almost over," the bully himself yelled across the hallway to Marty. Marty heard every word but chose to ignore Scott. But the arrogant pre-teen wouldn't take the silent treatment. He crossed his arms and growled, "Hey Kent! I'm talking to you! Look at me when I'm talking to you!"

Scott Gardner cockily strode across the crowded hallway, as if parting the Red Sea, while kids of all grades scrambled for their possessions to get out of his way. With every stride he took towards Marty, two or three children would hastily make way, like they were forming a gauntlet for the louse. Three of Gardner's "friends" kept in close proximity to him, staying near enough so as to not touch their general, but with enough distance to give him sufficient and much needed elbow room. Marty placed his hands to his face before turning around to face the big bully.

"Hey, look, I think he's upset," said Gardner, to uproarious laughter from his thugs.

"I think he's gonna cry."

Instantly, Scott Gardner pretended to cry like a baby, going so far as to suck his thumb and emit little baby noises. Some of the other children in the hallway laughed at the joke, a few from the pure hilarity of Scott's antics, but most out of pure terror. Not a soul in the entire school wasn't afraid of Scott Gardner. That is, with the exception of Marty's one and only true and life-long friend, his fellow sixth-grader Brenna Nelson.

Sure, Brenna had saved his neck before—several times, in fact. Marty recalled an incident just weeks prior, when Scott Gardner had picked yet another fight with him during recess. Apparently, the bully was short on cash this particular day, and, despite the fact the Kents were one notch below the middle-class barometer, Marty always seemed to have a nickel or two in his pockets, a fact Scott Gardner knew all too well. When Brenna Nelson intervened that day, Marty was both embarrassed and relieved: embarrassed that a girl would bail him out against the likes of Scott Gardner, and at the same time relieved that she did. Marty hoped with all his might for a repeat performance from Brenna today. He closed his eyes and wished for her to appear.

"Why don't you pick on somebody your own size?" The young girl's voice rang across the hallway, stopping each and every student in their tracks. Marty couldn't believe it. Brenna had indeed arrived, all 85 pounds of her, standing toe to toe against the towering image of Scott Gardner. Scott held a huge physical advantage over her, one of at least seven inches in height and 50 pounds in weight. The sight was really rather unusual, actually. Scrappy and confident Brenna Nelson, so unafraid and unwavering, peering upwards, into the ice-cold eyes of the school brut. Marty wondered why he couldn't stand up to Scott like Brenna did but deep down he knew exactly why. He was simply afraid. And to add insult to injury, he couldn't help but feel so self-conscious about his ugly black glasses, his pimply skin, and the extra 30 pounds he carried around his middle. He'd be no match for Scott Gardner, for the biggest battle he fought was internal, and he seemed to be losing that battle on a daily basis.

"What, are you here to save your boyfriend again?" sneered the bully.

Brenna glanced Marty's way, then looked back up at Gardner.

"So what if I am?" she said, crossing her arms defiantly.

"Oh, so you admit he's your boyfriend then?" Gardner chided, folding his arms to mimic the girl, while looking around the hallway at all the students clustered nearby.

"I didn't say he's my boyfriend," sneered Brenna. "I just want to know why you're always picking on him? What did he do to you, anyway?"

The bully walked over to Marty and put his big right arm around the plump youngster. "Why, what do you mean?" he playfully asked. "Chubby here and I are best friends, didn't you know?"

At poor Marty's expense, all of Gardner's friends bellowed with laughter. But Brenna Nelson was not amused as Marty struggled to pull away from Gardner's hold. Just then, Principal Irwin Principle turned the corner and observed the commotion.

"All right, what's going on here?" Principle shouted, quickly surveying the scene before him. He'd noticed, and was not surprised by any stretch of the imagination, that Scott Gardner was in the middle of the action. Principle rolled his eyes and prepared himself for what was about to come his way. He'd had his share of pranks, fights and practical jokes from Gardner over the years. The only thing worse than Scott Gardner, he deduced, was Scott Gardner's parents, especially his father, Joe. Considering all the victims he'd terrorized, justifying the bad things Scott Gardner seemed to pull on a weekly basis since his kindergarten days was simply out of the question. But his father, ever vigilant, continuously defended his son

11

and accused the school and other children of causing all the problems. He'd even gone as far as to threaten the school with legal action if his son was suspended one more time, not to mention warning Principle on a very personal level.

Principle had reached his sanity's peak with the Gardner's, yet in the back of his mind, he'd always been cautious since that day, two years ago, when he dealt with and dished out punishment to Scott Gardner. After all, he had his own family to protect, and Joe Gardner was a man not to be taken lightly when he threatened anyone. Unfortunately for Principle, the cunning and clever Scott was well aware of the clout of his relationship with his father, and, like all bullies in all walks of life, the kid used his own and his father's disregard for authority to his full and complete advantage.

"Look, it's Principal Principle!" said Scott Gardner, oozing sarcasm. "I'll bet you're gonna miss me when I'm gone, won't you, sir?"

The middle-aged man began to speak, then thought twice about the remarks he prepared to make. His mind wrestled with the current situation, but meanwhile, thoughts of being pummeled by Joe Gardner also occupied his imagination's deep, dark corners.

He decided, as he always did since the first time he'd been threatened, to error on the side of caution. After all, Scott Gardner would no longer be *his* problem from this day forward.

"Mr. Gardner," he said sternly, "I don't need to remind you this is the final day of school. Could you just this once comply with the school code of conduct, and give Mr. Kent ample room to gather his belongings?"

"Sure, no problem, sir," Scott replied with reverent hypocrisy. He stole a glance at Marty. Scott was toying with him now, but for the moment, Marty had escaped the evil boy.

"Good," said Principle. "Now I suggest you move along home yourself."

Scott smirked. "Oh, I'll be moving in just a few moments, sir. I want to go around and personally thank all my teachers for teaching me so much through the years." He was once more looking for a few laughs from his buddies, and they complied as usual, right on cue. "Think I'll miss you the most of all, sir."

Principle glared at Scott, pointing down the hallway behind him with his left hand, and surprising himself by maintaining eye contact with the youngster.

"I suggest you move along, *now*, young man."

Scott turned with a huff, deliberately brushing up against Marty as he passed him. Scott and his gang soon disappeared from sight, turning left down the long hallway. At that moment, Marty Kent felt only seething anger towards Scott Gardner. He wanted in the worst way to give back to the bully all he had dished out. He wanted to hurt him physically, beat him to a pulp. But Marty Kent knew the score, and he knew his physical limitations. He could only see himself as overweight, scared and weak, and the loneliness he'd felt for so much of his childhood once again seized him. Marty was just so disgusted with himself—the pimply skin, the rolls of fat, the hideously ugly black eyeglasses. He didn't understand why he couldn't do a simple thing like hit a baseball, or throw a ball, like the other boys. He couldn't even do one push-up, or complete the 100-yard dash without collapsing. *I'm a loser*, he thought, *I'm just a loser*.

He snapped out of his reverie and looked at his one true friend. For a moment he managed a smile, trying so desperately to hide the tears welling up in his eyes. "Let's go home Brenna," he said faintly.

CHAPTER 4

The young reporter couldn't get the meeting with Mayor Thomas out of her mind, making her particularly anxious for work today. She envisioned herself assigned to the story that would put Binghamton on the map, propelling the city of 69,000 into the national spotlight. She also knew deep down of the obstacles to be overcome. First and foremost, no story was brewing yet; Mayor Thomas had made that perfectly clear to her. Second, Kelly had not really proven her writing skills to anyone at the *Bulletin,* so why should she get the assignment over a veteran reporter who had much more of a feel for the area? Third there was Harry Whiting, perhaps the biggest obstacle of them all. She'd had it with all his tomfoolery, and she knew the battle would be all uphill even if Mayor Thomas was given a story idea worthy of her scrutiny.

Kelly pursed her lips, grabbed her pocketbook and shot out the door of the small flat she rented on the city's west-side. The time 10 a.m., two full hours before her shift would begin. Maybe, thought Kelly, she'd catch a quick meeting with Whiting, loosen him up a bit, get the ball rolling. This seemed the only thing she could do at this point as she climbed into her little red sports-car and headed for work.

The first stretch of the 10-mile drive wound through the working-class neighborhoods of the west-side. Fifty and hundred-year-old homes lined the old streets, the shelter of magnificent oaks providing ample shade. Old factories filled the skyline nearby, the ugly, gray smoke billowing from the stacks contrasting with the natural beauty

15

of the trees. Kelly passed the "Ritz Theatre," where a Tarzan movie was currently playing. She turned off Main Street onto Laurel and followed the long road to the end, where she'd turn right on College Street.

From there Kelly would pass her favorite place, Recreation Park, before heading towards Lourdes Hospital and the upper-class mansions of Riverside Drive. Another few miles and she'd connect to the Vestal Parkway, where *The Binghamton Bulletin* stood magnificently against the backdrop of a sea of old pines.

Kelly turned on College and gazed down the road to the entrance of Rec-Park, the name the locals had given it. Rec-Park was a beautiful, sprawling piece of property with all sorts of activities for people of all ages: a public pool, swings and slides, concession stand, walking and running paths, magnificent statues of famous Americans, tennis courts, a wonderful carousel and several baseball and softball fields. Even in the dead of winter, hundreds of people used the park, to ice-skate on the frozen-over and publicly flooded baseball field. Kelly would often stop off at the Park and take a stroll around to free her mind and simply watch people in a relaxed setting. She loved the Park and everything it had to offer. She looked at her watch. *Only 10:15.* She'd still have plenty of time to catch Whiting before her shift, she reasoned. She nodded once, then pulled into the single-lane entrance to the Park, quickly found a parking spot, and headed towards the center and the concession stand. Kelly was in the mood for cotton-candy, and what they served here was the best she'd ever had.

"One cotton-candy, please," she kindly asked the old man behind the counter. Kelly took it all in, whiffing at the cotton-candy, the popcorn, the hot dogs rolling on the grill. This place had reminded her so much of home, of the little concession stand around the corner from her south-Philly row-home. This little park sure wasn't home, but it was the closest thing to it Kelly knew in Binghamton, and for a moment, Kelly felt more than a bit homesick.

"That'll be fifteen cents," the cashier responded cheerfully. Kelly slipped him a quarter, retrieved her change, and headed towards the baseball field just below the entrance and down the hill from the stand.

It was a beautiful June day, the kind of day meant for long walks and absorbing everything one could see. Kelly took her time ambling down the narrow path leading to the ball field. Her leisurely pace contrasted with her usual hurried and brisk walking motion, and she enjoyed the relaxing feeling. She knew full well that she always seemed to be in a hurry to everyone around her, and she always exuded purpose in everything she did. She didn't seem to mind that people took her that way. After all, there always was somewhere to go, someone to meet. *I'm a reporter*, she thought, emitting a short giggle as she angled her mouth around the first bite of cotton-candy.

Kelly noticed the sounds of music coming from the direction of the carousel. Children were running wildly towards the sound, a signal that the next ride would be in three minutes. Several boys whizzed past her on bicycles, and for that one brief moment, Kelly Trapp felt 10 years old again, and the sensation brought her immense pleasure.

Several loud sounds of voices—arguing voices—lifted above the thrilling cries of the children headed for the carousel. Kelly looked around, finally focusing on the ball field below. She noticed one overweight youngster apparently being picked on by a gang of larger boys. Her pace quickened and her stride lengthened as she sensed danger for the boy, who was now being shoved around the circle of what looked like a kid-sized mob.

The boy bounced from person to person like a ball, and finally, after several shoves, fell backwards to the ground, holding his left shoulder as he hit dirt with a thud. Kelly tossed her cotton-candy aside, increased her trot to a full-fledged sprint, and began yelling at the top of her lungs, drawing the attention of those around her.

"*Hey! Leave him alone!*" she cried out. The group of boys looked towards Kelly, and, sensing her anger and urgency, quickly grabbed their gloves and balls, hopped onto their bikes, and headed in the other direction, towards the safety of the main road. Within seconds, Kelly reached the battered boy, who was being comforted by one lone girl who had stayed behind to help him.

"Oh my gosh, are you all right?" Kelly gasped, helping the boy to his feet. She turned towards the fleeing boys and yelled, "*Cowards!*" as they sped away.

Kelly dusted off the boy, noticing a few cuts on his arms and face. She saw big tears rolling down his cheeks and felt sorry for him. He tried to adjust his thick black eyeglasses to his face, but they'd been bent in the fall.

"Are you hurt?" she finally asked him.

"No, I—I think I'll be O.K." he stuttered. "Thank you for helping me."

Kelly nodded and looked towards the young girl standing quietly to the side. Fire raged in her eyes as she gently brushed the dirt from her friend's clothing. Kelly was pleased to see that a girl had stayed behind to help. She quickly assumed the two youngsters were related, though she noticed no physical similarities between them.

"Are you brother and sister?" Kelly asked, politely.

"Oh, no," the girl said through a huge grin. "We're just good friends."

"And you, young man, why were those boys picking on you?" said Kelly angrily. "I have a good mind to report them to the police, even contact their parents."

"No, you can't!" Marty blurted. Then he looked down remorsefully. "I mean, please don't," he said, much more quietly. "There's nothing anyone will do about it, anyway."

Kelly squinted her eyes at the boy. *He'd been through this before with these bullies,* she thought. *There's history here.* She held out her right hand to the boy. "Kelly Trapp," she said with a firm handshake. "I'm a reporter for *The Binghamton Bulletin*."

"Marty, Marty Kent," he replied. "And this is Brenna—Brenna Nelson."

"Hi," Brenna said shyly.

"Well, can I give you two a ride home or something?" asked Kelly.

"No, thanks," Marty replied. "We live on the other side of the park, next to Horace Mann School. We're used to the walk."

Kelly stood with her hands on her hips as the pair thanked her again, and headed up the hill towards home. As they reached the top, they again turned and waved to Kelly before disappearing seconds later. Kelly spun in the direction the bullies had taken for their getaway. She wanted so much to catch those rotten boys herself, teach them a lesson or two. She was a Philadelphia girl after all, street smart and tough and proud of it. She thought of Brenna Nelson and smiled. She remembered helping a young friend in similar circumstances years ago, on the hard Philly streets. That boy, like the one she'd just met, was overweight, pimply and non-athletic. He too had been used and abused by street bullies. Kelly recalled that boy, *so much like Marty*, she thought. She remembered the years of constant abuse he'd endured, of how those beatings and bullying affected the young boy's life in every way, even his aging parents. She'd heard he was still living at home with them, had no job or income, had grown to obesity, and lacked any skill at all to join the work force. He'd become reclusive, confined to his own home by choice. He had no friends, no hobbies, no contact with others outside of his home, an anti-social misfit born out of the awful bullying from so long ago.

What a sad reality, she thought. So sad that a teacher or a coach or some caring adult could have, *should have* interceded *somewhere* along the way to help reverse things for the unhappy boy. She thought of the many similarities there might be between his life and Marty's, and how she'd felt as a child, watching helplessly with anger as the bullies pushed the boy around. To see it happen again was nothing short of a nightmare. She could only hope that Marty Kent wasn't facing a similar "life sentence."

CHAPTER 5

Marty went straight to his room the minute he set foot in his house, tiptoeing up the twelve creaky stairs as quietly as possible. Years of ascending these steps had taught Marty where to precariously position himself on each stair to minimize the noise they'd produce. He didn't want his mother to see the scrapes from his altercation with the bullies until he could check them out himself, clean up the wounds, and possibly even shield them from her view. One wrong movement on the stairs would certainly alert her to his whereabouts, so Marty was his most cautious self as he crept up.

For the moment, he was in the clear. He accomplished his goal in a matter of seconds, clearing the top step to the landing. He continued to creep silently towards his room, but he noticed just then the washing machine's rumblings from the basement, and knew his mother was right next to the washer, probably folding or hanging clothes. In no way could she hear him, he thought, relieved, as he walked quickly to his room, closed the door and headed for the mirror on his dresser.

At first, the cut above his left-eye seemed harmless enough as he wiped away the dried blood with a paper towel moistened with a little saliva. "Not too bad," he said aloud, turning his attention to his scraped elbows. *Mom won't see these*, he thought.

Marty stepped into the bathroom down the hallway and thoroughly washed his hands and arms. Confident that his injuries were minimal to the eye, made his way back down the stairs where he'd greet his mother. He didn't feel like explaining the true story behind his wounds to her, and was ready with an old fashioned white lie just in case she noticed.

"Hi mom!" he called loudly above the noise of the washer.

"Oh, my, you startled me, dear!" responded his mother, placing her left hand over her heart and laughing aloud. "I didn't see you there."

"I just got home from the park," said Marty casually, positioning his face as far away from his mother's gaze as possible.

"Oh, you're home awfully early," she stated. "Is everything all right?"

"Sure, there was just nothing going on, so I came home early. What's for supper?"

"I'm making chicken tonight on the barbecue," said Mrs. Kent. It's a perfect night for a cookout." She paused for a moment, as if noticing her son's peculiar stance. "Are you sure everything is O. K.?"

"Yeah, I'm just bored," Marty replied, looking down. "I need something to do."

His mother continued folding clothes, half-listening to her son. It was only the first day of summer vacation, and already the dreaded boredom had found its way to Marty.

"Why don't you go play ball with the boys?" she asked.

"They're not playing today," he said. "Plus, I stink at baseball. Nobody wants me to play with them." He looked dejected.

Patricia Kent perked up just then. She placed the clothes on the hamper lid and walked towards her son. Marty kept his head down as she reached out to hug him. He accepted her embrace, burying his face against her middle, and clutching her as tightly as he could. She stroked his short brown hair, her own sorrow for her son's physical looks occupying her mind. She knew he'd been picked on several times by some of the boys at school; she'd even had some meetings with the principal and teachers, trying to get to the root of the problem. But after each meeting, the bullying only worsened. Such a terrible fate was an awful fact of life that some kids faced for a variety of reasons. For Patricia's son, it was the weight, the pimples, the glasses. She also knew she'd been pampering her son more than she should a boy his age. She'd tried changing her ways, but for every attempt at allowing Marty to fail on his own, there she'd be, smothering him with far too much support. Plenty of arguments had transpired in the Kent household over the subject, but she, too, felt trapped. Her only child was overweight, acne-ridden, non-athletic, and a dreamer at best, whose little world existed mainly of comic books and cartoons. She knew Marty was slower than the other kids; heck, she still coddled him with the notion that Santa Claus, the Easter Bunny and the Tooth Fairy actually existed. To her young son, life was a fantasy, and she'd done very little to help him face reality. In fact, she'd all but promoted unreality when it came to him.

"Marty," she said, doing her best to change the subject, "how would you like to go see the Optometrist in a few days? I hear they have those new wire-rimmed glasses. Plus, you haven't had an eye exam in over a year."

Marty thought it over for a moment. He didn't doubt for a second that his glasses were horrible. Plus, they had gotten bent in the fall at the park. He had also seen a few kids with the new metal rims, and liked what he'd seen. New glasses sounded to him like an extremely great idea. "Yeah, I'd like to get new glasses," he said softly.

His mom pulled away from their hug. She noticed he continued to look away from her. She quickly grabbed her son with both hands on the side of his head and asked, "Why aren't you looking at me?" Her answer came as she beheld the small cut above his left eye.

Marty had been caught in record time. His quiet trip up the stairs had produced nothing but the upcoming barrage of questions certain to come from her. But he was ready this time. Truth or no truth, he was adequately prepared for her questions.

"Where did you get that cut?" she cried. "It needs to be cleaned, right away!"

"I fell at the park," Marty said. "It's not that bad, really, it doesn't even hurt."

But it did hurt. Everything seemed to hurt him. His low threshold of pain had been a topic of many conversations between him and his father, a former quarterback of the local high-school team. "You gotta be tough," he'd tell Marty, reaching back in time to recall yet another heroic story of playing football with broken hands, broken toes, even broken legs. "Every time you get hurt, you gotta pick yourself up and get back in the game. Life is tough, young man, so you gotta be tough, too."

Marty's dad certainly wasn't as understanding as his mother. He had been the star athlete of his day, and the girls had flocked to him. His flowing brown hair, his dashing good looks, his ability on gridirons and baseball fields had been well documented, and Marty had been constantly reminded of his dad's exploits. Indeed, his father's heroics had contributed to his depression—the constant comparisons and expectations, the subsequent failures and disappointments. It had all led to a distant relationship between the two. In fact, his father had decided to let Marty "fend for himself" against the bullies at school. "A boy's gotta be able to stick-up for himself," he'd always say. Despite the occasional scrapes and cuts provided by Scott Gardner and company, Marty was on his own as far as his father was concerned.

Marty's pain was sometimes emotional, sometimes physical, sometimes both. His mother acted surprised, though, as she looked his way again. "Doesn't hurt?" she asked curiously. "Let's march right up to the bathroom and get you cleaned up. That cut needs peroxide."

The two climbed the stairs to the first floor bathroom, where Marty's mom cleaned the wound with peroxide. She warned Marty it would burn for a moment, but uncharacteristically, he didn't even flinch. She raised her eyebrows at this surprise, placed the cap back on the bottle, and peeled a Band-Aid over the wound.

"There," she said confidently. "All better."

"Thanks, Mom," he said. He looked past her, toward the window. "I need something to do. I'm really bored."

She paused. Nothing crossed her mind at the moment. She thought back to her own youth. Yes, she'd been bored from time to time during summer vacation. *Every kid experiences that*, she mused. But here, on the first day, her son was already feeling the pangs of boredom. *It's going to be a long summer*, she thought.

Suddenly, an idea popped into her mind. "Hey, why don't you grab a shovel and go into the backyard and start digging a hole?" she said enthusiastically. "They say if you dig deep enough, you'll reach China."

Marty had never heard an notion like that before. *Dig a hole to China?* he thought. *How interesting. Has it ever been done?* The notion sounded like fun to him, a great adventure in his own backyard. Marty's young and fantasy-steeped mind quickly imagined the scene: mounds of dirt heaped against the backdrop of his house, and Marty digging into the center of the earth, tunneling through mile after mile of dirt and rock. He envisioned himself dirty and grimy, tired—beyond tired, and climbing through the exit hole on the other side of the world, being greeted by thousands of cheering Chinese. Now he was being lifted out of the hole, amidst great celebration and the sounds of bands playing happy songs. Somehow, as he thought about it, Marty felt sure that an entire summer vacation would certainly be enough time to dig to China. All of a sudden, he found himself more excited than he'd been in a long time. Digging a hole to China sounded just right to him.

"Could I really, Mom?" he asked excitedly.

"Could you really, what?" she smiled.

"Dig a hole to China!" Marty beamed.

His enthusiastic response had caught Patricia Kent off guard. She had mentioned the idea in passing, facetiously, really. She hadn't truly weighed it out, and she never dreamed Marty would in any way be interested trying to dig to China.

But what's the harm in him digging just to be digging? she thought. By fall, the bulldozers would be clearing their land away for the new school, so it would matter little if the Kents' yard would now include one large hole. It'd be one less hole for the builders to dig. Patricia also knew her son well; she knew he'd soon tire once he'd begun digging.

In fact he'd probably give up just as soon as the slightest sign of fatigue set in, or once the first blister appeared. Yet maybe, just maybe, she could challenge him, not just with the physical aspect of digging, but also to dig up information on the earth and China, through encyclopedias and reference books. If Marty seemed excited enough about the idea, maybe he would benefit from a little learning—about something more than just his comic books. So...

"I don't see why not," she responded to his question. "But before you start digging, why don't you run down to the library tomorrow morning and take out a few books on China and Planet Earth in general. That might help us to know what to expect—plus, you'll learn something about the Chinese people—even how deep the earth really is. And you can start digging as early as tomorrow if you'd like!"

Marty mulled it over for a moment. He was eager to start his dig, but his mother's suggestion also sounded reasonable to him. He'd gather a few books together in the morning, then grab a shovel and start digging for the rest of the day.

Maybe I'll even start a diary, he pondered. After all, such a literary work would serve well to chronicle the day-to-day events of the world's youngest explorer: *Marty Kent of Binghamton, New York!*

CHAPTER 6

Despite having stopped over at Rec-Park to lend Marty a hand, Kelly Trapp still arrived 45 minutes early for work. She quickly looked around for Harry Whiting, wondering where he could be at this hour of the day. Whiting was forever bopping around the place, handing out assignments or creating work schedules in his office. But, as luck would have it, today he'd be coming in around noon, the same time as Kelly.

"Darn," she said to herself, finally settling in at her own cubicle. She decided to take the extra time waiting for Whiting to read and evaluate the recent stories in *The Bulletin*. *How boring*, she thought, thumbing through the past month's back issues. *There's nothing here exciting, nothing riveting, nothing to get people scurrying to their newsstands. No wonder circulation and ad revenues have gone down.* Such an occurrence was a difficult feat to achieve, she chuckled, as *The Bulletin* was the only daily newspaper in town. They'd often held long editorial meetings addressing the problems at the paper, but in Kelly's opinion, they needed more hard-nosed stories, more specials, more "in the field" reporting that uncovered stories just waiting to be found.

Somehow, her suggestions never seemed to reach beyond Harry Whiting, but how could they? He was the editor, after all, and the only person above him was publisher Joel Kincade. She'd often thought several times about it, had come dangerously close to, going over Whiting's head. But she knew these weren't the streets of

27

Philadelphia; street mentality wouldn't be tolerated around here. She'd accept the chain of command like a good little soldier, not jeopardizing her lowly status at the paper. For now, at least, she'd bite her tongue once more. But she knew her breaking point with the likes of Harry Whiting was precariously close to snapping, job or no job. She needed to be heard by someone who'd actually listen to her ideas.

Her thoughts were interrupted by her superior's casual stride into the room. Standing quickly, she said, "Mr. Whiting, I didn't see you come in." Then, jutting out her jaw, she said, "I'm glad you're here, sir. I'd like to propose to you an idea I…"

"Let it wait," said Whiting curtly, snapping her sentence in two. "Right now, I need you to go down to the public library. I need some research done on a feature we're gonna run about the founding of our town."

"Oh," Kelly muttered. "Does that mean I finally get to do the story?"

"No, just the research," he deadpanned. "Corrigan's doing the story."

"That's just not fair, sir," Kelly exclaimed, suddenly in a rage. "If *I'm* doing the research, it's only fair that *I* be the one to do the story."

Whiting eyed her long figure with his cold, dark eyes. His feelings towards her were blatantly obvious: he despised her as an outsider, for one thing, and her "city" attitude for another. Harry Whiting was so set in his ways, so rigid and downright nasty. He had no intention of ever awarding Kelly a story to report, despite his recent promises. She'd remain the "go-fer" he viewed her as, nothing more than a gatherer of news, never worthy to report on anything greater than city hall meetings. Deep down, Kelly knew this was true. Right then she considered quitting on the spot; but instead, she once more gritted her teeth, grabbed the assignment from Whiting's stubby little hands, and began to badger her boss. Her voice grew louder and stronger by the moment, filled with rage and anger and passion. Soon, "What's all the ruckus?" yelled a voice from the corner. As if he were some kind of hero making a grand entrance, Joel Kincade stepped into the room, standing as tall and straight as a field-commander in battle. "Is there something wrong here, Harry?"

Harry Whiting swallowed hard. Joel Kincade possessed a unique combination of charm and fear that commanded immediate attention and reverence. Whiting had always been second fiddle to Kincade. But for some reason unknown to Kelly and just as puzzling, he was almost always able to get his way with his superior. Now standing before the two most powerful men of the *Bulletin*, Kelly decided this would be the perfect time to let it all out. Whiting himself also reasoned this would be the perfect time to reveal the attitude of, in his opinion, an out-of-line reporter just begging to be reprimanded, suspended, even dismissed. Whatever would happen over the next few minutes was bound to change something for someone—perhaps all three of them.

Whiting started the fray by bellowing confidently, "It seems our Ms. *Trapp* here didn't like her new assignment. And every time she doesn't get her way, she's insubordinate, to boot. I've been meaning to talk to you about reprimanding and possibly even suspending her, sir."

Joel Kincade gazed around the room, mumbling something to himself. He looked at Whiting, then at Kelly, who stood quiet and still, uneasy. He paused again, raised his chin towards Kelly and finally asked, "Is that so, young lady?"

Kelly opened her mouth to defend herself, but Kincade continued to speak. "How are things going down at City Hall?" he asked.

"Fine, I guess" she shrugged, surprised at the question.

"*Really?*" he asked. "City Hall meetings always seem so boring, don't they? Kelly was shocked that he'd be so candid with her. She felt comfortable enough at that moment to respond just as openly as he had to her. "I'd rather be doing something else," she said, trying not to let Harry Whiting's presence deter her from going on.

"It's actually very boring stuff, but I've gotten in good with the Mayor recently. She has an idea for a heckuva story, actually."

"Oh, I know," Kincade remarked. "She's already contacted me."

Harry Whiting couldn't believe the conversation ensuing before him. He stood, appalled that Joel Kincade was being pleasant to Kelly Trapp, and that they were chatting pleasantly as if nothing had just happened. Yet he remained silent, covering his face with a poor excuse for a smile.

"Mayor Thomas is a good woman," Kincade said. "You'll learn much from her if you let it happen."

Kelly smiled, almost forgetting her place and who stood near her. Only when she heard "But sir!" emit from Harry Whiting's pudgy face did she snap back into reality.

Almost comically, Whiting began barking at Kincade, his words nothing but incessant complaining. Kincade held up his hand to silence Whiting. Obviously Whiting had been paying little attention to what Kincade had to say. It was the first time Kelly—or any of the other reporters, for that matter—had witnessed Joel Kincade actually use his power over Harry Whiting.

Whiting swallowed hard, looking puzzled and bewildered at Kincade. This was something new for him, too, and he didn't like the way it felt, didn't like the brief exchange Kelly and Kincade had just had together. But Joel Kincade looked pretty serious to him, and to the others around him, who'd been listening to the exchanges.

Kincade turned to face the remaining reporters. He opened his briefcase and pulled out a thick document, holding it up high for all to see.

"In my hand, I have the latest circulation figures for our newspaper," he began. He lowered the document and made eye-contact with each person on the floor. "Does anyone in this room know what it takes to get readers?" he sighed. Responding to his own question, he said, "Well, I'll tell you what it takes." He rolled up the sleeves of his shirt and continued: "It takes dedication and determination and ability. It takes drive and intestinal fortitude and moxie. It takes ideas and good old-fashioned dig-down-deep reporting. *That's* what it takes."

His comments seemed to take the entire newsroom off guard. He picked up his briefcase and studied the faces around him. *It's so quiet*, Kelly thought. *Quiet as a church.* Kincade had his audience riveted.

"Above all else," Kincade thundered, "above all else, what it really takes to get it done is *passion*." He clenched his fist tightly. "*That's* what I want to see a lot more of around here."

Kincade turned and walked slowly towards his office. When he came within a few feet of the door, he casually called out for Harry

Whiting to join him, never looking back for any sign of acknowledgment.

* * *

Kincade opened his door, flicked on the light, and disappeared deep into the great room. He removed his jacket, tossed it carefully over a chair and stared at the wall calendar. He took a pen from his shirt pocket, crossed a big "X" through the current day on the calendar, and then muttered, "Only a few more days."

Harry Whiting glared at Kelly, but his expression felt different to her now. The words Kincade had just uttered, albeit brief, had given her a lift and confidence, a reason to not be afraid any longer. She crossed her arms and held her chin high, as Harry Whiting stumbled down the hallway, entered the great office, and closed the door behind him.

The impromptu intrusion from Joel Kincade had energized Kelly even more than Mayor Thomas's plan for a story on Binghamton. Suddenly, running to the library for Harry Whiting didn't seem so difficult a task to her. *Kincade really dressed him down*, she thought happily. *He seemed to be on my side.* Kelly felt the little meeting in the hallway may have been a giant step in finally getting to report a real story. She thought about Kincade's words of advice for all the reporters: *Dedication, determination, ability, passion. Old-fashioned, dig-down-deep reporting. He'd said it for a variety of reasons,* she thought, *but mostly out of frustration.* The commotion caused by Kincade also delayed Kelly's trip to the public library. She stuck around her cubicle for about an hour, talking to fellow staffers about Kincade's remarks—and how he had made Harry Whiting look like putty in front of the whole office. In fact, Harry Whiting had been holed-up in Joel Kincade's office the entire time following the episode in the hallway, and when the meeting adjourned, he came away from with a look of utter despair plastered across his portly face. *There's too much to miss here today,* Kelly thought, a little disappointed that she couldn't stick around, but her sense of duty directed her back to the task at hand.

CHAPTER 7

The Binghamton Public Library had always fascinated Kelly. By her estimates, she'd frequented the old building at least a dozen times, always searching for information to assist *other* reporters. But it was all in the line-of-duty, she had to remind herself, and she'd gotten very good at it, even drawing compliments and praise from the old guard at the paper. For the first time in two years she felt more like one of them. Plus, this assignment could even draw her closer to the story she'd truly longed to write. *Maybe I'll find something out about Binghamton to help my own cause*, she thought.

"Good afternoon, Kelly," greeted the librarian. "Researching a story?"

Kelly smiled. "Morning to you Mrs. Springer. Oh, yes, I've got a decent assignment today. I need to find out some things about the history of Binghamton. Could you let me know where to look for anything you have on it?"

"Why, of course," the elderly woman said quietly. "We have a few books over in the Historical section. Fourth aisle, sixth row on the left."

"Thank you so much," Kelly responded. She walked to the area the librarian had directed her to, scanned the sixth row from top to bottom, and found nothing on the subject of Binghamton. She glanced from row to row, saw nothing yet again, and with growing impatience she walked briskly back towards the librarian's station, where Mrs. Springer was currently engaged in serving a young boy.

33

"Excuse me, ma'am," the boy asked politely. "I'm looking for books on China and the earth."

The woman scrutinized the boy over her half-eye reading glasses. *What a curious request*, she thought. Summer vacation had left the usually bustling library with quite a drop in attendance, and summer school hadn't begun yet. Even more odd was the content of the books the young boy was requesting. *China and the earth*, she thought. *Why would such a young boy be interested in such things? He should be playing baseball, or riding bikes, or doing whatever it is kids of his age usually do.*

"China and the earth, you say?" she asked, looking first at the young boy, then at Kelly, who stood nearby, half-listening to the conversation. "We have a few books on China in both the Historical section and the Geographic section. Could you be more specific on what it is you're looking for on the subject of *earth*?" she asked.

"Yes, I want to know how deep the earth is," Marty said confidently.

"How deep the earth is?" she repeated. "I do believe we have reference material in Geography." The experienced librarian removed her glasses now, leaving them dangling on a metal cord on her chest. "Are you doing some sort of project for school?"

"Oh, no ma'am," Marty replied politely. "I'm going to dig a hole to China, and I just want to see how deep it is to get there."

The woman chuckled under her breath, as did Kelly. The boy zoomed past her towards the location he'd been directed.

"Isn't that cute?" the librarian commented to Kelly. "I've heard of children digging holes to try and reach China, but in all my years I've never had one person request written materials on the subject."

Kelly said, "I hope he isn't too disappointed when he finds out how far China really is. How long do you think it'll take him before he realizes how ridiculous the idea is?"

The librarian motioned Kelly forward. Kelly looked around her to see if anyone was near, then moved as close to the woman as she could on her side of the front desk, at which point the librarian began to speak.

"You and I both know he'll *never* be able to dig a hole to China," the woman said. "But it's important for him to learn, and to fail on his own terms. Plus," she grinned with a twinkle in her eye, "how do we really know he *can't* get to China just because it's never been done before?"

The comment took Kelly by surprise. Sure, she believed in the will of the human spirit; all sorts of examples in history proved it. But digging a hole to China? She dismissed the idea, focusing on her main objective. "I can't locate any of the reference books on Binghamton," she said.

"Are you sure you looked in the correct aisle?"

"Very sure, fourth aisle, sixth row on the left."

The woman briefly left her station with Kelly trailing behind. Together they walked to the correct reference area, the librarian shuffled about some books, then located the materials in question. "I'm so sorry these were out of order," she said. "Sometimes the kids move things about and we simply overlook them."

"Thank you," said Kelly.

She gathered two books on her subject, then spotted the boy, who was looking for his materials one row over. She had not taken a good look at him earlier, but now she was sure she recognized him, and she eagerly approached him.

"Well, hello!" she said to the boy, who looked up at her, wide-eyed. "Remember me...Kelly Trapp, the reporter? I sort of rescued you at the park the other day."

"Oh, hello," said Marty.

Kelly noticed the books in Marty's arms and smiled.

"So, you plan on digging a hole to China?" she asked.

"Yeah," Marty replied, quite serious. "I'm gonna get started right away, and get there by the end of the summer. I *have* to reach China by then, 'cause they're tearing down my house."

His last remark sparked Kelly's interest. "Who's tearing down your house?"

"The city is. It's for the new Horace Mann School, and our house is in the way."

"I'm sorry to hear that."

"Yeah, me too, sorta."

Kelly examined the boy's face and thought she detected sadness. *I'd be sad too,* she mused, *if my house was being taken away.*

"That's quite an ambitious undertaking you've decided to do," she said aloud. "Is anyone going to help you?"

Marty paused. "Well, I think my mom will help me some, and Brenna will like the idea. She'll help too. But mostly, I'll be the one doing the digging."

"Well good luck to you, then!" said Kelly, ambling away.

Marty checked out his books and headed home. Kelly waved to him through the window as he hustled on past her. She then took her own reference books on Binghamton and settled into a quiet area in the far corner of the library, enjoying its uninterrupted peacefulness. She'd always done her best thinking without the distractions associated with the hustle and bustle of the newspaper world. She opened the books on Binghamton, but somehow, couldn't get her mind off Marty and his hole to China idea. As she thumbed through the books' pages, the silly notion of digging a hole to China seemed about as real to her as finding something – anything—to write about. *The mayor's right*, she thought. *There just seems to be nothing of historical importance to draw people to Binghamton.*

CHAPTER 8

The two shovels owned by the Kents had both seen better days. The winter shovel, the first one Marty picked up, had been curled at the ends from the wear and tear of hundreds of inches of snow, shoveled over the years from the icy-hard pavement of the Kents' front sidewalk. Marty himself had lobbied for a new one just this past winter, but, as usual, the Kents had little money for such things. *"It'll do for another year or two,"* his father had told him.

The garden shovel, a 40-year-old hand-me-down from Marty's grandfather, had a similar history, only it did have some life left in it. It too had been bent at the ends, the handle was loose, and most of the metal had turned a rusty orange color. Marty pulled it out of the corner of the small storage shed in his backyard, gripped the handle with his right hand, and held the shaft with his left. It felt good to him. Not too heavy, not too light. Just right, actually. He temporarily let go of the shovel with his left hand, grabbed a pair of garden gloves situated on a shelf about eye-level to him, and made his way outside to begin his dig.

It was only seven a.m. and the neighborhood was fairly quiet. A few cars passed by Marty, the people inside offering friendly waves, but Marty didn't return the gestures. He was so focused on his quest, so tuned in to his work, he failed to notice anything around him.

Marty stood near the center of the yard, scanned it in every direction, then thought, *This looks like a good spot to start.* He firmly gripped the shovel's handle with both hands, and began piercing the land with the blade of the shovel.

The shovel's blade carved a wedge of ground about six inches deep. *That felt good,* Marty thought excitedly, pulling the shovel up from the ground with a couple of mighty tugs. He swayed backwards on the second pull, stumbling, then falling to the ground. He laughed at himself just then, picked himself up and dusted himself off, and drove the shovel hard once more in the vicinity of the first drive. *I like the way this feels,* he mused, and he began to dig the usual way. His left foot pushed the blade into the ground, and with renewed energy, he tossed the first mound of earth and grass eagerly to the side. One by one, the small loads of dirt filled Marty's shovel, and within a few minutes, he'd starting panting. His brow had become moist, for he'd been perspiring and working hard. Marty hadn't noticed the aches forming in his arms and legs, the push and pull and strain that comes with lifting heavy weight in such a short period of time. He focused solely on the hole, his adrenaline pumping through his veins, his little heart racing from the lack of exercise over his young life.

Suddenly he grew aware of the strain. His arms tightened, his legs wobbled. He placed the shovel down, wiped his brow with his dirty gloves, and for the first time took a good look at his work.

He had excavated quite a decent amount of earth, he thought, and it lay piled in a heap about a foot high, its contents forming a small cone. He peered into the hole. By his estimates, it looked about three feet deep and perhaps two feet wide. Bugs and worms squirmed in both the hole and the earth dug from it. The soil was rather soft so far, and the task had been fairly easy up to this juncture. Marty remembered the picture book he'd studied the night before. The earth was made up of crust, mantle and core. The outer layer of crust was rather soft, he'd discovered. Though he'd only been digging for 20 minutes, his young mind commanded his body to move forward. *I've gotta keep digging,* he thought.

"Hi, honey!" waved his mother from the top step of the back porch, approximately 60 feet away. "How's it going so far?"

She came down the four stairs and walked towards Marty, greeting him with a big smile as she approached the mess he'd made.

She looked into the hole, surprised to see the depth he'd accomplished so far.

"*Wow!*" she proclaimed. "That's pretty deep! How long have you been out here?"

Marty looked at his watch. "About a half-hour," he replied.

Mrs. Kent put on a proud, motherly grin, not only to show Marty how impressed she was with his beginnings, but to provide encouragement. Deep–down, she longed for Marty to dig as far as he could; she didn't want him to quit or fail. But she knew him all too well. He'd failed at most everything he had tried before. He was a quitter, and had proven that over and over in the past. But something about this particular idea really seemed to have captured his imagination. He seemed more confident, more assured, unlike anything his mother had ever seen before. Such a display provided a rare yet cautious moment of cheer for her.

"Why don't I go and borrow the Dickerson's shovel?" she suggested. "Two of us could get a lot farther together, don't you think?"

"Sure mom," Marty said, liking the notion. "I was thinking about going over to tell Brenna after lunch. I know she'd like to help out, too. She'll think it's a neat idea."

"Well then, that's that," his mother said. "I'll go get dressed and borrow that shovel. I can't wait till your father gets home from work. He'll be excited, too!"

Marty didn't share the same confidence in what Dad would think when he was introduced to Marty's project. He couldn't remember one solitary day of his 12 miserable years on earth when his father had been proud of something he'd accomplished. He drove the shovel's blade as hard as he could now, slamming into the ground with even more force than his initial thrusts. *That does feel good*, he thought, and he kept on digging.

CHAPTER 9

The four-eighteen whistle signaled the end of the day for the first of three shifts at the factory that employed Donald Kent. His 17 years of assorted duties at the plant had produced moderate pay increases, terrific health benefits, and job security. He didn't exactly enjoy his work—for the most part it was usually quite tedious—but the pros of his employment outweighed the cons, so he pressed on. The four-eighteen whistle had reminded him of that each and every day since the accident had occurred 19 years earlier.

Daydreams of a time gone by played on him consistently, and they were happening now to him as he gathered his belongings and headed for the parking lot. *If only it hadn't happened,* he thought, *I'd still be the hero.*

He had made his mark in the triple-city area of Binghamton, Johnson City and Union-Endicott on the playing fields of high school football and baseball, as well as on the basketball courts. His plethora of accomplishments, and the subsequent records he'd produced, had stood the test of time. When he was quarterback for Binghamton Central High School, his last second 60-yard heave for the winning touchdown stunned arch-rival Johnson City, propelling the Bulldogs to their one and only state championship. His 55-point performance in the Southern-Tier Athletic Conference championship basketball game—the most points ever scored by a high-school player from the area at the time—sent Central to a second state championship. In the spring of that same year, his extra-inning, game-winning home run over an equally stunned Maine- Endwell team vaulted the Bulldogs into yet another state championship. Against all the odds, the Binghamton Central Bulldogs had pulled off the amazing trifecta of being crowned state champions in all three major sports in the same year. Donald Kent indeed *was* the big man on campus back then.

Dozens of well-known colleges from all over the country had tried to recruit him. His fame was destined to zoom from the local haunts of the Susquehanna Valley to the national spotlight. He'd been guaranteed a full scholarship from each of the schools; the choice of which had been his to make. That was 1949, World War II had ended four years earlier, and the nation was at peace. The war draft had still been in place, but college was a young man's ticket out of selective service. Life couldn't have been better for the young man with such a bright future—until fate stepped in and changed it all.

In the summer of that fateful year, 1949, a freak accident during a pickup baseball game changed the course of Donald Kent's life. He blew out his left knee while sliding into second base—a feat he'd performed hundreds of times before. He remembered the exact moment all too well. It replayed in his mind every day like a broken record, at times teasing him into believing *it never happened.* He remembered the popping sound, the excruciating pain, the look of disbelief on his friends' and family's faces as he writhed in anguish on the ground. He remembered the arrival of the ambulance, the trip to the hospital, the emergency surgery he needed right away…

His deepest memory of the entire episode had permanently etched its dark message the moment Dr. Bradley had spoken the words. He painfully recalled the sobbing of his mother, seated at the foot of his hospital bed, the forlorn look of dread plastered across his father's face. And Dr. Bradley seemingly looked for just the right words, then softly spoke, the haunting, horrible, nightmarish sentence: *"Son, you'll never be able to play competitive sports again…"*

But Donald yearned to play sports again—was so sure he would—but old Dr. Bradley had been right on the money. The injury never allowed him back onto any field or court. Golf and bowling had to replace his aching need for strenuous competition.

He'd excelled at both sports, even thought about touring professionally on the bowling circuit, but money and responsibility always seemed to get in his way. A life so full of promise and fame had been reduced to a mundane existence in a factory.

The old-timers knew his accomplishments, even reminded him of the memories they recalled from his star athlete days. He loved the praise, and that and only that seemed to draw him back into life. But he lived in the past, no doubt about it. By age 20, he'd married his high school sweetheart, Patricia. By 23 he'd bought his first and only house. At 25, the first and only child arrived, and Donald Kent saw an opportunity so many fathers like him had seen before. He imagined his son, this new entry into the world, as Binghamton Central's next star athlete. His son, too, would lead his teams to championships, break records his own father had established, and go on to fame and fortune both in the college and professional ranks. The kid would have it made.

A built-in natural athlete father would provide a sure bet for the big ticket. It would only be a matter of time before the vicarious life he fashioned in his mind for his son would come to fruition. So when the first signs began to appear that such a life would probably never take shape for his son, Donald grew distant. The father/son relationship he had envisioned became nothing more than pure fantasy. His son couldn't hit a ball, he was the slowest runner in his class, he even threw the ball like a girl. This unfortunate turn of events, Donald came to believe, was just another cruel trick played on him by someone or something seeing to it that his life stay a shameful misery. His wife wanted more children, but he had seen enough. Marty would be the only child in the Kent household.

And Donald Kent, the aging boy wonder of Binghamton, the boy who had been picked as the "Athlete of the Half-Century," would be left with more questions than answers about the peculiar circumstances he faced every day of his unfair life.

He now parked the car directly in front of his house on College Street. In the schoolyard next door, several neighborhood kids, boys and girls of all ages, were playing wiffle-ball. Donald placed his hand over his eyes to shield the sun, looking within the group for Marty. He shook his head. *Nothing more than wishful thinking.* He knew Marty wasn't playing ball. *He's probably inside,* Donald thought, *watching cartoons or reading comic books.* He grabbed the latest copy of *The Bulletin* from the sidewalk in front of the house. Then he

43

noticed from the corner of his eye what looked to be dirt being thrown from a hole somewhere in the backyard.

He walked back there, approached what looked like a growing hole and gazed at it for a moment, amazed. At last he stammered, "Hey, what's going on, Marty?" He peered into the hole, which appeared to be about five feet deep and contained both his son and Brenna Nelson. "Hello, Brenna," he said, even more surprised at her presence.

"Hello, Mr. Kent," Brenna said cheerfully.

Donald stretched out his arms in the direction of the big dirt pile that had continued to grow even as he'd watched the two dig, and walked closer to the hole's edge. "Uh, why are you digging a hole in the yard?" he said.

"Dad!" Marty exclaimed, putting down his shovel and wiping the sweat from his brow. "I'm glad you're home. We're digging a hole to China! What do you think?"

Huh, Donald thought. *What kind of crazy scheme is this? Digging a hole to China?*

"Whaddaya mean digging a hole to China?" he cried. "Does your mother know anything about this?"

"I sure do!" Patricia said, answering him unexpectedly. She'd anticipated his arrival and crept up behind him to see his initial reaction. "They've gotten quite far for the first day of digging, don't you think?"

Mr. Kent looked at the hole and dirt produced from Marty and Brenna's efforts, still more than a little confused by it all. He looked at his wife, then at Marty and Brenna, and finally at the hole.

"You two did this – all by yourself?" he asked skeptically.

Marty nodded. "Mom helped a little, but we did all the rest."

"Must be pretty tired," his father grinned for want of anything smarter-sounding to say. "That's an awful lot of dirt for two kids to shovel."

It was the closest thing to a ringing endorsement Marty's father could seem to muster. Marty cringed slightly. He knew it – his father would never come right out and actually give his blessings to anything like this. It wasn't his kind of thing. Instead, he'd probably excuse himself in a moment and retire to the private confines of his bedroom, where he'd offer his *opinion* to his normally very submissive wife. Marty could see it all coming: His dad would find a way to convince his mother that what Marty was doing should be forbidden, and should cease immediately.

But this project was different than any other, Marty thought, and he tried hoping that maybe this time his father would realize it. Marty *really* wanted to dig this hole – his hole to China.

Just then he heard his father say sternly, "Patricia, could I see you for a moment inside?"

"Certainly, dear," Patricia replied. Marty's heart sank in his chest. His shoulders slumped as if someone had just removed all the supporting bones. He watched at his mother now be called away for the Grand Inquisition. She turned to look at Marty, blew him a kiss, then winked the most reassuring wink he'd ever witnessed. "I'll be back in a few minutes, you two," she said confidently. "Go ahead, just keep on digging."

The two diggers paused for a moment. They listened to the sound of the screen door slamming against the siding. They looked at each other, then grabbed their shovels and continued a fierce pace of digging and tossing dirt. A strange feeling of peace crossed Marty's heart just then. Not only did he feel so right in the noble cause of this dig, he believed that for the first time in what seemed like an eternity, his mother was somehow going to get her way.

CHAPTER 10

As usual, Kelly's ride home from work included her slow drive past Recreation Park. Although she made her living forming words into stories, she never could quite explain the pull the park held for her. *It's like a magnet*, she thought, slowing to well below the posted speed on Laurel Avenue.

As she watched in passing the little groups of people enjoying the park's many activities, she reflected on how busy her mind had been at work the past few days. She remembered again the meeting in the hallway with Kincade and Whiting, the mayor's idea of a story on Binghamton, the trip to the library and the chance encounter with Marty Kent. That very thought struck her as she turned the corner onto College Street. She recalled Marty telling her he lived in the vicinity of Horace Mann School, and there stood the old brick building, directly to her left as she straightened the steering wheel. It would be only minutes away from her direct route home from work, and curiosity overcame her: She wanted to see for herself if Marty had actually starting digging his hole to China.

She slowed to five miles-per-hour, scanning both sides of the street for any signs of Marty or his hole. The neighborhood's old homes and properties were fairly well maintained; only a few eyesores stood out against the others. She passed the school and the schoolyard, glanced right, then left—and thought she saw something flying out of the ground as she passed the first house on the left.

She checked her rear view mirror, placed the car in reverse, and slowly backed up a few feet to get a better look at what was going on.

For a moment, she saw nothing resembling a boy digging a hole. *My active imagination,* Kelly thought. She put the car back into drive; but just then she spotted a large pile of dirt rising, then falling to the ground in the backyard of the green house on her left.

She quickly found an open spot a few car lengths ahead, hurriedly parked her car and headed for the house. *Why am I doing this?* she thought. Maybe it was to see for herself how far he'd gotten. *No,* she thought. She simply wanted to check on the kid, make sure he was all right. She even hoped the bullies that had pushed him around at the park would be nearby. Maybe she'd get an opportunity to tell them a thing or two. She'd sort of fallen for Marty, and felt sorry for him. She didn't want him to become like the kid she'd known back home. She'd felt sorrow and guilt for what she learned that kid had become. Maybe she could strike up a friendship with Marty. He seemed to be the lovable type, after all. Whatever her fascination with the whole thing, she knew she'd feel better just seeing him again.

"Well, hello down there!" Kelly yelled into the hole – and suddenly she flinched, amazed at what she was seeing. *That hole has to be eight-feet deep,* she thought, *and six-feet wide!* "It's me, Kelly Trapp from the paper!" she called out.

Marty and Brenna glanced up from the darkness of the hole, literally covered with filth from head to toe.

"Oh, hi, Kelly," said Marty. Brenna followed with her own hello. "We started digging the hole to China," said Marty proudly. "Look how deep we got so far!"

Kelly was impressed. Pleased *and* impressed. A warm feeling overcame her as she squatted to get a better look. She observed the huge mound of dirt to the side of the hole, and wondered exactly how they'd been able to heave load after load up and over the slope. *That would take some strength,* she thought. Her musings took her to the next step—*a reporter's instincts.* Exactly how would they continue to dig, heave the dirt over and crawl back out? She wasn't sure at this point if they'd engaged any adults to help them get past the initial idea of simply digging a hole. If Marty and Brenna were as serious as they appeared to be, they'd have needed some assistance planning it out.

"That's pretty deep!" Kelly remarked. "Are any adults helping you?"

Marty looked at Brenna, shrugged his shoulders matter-of-factly, and said, "My mom said she'd help, but I don't think we'll need her to. We're doing good all by ourselves."

"Yes, yes you are," said Kelly. She suddenly remembered what Mrs. Springer, the librarian, had told her: *Let him fail on his own terms.* The advice may have sounded right to Kelly at the time, but something inside her wanted to help Marty. She fashioned a grin at the children, and stood up. "Is your mother home, Marty?" she asked.

"She's inside the house," he replied.

"Do you think it'll be all right if I introduced myself to her?" Kelly inquired.

"Sure," said Marty. "She likes company."

Kelly walked to the front of the house, up the four stairs to the porch, and rang the bell once. She wasn't quite sure what she'd say when Marty's mom answered the door, and felt a bit out of place as she waited for someone to answer.

The door slowly creaked open. "Yes, may I help you?" said a woman's kind voice.

Kelly was surprised to see a slender, dirty-blonde haired woman at the door. She'd assumed Marty's mom would be overweight, even obese. She'd pictured her having greasy, stringy black hair, with thick, plastic eyeglasses and an oversized sweatshirt on.

Maybe Marty's dad's the overweight one, she thought.

"Mrs. Kent?" she asked, collecting herself.

The woman smiled. "Yes, I'm Mrs. Kent."

"My name's Kelly Trapp. I'm a reporter for *The Bulletin.*"

"A reporter?" Patricia Kent wore a puzzled look on her face. *Why would a reporter for The Binghamton Bulletin be at her door?* she wondered. She suddenly remembered she'd been warned that the press would probably be around, asking questions about the leveling of Horace Mann School, and, more importantly for the Kents, their home. She smacked herself lightly on the forehead with the palm of her hand, opened the door, and stepped outside.

"I'm sorry, Miss Trapp," she said. "I had no idea you news-people would be around so soon. We're sure gonna miss this place, you know. It's always been our home. We love it here."

49

Kelly was confused. "Am I missing something here?"

"You *are* here to do a story on Horace Mann School and eminent domain, aren't you?"

"Eminent domain?" Kelly questioned. "Oh, no, not at all," she said. "I did hear about the new school going up here, but I'm not here on any official business, really."

Now it was Patricia's turn to be confused. "You aren't?"

"No, I'm not. I just dropped by to see how Marty was doing with his digging."

Patricia's eyebrows shot skyward, "Well, how on earth did you know Marty was digging?"

"I ran into him at the library," said Kelly, "and I sort of intervened a few days earlier to help him against some bullies at Rec-Park."

"Oh, so that's what happened..." Patricia said.

Kelly suddenly felt like a snitch. Marty's mom seemed as if she knew nothing about the episode at the park. "You didn't know about the scuffle Marty was in, did you, Mrs. Kent?" she asked sheepishly.

"Maybe you'd better come inside," Marty's mother replied with a healthy smile.

Kelly hesitated. "Are you sure?"

"Absolutely sure," said Patricia, motioning Kelly inside. "Anyone who helps my son I owe something to. I'll make a pot of coffee, and maybe we could visit for a while?"

Kelly had no plans for the evening. She rarely did have something to occupy her night hours. Her work schedule made meeting adults her age difficult, for the most part, so Patricia's invitation sounded good to her.

"I guess I could stay for a while," she said, giving herself an out, if one was needed.

"Good, good, then come on inside," Patricia said. "We'll go sit on the back porch and watch the kids' progress."

Kelly's afternoon spent with Patricia Kent spilled over into Patricia's invitation to and Kelly's acceptance of dinner, and their time together continued through the evening and into the early morning hours: The pair had struck an immediate bond with each other.

Kelly learned so much about Patricia, Marty, and Donald Kent. She learned the tragic and heartbreaking story of Donald Kent's knee injury. She learned how the two had been high school sweethearts, how Patricia had staunchly remained the good wife, despite the growing separation she'd felt between her and Donald over the past few years.

Kelly learned how badly Patricia Kent wanted another child—a girl she'd hoped – and how her husband had eliminated the idea from the realm of possibility by taking up refuge in the guest room every night at bedtime. Kelly learned of the constant battles Marty fought with the bullies, about his weight, and his father's coolness toward his son.

She learned about the real meaning of eminent domain, and how it so affected Marty's father, who wanted no part in leaving his dream home.

Kelly learned that the Kents couldn't afford a lawyer to fight for their home, that it was only a matter of time before they'd have to leave their home, for the clock was ticking towards its target date. But Kelly couldn't believe how positive Patricia Kent sounded, despite all the setbacks and problems she'd still be facing tomorrow and beyond. Kelly felt honored that this woman, this stranger, would open herself up in the way she did.

Kelly also shared her own little battles and her former life in Philadelphia. She recounted how her parents had divorced when she was Marty's age, how her alcoholic father had provided nothing for her, emotionally or financially. She shared the pride she felt towards her mother, who'd worked two jobs and put Kelly through college. She shared the problems she faced at *The Bulletin* with Harry Whiting. Not much to be told was missed that night. And when the time came at last for Kelly to leave, she and Patricia embraced like sisters, and Kelly felt happy as she waved and drove away from sight – she finally had a friend outside of Philadelphia.

She also felt that maybe something could and should be done about the Kents' house, which was in danger of being leveled. After all, Kelly was a reporter. She even knew the mayor on a personal level. *There must be something I can do,* she thought. Her mother, Paula, had taught her early on in life to act, not react, against bad people, things and events. *Never give up or lose hope,* she'd say. *If there doesn't seem to be a way out, then find another way in.*

51

Gary Kaschak

Kelly pulled into her spot on Clinton Street. She ambled the short distance to the old building she resided in, and went inside. She'd been so used to coming home to an empty apartment, yet she rarely felt alone. She enjoyed her own company, her music, her magazines, even writing letters to friends back home. She really didn't have much of a life, she thought, but she enjoyed it nonetheless. She didn't particularly care for the bar scene, especially being a single, almost always unaccompanied female. She had no present religious affiliations, though she'd been raised Catholic, even attended Catholic school in Philadelphia. She still held onto many of the beliefs she'd been taught as a child, but she rarely attended Mass. Easter and Christmas remained mandatory to her, however.

Tonight was nice, she thought as she settled into her bed for some much-needed sleep. In the morning would be a meeting at city hall she'd attend—only this one would be different from the others. Townsfolk would have an opportunity to present the mayor with ideas for her *Boost Binghamton* idea. They had been expecting more people than usual for this particular gathering; they'd even moved the time to early morning in anticipation of a large crowd. Kelly looked forward to the change in venue, as well as to taking the opportunity to speak with Mayor Thomas about the Kents' plight concerning their home. She eagerly anticipated hearing the residents' many ideas about bringing popularity and fame to Binghamton. For the first time, Kelly felt like a very small part of this community.

CHAPTER 11

A decent number of townsfolk showed up for the meeting at city hall. The auditorium wasn't filled to capacity, but the count at least tripled the usual number of 50 or 60 people who regularly attended city hall meetings. Kelly fought through the crowd of people milling about, exchanging stories and ideas. Most toted written materials, graphs, and even drawings. Kelly decided to interview a few attendees just minutes before the start of the meeting. *Just in case,* she thought.

The first two people Kelly spoke to had decent, however not original, ideas. An elderly man sporting a baseball cap advertising the unit he fought for in World War I planned on suggesting a War Memorial. "Binghamton doesn't have one," he'd told Kelly. Kelly certainly agreed that one should be erected, but she doubted Mayor Thomas would share in the veteran's enthusiasm, at least for this particular suggestion. No doubt, though, it was a noble cause, and worth pursuing, so she had both complemented and warned him about its likely reception by the mayor.

An elderly woman planned to propose a shrine honoring the longevity of the oldest factory in Binghamton: Endicott-Johnson, the shoe-store founders, a truly American tradition. Certainly, Kelly knew, "E-J" was both a tradition and a staple throughout the triple-cities, a company familiar to almost everyone in the area, and they had provided employment for thousands over the centuries. Yet Kelly doubted that Mayor Thomas would be particularly excited by this

53

proposal, as it didn't seem to have enough "kick" to draw in outsiders. *This may be a long day,* Kelly thought, as she excused herself when the meeting came to order.

As the meeting progressed, Kelly saw that her predictions were right on the mark. One weak idea after another took up the entire morning, and although Mayor Thomas maintained her political cool through the lengthy ordeal, Kelly could clearly see that she was disappointed, and with good cause. As it turned out, the two locals Kelly had happened to interview prior to the presentations had the best ideas. But as Kelly had foreseen, the mayor's reaction was merely lukewarm. By Kelly's notes, exactly 40 people made presentations in front on the mayor and her staff. Kelly had eagerly scribbled notations early on, but soon she began to feel disappointed as the flow of ideas lost its momentum. To distract herself, she reflected on her own problems at the paper, repeatedly thinking back to Joel Kincade's remarks in the hallway about passion and discipline and intestinal fortitude. *Intestinal fortitude,* she thought. *Guts. That's what he wants out of his reporters. Someone who'll take a chance.*

Her thoughts returned to Marty and the hole to China. *Hmm, maybe I can write a story on* that, she pondered. She rubbed her chin, gazed at the ceiling and began to piece together a story–line. She even envisioned a headline banner with her byline below it...

But would it be a story that would strike anyone's interest—or would readers just brush it off as some childhood silliness? Worse yet, would Harry Whiting not only give Kelly a resounding *no* when he heard her idea; would he laugh her out of the building altogether? Kelly would have to mull these issues carefully before she'd dare pop the idea to Whiting. *I need to give it some more time,* she thought. *I mean, what if Marty gives up his dig before the story even comes out? Then I'll really look foolish around here.*

Kelly decided she'd give Marty at least a few more days and see just how determined he was before she approached Whiting. But in the meantime, she'd begin writing the story on her own, even conduct some research on China and the earth. *A hole to China – it could be a cute story people might like*, she thought.

Suddenly, snapping Kelly out of her reverie, Mayor Thomas said sharply, "I thank you, ladies and gentlemen, for coming here today.

We will be reviewing all of these fine presentations, and will update you all at the next city hall meeting. Now, I can't say for sure we'll choose any of these ideas. However, I was very impressed with many of them. Again, thank you for coming, and have a most pleasant day."

The sounds of shifting chairs and the sudden outbreak of voices was Kelly's cue to interview the mayor. She'd want a few more quotes on the mayor's thoughts, but was quite sure the mayor had just shared her opinion pretty fully. Fortunately, Kelly knew that Mayor Thomas was comfortable enough with her to at least state her honest thoughts, both on and off the record.

Kelly approached the podium as the mayor began collecting her belongings and shuffling papers about. "Mayor Thomas, could I have a few minutes with you now?" she asked.

"Yes, *now* would be the best time," the mayor answered emphatically. "Let's go into my office."

The mayor's office was situated directly behind them. The mayor excused herself from the crowd, waving and smiling and continuing to shake hands all the way to the door of her chambers. Kelly waited inside as the mayor continued to engage in the expected political rigmarole. Mayor Thomas then entered the office, and in a theatrical pose, pushed her back against the door, stretched out her arms against it, and squatted a few inches. Kelly laughed at her antics, glad that the mayor now felt relaxed enough to express her true emotions.

"Somebody please shoot me!" cried the mayor. She wasn't directing her cry for help to Kelly, but she struck quite a nerve in Kelly anyway. *I like her sense of humor*, Kelly thought, stifling a smile as the mayor invited her to have a seat.

"These people mean well," began the mayor. "But really, as I told you before, what is there in Binghamton to work with? I'm afraid I've opened up a can of worms here." She paused. "May I ask you, Kelly: Did any one of those presentations seem worthy or spectacular enough to even think of pursuing as the thing people might remember Binghamton by?"

Kelly pondered a moment. "Well, I thought the idea on Endicott-Johnson was the most promising of all. But I agree with you. I really heard nothing that seemed interesting enough to draw people to actually visit Binghamton."

"Yes, yes, you're quite right," Mayor Thomas sighed. "I suppose we should at least consider that one. It would be interesting to our own people, if no one else."

Kelly sensed a moment of resignation in the mayor. *She really wanted this to work*, she thought, *but it didn't.*

"Mayor Thomas, would you mind if I changed the subject for a moment?" Kelly said, picking up her pen. "I need your advice on something."

The mayor looked up over her reading glasses at Kelly. "By all means, young lady, I'd be glad to help you out if I can."

"I have an idea for a story, and I'm not so sure how to approach Harry Whiting with it."

"I see. Go on."

"Well, I've been at *The Bulletin* for two years, and all I get is the bottom of the barrel assignments," Kelly groused. Then, embarrassed, she thought about what she'd just said, covered her mouth with her hands and blurted out, "Oh, dear, I'm so sorry, Mayor. I didn't mean to offend…"

The mayor raised her hand, cutting Kelly off in mid-sentence. "Never mind, dear. I'll take no offense to that statement. You're a young woman who wants to do something fresh and fun. I completely understand. Now, about that idea for a story?"

"Well, I'm not so sure Mr. Whiting will take the idea seriously."

The mayor rolled her eyes. "Does any suggestion other than his own ever sound good to him?"

Kelly smiled. "No, not really."

Mayor Thomas eyed Kelly, seeing so much of herself in the young woman. Kelly was still raw and green, but the mayor found the drive and passion she sensed in her quite refreshing.

"Why don't you tell me your idea; then I'll offer some advice if I can." Mayor Thomas thought back to her days at *The Bulletin*. "I do have some idea of how things work down there."

Kelly took in a breath. "Well, I met a young boy recently."

"Uh, romantically interesting? How old?"

"No," Kelly grinned, "nothing romantic. He's twelve."

The mayor nodded for Kelly to continue.

"To make a long story short, he's got his problems," Kelly began. "He's very self-conscious about his looks. He's overweight and has a few blemishes on his face. His father almost pretends he's not there, and he's always being bullied by these boys..."

"Sounds very sad," said the mayor. "Is that the story?"

"Oh, no," Kelly quickly assured her. "The real story is that he's decided to dig a hole to China."

"*Dig a hole to China?*" the mayor laughed. "I suppose we've all contemplated doing that at some point in our youths."

"Yes, I agree with you. But this kid's idea seems different."

"Oh, how so?"

"Well," said Kelly, "he's checked out some books on China from the library – and he's started digging. He's dug pretty deep already."

"How deep?"

"The last time I looked, he was about ten feet down."

The mayor chuckled. "I'm sure he's soon going to tire himself out. So why do you think this would make such a great story?"

Kelly paused for a moment. She had asked herself the same question many times since the idea came to her. Maybe she just wanted Marty to succeed, to go as fast and far as he could before he quit. She knew he'd eventually have to quit digging; everyone knew digging to China was well beyond the realm of human possibility. Maybe she just wanted to stay close to Marty, to protect him against the menacing bullies. Whatever the reason, Kelly had a hunch that Marty's dig held some semblance of a story behind it.

"It's a great human interest story," Kelly offered at last. "Plus, the city is leveling their house in the fall. If the kid keeps digging through the summer, it could make for great drama."

"What do you mean the city's leveling their house?" asked the mayor.

"The family lives on the West Side, next to Horace Mann Grade School."

"Ah!" The mayor was quite familiar with the subject. She herself had attended the old school, and memories of her childhood flooded her senses every time she heard anyone utter the name, *Horace Mann.* "This boy and his family live right there, near the school?" asked the mayor sadly.

"First house on College Street." Kelly replied.

When it came to this particular issue Mayor Thomas had taken a position solidly "on the fence," and she confessed to herself that nostalgia clouded her thinking here. One part of her badly wanted to maintain the old school, while the other knew deep down it was probably time to shut its doors forever, not move to expand it. She felt a good deal of sympathy for the handful of residents who'd need to have their homes demolished to make way for the school's sparkling new building, but until now, she'd not known any of them personally, nor any of their personal business.

She straightened herself in her chair and looked at the young woman sitting across from her. "You know, Kelly, the real story you're looking for may be the school and the leveling of the neighborhood."

Kelly frowned. "What do you mean, Mayor Thomas?"

The Mayor pushed herself back as far as she could in her chair, placed her arms behind her head and rocked gently a few times. "Kelly, you are a reporter, and in my estimation, a darned good one. What I tell you here *must* remain off – completely off – the record. Do I make myself clear?"

"Yes, yes of course," Kelly nodded.

"I've been quite surprised that this business involving Horace Mann School has literally gone unnoticed by the press. Oh, they've run a few things here and there, but really nothing to speak of in the way of news.

"Now I must say that the people in that neighborhood put up a short fight in the beginning. But when we explained to them the procedures involved in eminent domain, they backed off. We explained that a lawyer may have postponed everything for a while, but eventually they'd be the ones to foot the bill when the inevitable occurred."

The mayor paused again, then said, "You've been over there, Miss Trapp. I'm sure you can see for yourself that most of those folks probably could never afford a lawyer to fight for them."

Kelly nodded agreement. "What are you suggesting I do?"

"I'm not suggesting anything specific," the mayor answered. "However, it seems to me there's an opportunity here to run a story on *The Hole To China* from a unique perspective – that of a kid who's about to lose his home. It's kind of his way of making his mark before he's forced to leave."

Kelly's eyes widened. "Funny, that's exactly the angle I was hoping to take!" She paused, then said, "Mayor Thomas, forgive me, but if I decide to do the story from this angle, I may need to ask you some questions about eminent domain."

Mayor Thomas had to think this through. She was quite sure Kelly had no idea she was challenging city policy. This story would merely be Kelly's opportunity, provided conveniently by the mayor, to prove her worth as a field reporter. Though Mayor Thomas had always been considerably cautious about the administration of city matters, she felt confident that the information she'd just shared with Kelly would remain private.

So, said the mayor matter-of-factly, "Guess a reporter's got to do what she's got to do."

Kelly stood up and extended her right hand. She wondered what would prompt the mayor to point her toward such an enormous lead. The city had undoubtedly spent thousands of dollars helping the school plan and develop its new building. Plus, leveling the old school would have to be extremely costly to the taxpayers, who'd be subsidizing the project.

The mayor suddenly suggested: "I think you should begin telling your story with the boy digging the hole. And right now I wouldn't even bother with Whiting if I were you.

You may never get anywhere with that jerk. You should just go straight to Kincade with the whole thing."

CHAPTER 12

Kelly still wasn't certain how she would handle her potential *Hole To China* story. But she suspected she'd gotten some savvy advice from Mayor Thomas. Still each time she'd considered going straight to Joel Kincade, she'd hesitated to get up from her chair and approach him.

She did, however, do some homework on the leveling of Horace Mann School. She talked to the two reporters at *The Bulletin* who'd handled the preliminary story, gleaning as much information as she could from their notes and stories. She began to spend all her free time either at the library gathering additional information, or stopping off at the Kents' to stay up on Marty's progress with the dig. And progress had been made on two fronts.

First, Patricia had reported to Kelly that her "conversation" with her husband about Marty and the hole had produced "better than expected results." In fact, he'd shown a bit of emotion, even some interest, but solely for his own reasons. He knew Marty would eventually fail, but he was interested in watching his son exert himself physically, to see how far he was capable of pushing his body. He was also anxious to see Marty's psychological handling of losing at something in which he greatly longed to succeed. It reminded him of his own personal trauma, suffered years ago, when the sports he loved to play so much were snatched away from him in an instant. His curiosity as to how his son would handle the approaching adversity was ever-growing.

The dig itself had produced wonderful results. The diggers had attained a depth of 12 feet by the end of the second day; now they required a ladder to be lowered into the hole so they could enter and exit. By day three, Marty and Brenna reached 20 feet, and had slowed considerably for a number of unforeseen reasons. Though Marty's mother had suggested from the beginning that they dig a wide enough opening to support two people shoveling dirt, the new problem of exactly how to get in and out of the hole posed two huge problems. The ladder was only 16 feet long, four feet shorter than the depth they'd achieved thus far. Marty and Brenna had still been able to reach the top by crawling the final four feet, but it became quite apparent that they'd need a longer ladder by the next phase of digging.

Shoveling and tossing was now out of the question as well. The height involved in throwing heavy dirt up and over an enclosed area was working against them. Of every shovel full of dirt they tossed upward, half would tumble back into the hole. Soon they retrieved a few small plastic buckets, lowered them into the hole, filled them with earth and carried them up the ladder and onto the massive dirt mound.

On a lighter note, the mound itself had begun to attract passers-by. Cars stopped in the middle of the street, neighbors curiously approached the hole, and most of the onlookers' reactions encouraged the kids to continue on. Kelly Trapp made sure to enter this important fact in her ever-growing notes, even stopping a few people to ask their opinions of Marty's hole to China.

"Excuse me, could I have a few words with you?" Kelly asked one middle-aged woman who'd stopped to observe the goings on.

The woman had lived in the neighborhood her entire life. She knew who was who around the block, and who were strangers to the area. She eyed Kelly cautiously. "I'm sorry, have we met before?" she said warily.

"No, we haven't," Kelly replied. "I'm a reporter, and I'd just like to ask you a question or two about the hole the boy's digging."

"Why, are you doing a story on it?" the woman asked.

Kelly grinned. "Possibly."

The woman's concerns quickly faded. She'd never been interviewed before, never had her name in the paper for any reason. In fact, nothing out of the ordinary ever seemed to happen in this neighborhood, she said, and the boy's hole might perk things up. "Ask your questions," she said cheerfully.

Kelly smiled. She drew out her pad and pen and began the interview: "What do you think of Marty's quest to dig a hole to China?"

The woman's memory flashed back 30 years, when, as it turned out, she'd made her own failed attempt to achieve the same goal. She recalled the excitement, the anticipation and the actual digging. Sure, she said, she hadn't gotten far, but the thrill of digging a hole into forbidden territory had been etched in her mind for all these years.

"I think it's something most kids want to try at least once," she said. "It actually reminded me of when I tried digging a hole to China with all the neighbors watching."

"Do you remember how far down you got?" asked Kelly.

"No, not really. I don't think we got too far before we gave up, but we were all excited, I can tell you that. That's what I remember the most."

Kelly asked a few more questions, thanked the woman and proceeded to a second neighbor who was hovering over the hole, talking to Marty and Brenna. The same questions produced similar answers. A few more neighbors continued their parade past the hole, and from every person Kelly spoke with, she determined several undeniable facts: Marty had aroused the neighbors' interest, and he and Brenna had unintentionally set-off lots of vivid childhood memories.

These people are really pulling for him, Kelly thought. *This will indeed make a good story.*

Kelly's interviewing continued with the project's "founders," Marty, Brenna and Patricia. She assembled an array of wonderful comments from the trio, *Enough to make a great story,* she thought happily. Excited and impatient from what she'd learned at the hole, Kelly decided to head back to *The Bulletin* and write the story, right then. She couldn't wait until tomorrow. Her creative juices were flowing, and she needed to get her thoughts down, *right now,* she thought. Plus, another editors' meeting was scheduled for mid-afternoon. *Perhaps I can present my story to Harry Whiting in the morning before the meeting starts,* she mused.

CHAPTER 13

"This is phenomenal, simply sensational," said Mary Jaggers, the paper's veteran columnist. She placed her hand to her heart and laid the paper down on her desk. "I especially love the way you've woven together the two stories—of the hole and the leveling of the school. It's quite impressive, actually. Have you shown this to Whiting yet?"

Kelly Trapp reached over and retrieved the document. She banged the papers together on the desk like a deck of cards, to straighten out the pages. Her forlorn look gave Jaggers the answer she'd expected.

"Every time I make a suggestion to him, he just cuts me off," Kelly retorted. "What's his big problem with me anyway, and why doesn't Mr. Kincade do something about it?"

"Whiting feels threatened by people with personality," quipped Jaggers. "As for why Joel Kincade lets it happen, well, there's been talk around here for years, you know."

"Talk? What kind of talk?" asked Kelly. "I've never heard anything said about it."

Mary Jaggers glanced around the area. She pulled Kelly closer and said softly, "There's been talk for years that Joel Kincade owes some kind of favor—a big favor – to Benjamin Whiting, Harry's father. I've never been able to really find out much more about it, but it stands to reason that it must be something big, because that drone of an editor's needed to be replaced for a long time."

"But why wouldn't Mr. Kincade just replace him if that's what's good for the paper?" asked Kelly.

"Principles," replied Jaggers. "Mr. Kincade is a man with principles and standards that can't be measured. I'm sure whatever the favor was, it was something quite important, indeed. Don't think for a minute that Kincade's not completely aware of the way Harry Whiting treats us all. In fact, I'm sure he aches from it."

"I don't get it," said Kelly.

"Understood," said Jaggers. "But it wasn't always like that with Harry; actually, he started out as a pretty good editor for his first eight years. But something's happened in the past two years, ever since his father died. Oh, don't get me wrong; he's never been a very nice man, but like I just said, he's gotten worse since his father passed on a couple years ago. He went from bad to worse since that day." She paused and said, "I think things will be coming to a head any day now."

"Why do you say that?" Kelly wondered aloud.

"Have you seen the big calendar in Kincade's office?" asked Jaggers.

"Yes, yes I've seen it," said Kelly, plainly puzzled.

"Have you noticed all the 'X's' he draws through each day as it ends?"

"Yes, I've seen those," replied Kelly. "What's any of that got to do with this?"

"Just a hunch on my part," said Jaggers. "Because today's date on the calendar is circled in big red marker."

"So, that doesn't prove anything unusual," said Kelly. "Maybe Mr. Kincade has it circled because of the big editors' meeting."

"I thought of that," agreed Jaggers. "But I don't think that's it. Mr. Kincade has been crossing out days for nearly two years now, ever since the day Benjamin Whiting died. I think I'm the only one who's noticed the connection, but there is one, I'm telling you.

Plus, Mr. Kincade didn't even know the meeting was planned for this day when he began checking off that calendar. It's more coincidence than anything that the meetings and the circled day just happen to be today. I'm telling you, something big is going down, and it's going down today."

The two women spoke more on the subject for several minutes, then returned to the original reason they'd come together, to discuss Kelly's story. Mary Jaggers picked the document up from the table again, looked at the story's lead again and handed it to Kelly.

Kelly said, "So you think I should give it to Whiting anyway?"

Jaggers sighed. "As much as I despise the man, he is still the editor here, at least for now. Perhaps if he doesn't go for it, then you could try to approach Kincade. I'd just be careful if I were you. Whiting's been known to make life miserable for anyone who crosses him. He's just that way."

Jaggers squinted her eyes and curled her lower lip over her top one. The veteran reporter had said the last few words more like advice than a statement of opinion. Kelly nodded and understood. The opportunity for something to finally break for her was at hand, she sensed.

"I'm going to give him one more chance," said Kelly. "But after that, I'm done with him."

But Kelly was no martyr, and now more than before, she felt tentative. She had finally begun to enjoy Binghamton, some of the reporters had started to take to her, and she'd grown close to Marty and his mom. Even the mayor was beginning to make her feel special, and the story—Jaggers had confirmed that *the story* had promise.

Kelly thanked Mary Jaggers and confidently left her office. *Maybe I'll show this to a few more staffers*, she thought, and she began to circulate her story to a few trusted and seasoned reporters.

From everyone to whom she showed it, the reactions to Kelly's story were the same as those of Mary Jaggers': *Compelling, dramatic, compassionate;* they used those kinds of adjectives to describe her work. But the reporters also knew what she was up against with Whiting, so they just wished her luck, and went back about their own agendas.

By noon, there was still no sign in the office of Harry Whiting or Joel Kincade. The editorial meeting had been planned for two o'clock in the conference room. This assembly would be quite unlike those Kelly had observed from her inferior vantage point. This meeting was *The Big One*, a collection of the top brass of the *Gannett News Group*. In fact, it was more than just an editor's meeting, you could more accurately call it an *editors'* meeting. Editors from all over New York State would be gathering together to discuss the whole syndicate's business of news. Representatives from Syracuse, Utica, Albany, Buffalo, New York City and other prominent cities in the state had arrived. Two-and-a-half days of discussions on ratings, circulation, advertising, delivery service, and literally everything else on the subject would take place, between the top minds from each paper in the syndicate.

Now a rumor was floating around that Joel Kincade was particularly interested in Binghamton circulation problems. The steady decline in readership had dropped advertising rates to a post-war low. Fewer companies were posting ads with *The Bulletin*, and those who dared were now enjoying steep discounts. Small talk swirled of impending layoffs to non-essential staff outside of the newsroom. Even long-standing reporters were feeling the pressure of early retirement proposals. That Joel Kincade was ready – and needed—to make some sort of fiscal move to keep the paper in the black was no secret. Kelly remembered the big red circled date on the calendar in Kincade's office, and doleful thoughts crossed her mind. Maybe Joel Kincade was selling the paper, or retiring, or, worst possible scenario: announcing layoffs. Given her lowly status at the paper, might Kelly be among those losing their jobs?

What else could it be? she thought, as her thoughts returned to Harry Whiting. Despite the growing tension of what the next few days could bring, Kelly couldn't resist the urge to confront Whiting the minute she spotted him. He'd have time to listen to her story idea, she hoped, and even possibly be able to scan and evaluate the content. She'd prepared two parts to the story, and she was ready to show him both, if necessary. Part 1 would be enough, she figured, to at least get some kind of reaction from him.

At 1:15, Harry Whiting entered the building looking very nervous. To Kelly, he appeared absolutely miserable. *He's in another bad mood*, she thought, trudging over to him just as he was settling into his office.

"Mr. Whiting, could I have a few minutes of your time?" she asked as politely as possible.

"What is it *now*, Miss Trapp?" Whiting spewed disgustedly.

"I know you have a big meeting today, sir, but I was wondering if you could take a look at a story I've written?"

"A story?" said Whiting incredulously. "What story? I never assigned you any *story*!"

"No, you didn't, sir," Kelly said calmly. "I did the story on my own time."

"On your own? Why would you do such a thing?"

"Because it's a story worth reporting, sir. I think our readers would like it."

Harry Whiting sat in his chair, kicked his feet up on his desk. "Close the door, Miss Trapp," he ordered.

Kelly shut the door behind her. She timidly placed the story on Whiting's desk and slid it towards him. He quickly glanced down at the papers, then abruptly slid them back across the desk. "Let's get something straight, Kelly," he fumed. "I don't care if this story is ever read by our readers. In fact, who are you to tell me our readers would like this story?" He grabbed the document and clumsily leafed through it.

"What is this?" he said, amused. "A story about some local boy digging a hole to China? That's about the dumbest thing I've ever heard! And you believe that this garbage is *newsworthy*? Ha!"

For a moment Kelly considered telling him how much the veteran reporters in the office had liked it; but she realized that with the mood he was in, hearing this would probably only make him angrier. She gathered her story into her chest, watching the arrogant man laugh at her and her idea. She got up, angrily opened the door, walked out, closed it behind her, and stumbled to her desk. All eyes in the newsroom followed her.

Her ears still rang of Whiting's uproarious laughter.

He's having a grand old time, she thought, lowering herself into her work station.

Mary Jaggers suddenly appeared by Kelly's desk. "How'd it go in there?" she asked.

"Just like we expected," Kelly answered. "He only read a few words and laughed at it. He never even gave it a chance."

Jaggers frowned. "It figures. Now what are you going to do?"

Kelly paused. "Well, I did say I'd give him one more chance before I approached Mr. Kincade."

"Yes, you did."

"Well then, that's exactly what I'm going to do next."

"Hm," Jaggers muttered. "If I were you I'd let it wait a few days—you know, with the meetings and all."

"Yeah," said Kelly dejectedly. "Guess I'll have to wait till Monday morning."

"Good luck then, Kelly," Jaggers said, patting Kelly's shoulder. "Again, I think it's a great human interest story, so well-written and concise. He really doesn't know what he's missing. This story needs to run."

"Thank you so much, Mary," said Kelly. "That means a lot to me, really."

Jaggers smiled at Kelly and returned to her own work station. Kelly looked out into the newsroom at her fellow reporters. So many of them, just like she, had felt Whiting's wrath over the years. *He's a vindictive dictator who hides things well*, she thought, surprised that the likes of Joel Kincade hadn't discovered that fact with the paper's sinking ratings.

Over the next hour, the contingent of editors began to arrive for the initial meeting, paraded through the newsroom by a welcoming committee. Some stopped at the cubicles of old friends, while others poked around the various areas of the main floor. By two o'clock, they were ushered to the big conference room in back, to begin the meeting.

Kelly spotted Joel Kincade just then, to her left. He cut a magnificent, fatherly figure, towering over each colleague he greeted. Kelly strained to listen to his salutations. His speech was so eloquent, his delivery so refined—he seemed to Kelly like a real wordsmith if one had ever lived.

At that moment, she decided that waiting until Monday would take away her edge. She needed to speak to him as soon as possible, and what's more, she reasoned, he needed to hear what she had to say. *I can't work under these conditions anymore,* she thought.

In the conference room, Joel Kincade began by briefly introducing each person attending the meeting. He stood at his head position at the far end of the giant conference room table, informing those who'd gathered of their individual past accomplishments. The editors enjoyed this nice touch to begin the grueling three days of meetings.

Harry Whiting, sitting directly to the right of Kincade, looked a bit nervous. Through most of his 10 years as editor, *The Bulletin* had been able to at least maintain its readership and sponsors, but now the ratings had sunk and people—especially Joel Kincade—were noticing. At first Kincade had given Whiting a little slack, placing some of the responsibility on his own shoulders, but he didn't really apply any pressure. Now Kincade was growing increasingly concerned with each passing fiscal quarter. The population of Binghamton and its surrounding communities may have shifted somewhat more to the suburbs in the past few years, but where were the readers going? Kincade had begun to put the squeeze on Whiting, imploring him to motivate his reporters to become *news-seekers*, not just news-gatherers. *There's such a big difference*, he thought, as his introductory comments now centered on Harry Whiting.

The first hour's agenda went right to the heart of the matter for Kincade. A group discussion on how to get and keep readership headed the list. Kincade opened the floor for ideas, and the group brainstormed, discussing the things that worked and those that didn't. By the end of the dialogue, Kincade, as host, had the final words to say on the matter.

"Ladies and gentlemen, thank you so much for sharing your stories, your ideas, your insights. Let's summarize."

Kincade glanced at the few notes he'd scribbled down. He sat back in his chair and looked around the room. Nothing he'd just heard had surprised him. He'd been in the news business his entire adult life, more than four decades, and he knew what worked and what didn't better than anyone in the room. His passion for news and stories had followed him throughout his career. What a peculiar feeling, he thought, to be for the first time in his career on the way down. Suddenly, he felt both vulnerable and energized: vulnerable from the sagging ratings, but energized by the opportunity to turn things around.

"I've listened very closely to what you've all contributed today," he began. "But when it's all said and done, it all comes back to one thing, and one thing alone." He held up his right index finger and pulled himself forward in his seat.

"It's the same thing, really, for all business," he continued. "The *basics*, ladies and gentlemen, getting back to the basics. We're in the news business. We generate news and stories for the world to read. That's the basic principle, very simple. Find a story, write a story."

Heads nodded across the table.

"Now, most of you know the woes we've experienced here lately," Kincade went on.

"Some of you happen to be in the same boat, trying to fix something, and nothing is working. Well, I'm here to say you've really got to start listening to your reporters." He gazed at Whiting, keeping fixed on him for several seconds as he spoke. Whiting squirmed uneasily in his chair. He couldn't believe Kincade seemed to be directing his opinion toward him, singling him out. It made him uncomfortable, yet he couldn't understand why Kincade kept looking at him. *I listen to my reporters,* he thought. *They just don't do a good job reporting the news.*

One editor asked. "Kincade, just what do you mean, listen to our reporters?"

"What I mean is this," Kincade began again. "Don't just assign a story, *look* for stories. Good reporters shouldn't be saddled in an office all day waiting for the phone to ring. They need to be on the streets, talking with those in the know. That's how news is made. A good reporter should be hungry and driven so hard by a story, that they never look at a clock to check when it's time to leave for the day. On the contrary, they should always feel as though there's not *enough* time in the day. They should have passion and drive and intestinal fortitude, with a dig-down deep attitude."

Kincade remembered back to his own days as a passionate reporter, always hungry to produce interesting and provocative news. Now, gloriously, the feeling was returning to him. All right, maybe he'd "mellowed" some over the past few years, maybe he'd even accepted a certain amount of mediocrity. But that wouldn't do any more. He felt young again, suddenly inspired. He looked at Harry Whiting, and instantly the pieces began to come together in his mind – he knew the reasons for the decline of *The Bulletin*, and he knew what needed to be done to remedy things.

Gentle applause from the table caught Kincade off guard. He placed his right hand to his brow, slowly saluted his colleagues and announced that he thought a short recess would be in order.

An instant later, amid the ensuing chair-scraping, here was that young reporter, Kelly Trapp, bursting into the room, waving a sheaf of papers in the air. Breathless, she announced, "I'm sorry to disturb your meeting, Mr. Kincade, but this just can't wait any longer."

Harry Whiting's jaw dropped like a lead weight, as did many others' in the room. He couldn't believe the arrogance and rudeness this woman was displaying. *That's the last straw*, he thought. *Kincade will be appalled by this intrusion, and he'll fire her on the spot.*

"What do you think you're doing in here?" Whiting shouted.

Kelly ignored Whiting and looked straight at Kincade. She handed him her story, folded her arms and threw back her shoulders. The room full of editors sat in stunned – silence, waiting for Kincade to speak.

"What is this, Kelly?" he asked gently.

"It's a story I've written about a local boy," she replied firmly.

Kincade glanced at Whiting, then back to Kelly.

"I see," he said. "Perhaps you could summarize in 30 seconds exactly what it is I need to know about this particular story."

Whiting felt very hot all of a sudden. He could feel his blood pressure rising and his heart begin to race. He couldn't believe that for the second time in a week, Kincade was behaving nicely towards this Kelly, especially considering the current conditions. But he was still confident that the axe would be falling on Kelly any minute.

Kelly began, "It's a story about a boy whose home is about to be demolished. But before it is, he wants to dig a hole to China."

A collective chuckle filled the air, but Kelly wasn't amused; in fact her burning gaze actually silenced the audience of editors. She looked back at Kincade, who was thumbing through the document.

"A hole to China?" he repeated with just a hint of a smile.

"Yes sir, a hole to China," Kelly said, standing steadfast.

Kincade peered at Whiting. "Harry, have you seen this story?" he questioned.

"Yes, I saw it earlier," Whiting responded. Now was his chance to humiliate this young woman, and he was going to seize it. "I've already told her it's a ridiculous idea for a story." He glared at Kelly, his eyes seething with anger. "Young lady, you have some nerve barging in here like this."

Kelly looked past Whiting, straight at Kincade. "But that's just the point," she snapped.

"The point?" Kincade echoed.

"Yes sir, *your* point," Kelly said. "You recently told us reporters that determination and intestinal fortitude are what it takes to make news worth reading."

Kincade raised his chin. "Please go on."

"You told us to take a chance, to go out and find a story," Kelly continued. "You asked for us to dig, deep-down, sir. Well, not only have I done that, but digging deep down's exactly what my story is about."

Kincade smiled. "You mean, about some boy who's digging to China?"

"Yes sir, about a boy who's digging to China," Kelly shot back.

Utter silence befell the room. Kincade pondered Kelly's remarks for a few seconds.

"What makes this story so special?" he finally asked. "Doesn't every kid want to dig a hole to China?"

"Yes, every kid does, sir," said Kelly. "But for one thing, this kid's already dug about 20 feet deep, and his digging's tied in with the other angle—the leveling of his home."

"What do you mean?" Kincade inquired. "Who's leveling his home, and why?"

Kelly knew this would take more time than she'd already been granted; Kincade really needed to read the entire story to get a clear perspective on things.

She said, "Sir, I don't want to take up any more of your time. But may I ask you to take the story and read it, and then draw your own conclusions about it?"

Something about this whole display of sheer gumption intrigued Kincade. On the surface, the story sounded like a simple, bottom of the page filler. Perhaps a photo of the boy standing in the hole could accompany it, but it certainly couldn't merit anything more.

Just then a knock directed the attention of the room from Kincade to the door.

Kincade's orders, had been for no interruptions aside from a true emergency, and Kelly had already breached those. Annoyed, he asked the man closest to the door to open it.

Mary Jaggers stood in the doorway and said, "Excuse me, all of you."

Kincade, clearly surprised, asked, "Mary, what can we do for you?"

"Well, sir," Jaggers said quickly, "I know why Kelly came in here – and I came in after her, to support her."

Whiting felt like gagging. Now his top columnist had turned on him, too! Things were unraveling at supersonic speed...

"Oh, I see," said Kincade. "Have you read her story?"

"Yes, I have, sir," Jaggers replied.

"And what did you think?" Kincade pressed. He had the utmost respect for Mary Jaggers. Her writing had won many awards; her column had stood the test of time. In fact, her column was the main reason *The Bulletin's* readership hadn't declined even more.

Jaggers said, "It's truly a wonderful story, sir. I know you'd like it...and so would our readers."

Kincade eyed her suspiciously. "They would, would they?"

"Yes, indeed," said Jaggers. "It's intriguing, riveting and full of heart, and if I might say so, sir, it could easily become a continuing story, and run as long as the boy keeps on digging."

The people in the room laughed at the comment. Kincade grinned. "Perhaps it could," he said. He looked straight at Kelly. "And what do *you* think, young lady?"

Kelly raised her eyebrows and said, "I've thought of that, and I'm ready to move on with follow-up articles, sir. In fact, I've already written the second one."

Kincade bellowed triumphantly, "Now, *that's* what I like in a reporter! Folks, this is exactly what we've been talking about today!"

Kincade picked up the story again and began to read the first page. After a few moments, he placed the papers back down, and turned once more to Mary Jaggers. "You truly give this story your seal of approval?"

"Indeed I do," she replied.

"Well, I like it myself, and I trust your *gut*," said Kincade, eyeing the wilting Whiting.

"My likes and your word are as good as gold to me."

Jaggers smiled, winked at Kelly, then swiftly exited the room.

Kincade turned to Whiting. "Harry, I'd like to see you in private for a few minutes during this break. As for you, Kelly, I want you to go find Nick Flanders."

"Flanders?" Kelly gasped. "Isn't he a photographer, sir?"

"Yes, he is," Kincade answered. "I want you and Flanders to go down to the site. Tell him my orders to him are to take a few photos of the hole and the boy."

"Does that mean we're running the story?" Kelly asked.

The room fell utterly still. Kincade folded his hands together on the table. This was how he used to like things, how he remembered the thrill of *the story*, and now he could see the same look he used to have, in Kelly's eyes. He liked the feeling of being *the one* in charge, and here again, he was. *Just like the old days*, he thought. He looked deeply at Kelly. *Hungry eyes. That's what's needed around here.* He was deliberately rebuking Harry Whiting with this move, he knew Whiting would be feeling foolish and humiliated in front of his peers, but Kincade didn't care—things were clearing up for him now as he envisioned the big red circled date on the calendar in his office. He'd always left story decisions to his editors in the past, he'd kept his distance somewhat, he'd prided himself in delegating, but things had been going wrong for too long now. He'd always trusted his gut in the past, that intangible that can't be measured or weighed, and this time his *gut* was speaking to him loud and clear.

"Yes," he said with finality. "We're running the story."

CHAPTER 14

Part one of Kelly's story ran at the bottom of page three, in the *Community* section of the paper. Alongside the headline, *City Boy Makes His Mark,* was a photo of Marty, standing with his shovel over his shoulder, in front of the great mound of dirt he'd produced.

It was Kelly's first time seeing her by-line for *The Bulletin.* She read the story a dozen times with the excitement that *her words, with her name,* were circulating throughout the triple-cities.

She received permission to take as many copies of that edition of the paper as she desired, and she spent the first night dishing off one copy after another to relatives and friends. It had finally happened for her, and the feeling was one of immense pleasure.

She also received several phone calls from area residents and readers who'd taken to the story and wanted more of it. Kelly was pleasantly surprised to be receiving such fanfare over *her story.* After all, a very big part of the account she'd written was pure fantasy, yet *exactly* that inspired the calls. The avid readers told Kelly she'd taken them back in time to their own youth. She heard stories from strangers who'd also believed digging to China was possible, memories of where they were when they tried, what friends tried with them and how deep they'd gotten. They were pulling for Marty, wanted him to go as deep as he could—deeper than they'd ever gone. One call after the other came in, all with the same message: They were rooting for the kid, and surprisingly, against demolishing Horace

Mann School and leveling the neighborhood homes for a new building.

The constant phone calls Kelly received brought huge amounts of attention to her desk. Staffers who'd experienced Kelly's misfortune with Whiting for two years were rooting for her as much as the community seemed to be rooting for Marty, a fact that didn't go unnoticed by the ever-present Mary Jaggers.

"Kelly, this is pretty impressive," she remarked one day. "All these calls over your story!"

"I can't believe it myself!" Kelly agreed. "These people seem to have fallen in love with this story. They all want to tell me about their own experiences digging holes to China."

Mary nodded. "Yes, it's created quite a stir."

Mary Jaggers' mind raced fast-forward. She knew a good story, and she knew the opportunity this story was spawning was happening at that very moment. Her experience in such matters had been the main factor in her own personal climb up the narrow ladder of a reporter's career. She decided mentoring Kelly was as significant as if she were writing the story herself, and she was quite content with that role.

Along with the early success of Kelly's story came the daily drama of the editorial meetings. As Kincade had requested, Harry Whiting met briefly with his boss just minutes after Kelly left the office following her editors' meeting intrusion. Harry Whiting's absence after the meeting also didn't go unnoticed. The official word was that Whiting had taken a few days off for some much needed *personal time*. In the interim, reporters were told to "find good stories" until the editors' meetings ended and some semblance of order returned. But even if all this hooplah turned out to be temporary, Kelly thought, whatever was happening had provided a huge spark the place hadn't felt in years.

The editors' meetings concluded on Thursday afternoon, but prior to leaving, many of the visiting editors stopped by Kelly's desk to deliver a variety of messages. One wished her luck, another commended her on having *guts*, while a third actually thanked her for what she'd done.

"I'm sure you have no idea what you've done for us," said Clyde Walton of the *Syracuse Herald*. "Your little interruption a few days ago sparked quite a discussion among the group. There was a real surge of energy. I could feel it, we all could."

The man looked around the room and came closer to Kelly, his voice lowering dramatically. "Your publisher was the most – impressed of us all. I've known Joel Kincade for 30 years, and I've never seen him so inspired. He's like a young reporter again."

He thanked Kelly, grabbed a copy of the edition that contained her story and headed home with the others. Kelly thanked and said good-bye to them all. She just couldn't believe the amount of good fortune now coming her way—*in droves.* She sat down to review her notes...

Some time later, one of the couriers delivered a memo: *Mandatory staff meeting for all employees, company cafeteria, tomorrow morning, 8:00 sharp.*

Kelly looked up and watched the courier drop the memo into every bin. She held the paper in her hand, especially pleased to find it signed by none other than Joel Kincade.

CHAPTER 15

At the very top of the array of character traits Joel Kincade possessed was punctuality. If a meeting was scheduled for 8:00, he didn't mean to start it at 8:01. In his world, time was everything. A paper must always get out, and another one tomorrow, and another the next day – *on time*. He had no time to dicker and dabble.

In the short span between employees receiving the memo announcing the meeting and the actual meeting itself, more rumors spred as to its nature. Some said Kincade would be announcing layoffs and needed to hold the assembly to prepare those unfortunate souls who were about to lose their jobs. Others said it was just a follow-up, to share information from the three-day editorial meetings; while others believed Harry Whiting was about to be fired, and Joel Kincade would be announcing a new editor of *The Binghamton Bulletin*.

Whatever the reason for the mandatory meeting, the energy level that surrounded it seemed to be at an all-time high, from Kelly's perspective. Even old-timers like Mary Jaggers felt the same. This was the first mandatory meeting Kelly would be attending, and the first of its kind in over two years. Something *big* was up.

The company cafeteria was the only room in the building large enough to hold all its 150 employees. A microphone had been wired upon a podium near the food service area, where Joel Kincade now stood patiently, ready to speak. He was dressed in his usual white Oxford and tie, but his shirt sleeves were rolled up just below his elbows. He'd been talking to a few staffers, and several appeared nervous and apprehensive to Kelly.

The electrician handed the microphone to Kincade, told him it was ready, and sat down in the crowd of very, very quiet people.

As Kincade began talking, Kelly noticed Harry Whiting was absent. *Maybe he has been replaced,* she thought. *After all, this is a mandatory all-staff meeting, and he should be here.* She envisioned life at *The Bulletin* without Whiting around to pick on her and pretend to be so high and mighty. *That would be great,* she thought, then turning her full and undivided attention to Joel Kincade.

"I thank you all for being here, and being here *promptly,*" Kincade began. Several people laughed as he placed the emphasis on *promptly.* "I'm not going to take up a lot of your time, after all, we do have a paper to get out."

Kincade made eye contact with many of the "older" employees, some he had even hired himself. He possessed a magnetism unlike any other man's Kelly had ever seen.

When he spoke, people felt comfortable, self-assured; they knew they'd be getting the straight stuff, right from the start. Kincade had never been known to mislead anyone, he never sugar-coated the issues. Truth, above all, he portrayed in what he stood for, how he lived his life, and how he'd expected the same from his employees in return.

"As most of you know," he continued, "over the past three days we've hosted the annual New York State Editors' Meeting. It's designed like all other meetings, really: an opportunity to learn from others sits right there at the top of the agenda.

"Now, most of you also know the current state of our company. Our ratings are down, including our circulation in both subscribers and newsstand sales. It's an oddity, actually.

Since we're the only game in town, news-wise, it's a difficult thing to fathom from the direction we've been heading in. And can you imagine where we might be if another newspaper just happened to be in town?"

Kelly nodded, as did many others. She'd thought about that from time to time as well, and asked herself the same question Kincade had just posed them.

"Well, one day, we will have a competitor," said Kincade. "There's talk of a national daily paper coming in, with big money supporting it. It sounds far-fetched, but we'd better imagine that the talk's true."

Kincade allowed a few seconds for the thought to permeate his listeners' minds.

"And if it is true, then I'd venture to say we may soon be in pretty deep you-know-what." The room filled with uneasy chuckles but fell silent as Kincade went on.

"As a matter of fact, in that case we'd have two choices to make in the matter. The first would be to stand by and do nothing, and watch the slow death of our great paper. The other would be to make some changes, pay more attention to things, and do the things a business needs to do in order to not only *survive*, but to *compete* and *thrive*. I don't know about you, ladies and gentlemen, but I choose to *compete*...and compete we will!"

Excited chatter erupted from the audience, but Kincade silenced it, saying, "That's why, starting today, we're going to begin to operate this newspaper *as if* this competitor already exists and is doing business right in our back yard."

"How are we going to do that?" called a voice from the crowd.

"Simple, really," said Kincade. "We're going to get back to the sound and solid things that worked in *my* day. We're going to hit the streets, we're going to talk to the right people, make our connections where the news is, not wait for it to come to us. What's more...we're going to be *accountable* for the stories we produce."

A giant cheer arouse from the crowd as Kincade continued to speak. The wheels turned simultaneously with his acknowledgement to the reaction. He had hoped for just this type of fervor from his people. When things settled down, he continued.

"In order for this to happen...to help snap everyone out of this...this hibernation we've been in, we're making some personnel changes." Kincade noticed the smiling faces transform into looks of sheer terror. He'd anticipated this reaction, and though his intention was to make just one vital personnel change, he thought it good for the staff to collectively feel, albeit for a few seconds, the potential loss of their employment. *This group's been needing a wake-up call,* he thought.

"I know what you're thinking," he said aloud, "but rest assured, there's only one personnel change we're making...at this time.

"You've undoubtedly noticed the absence of Harry Whiting from this meeting. Well, he's not here because he was excused from these festivities—in fact, he's been excused *permanently*. You won't see Harry back here at all, from here on."

Spontaneous applauding broke out from many in the crowd, and most loudly from the crew of reporters. But Joel Kincade held up his hand just as the first signs of clapping ensued. "There will be none of that around here," he said. "Harry Whiting is gone, and that's all you need to know. But there will be no bashing of him by anyone here— do I make myself perfectly clear?"

The buzz subsided, and even the reporting crew nodded.

"Good," said Kincade. "Then it's time to move forward, together. Effective immediately, the new editor-in-chief will be handling many of the duties Harry performed, but will be delegating many duties as well. That's because the new editor wants to concentrate one hundred percent on gathering news."

"Who's the new editor?" several people called out.

"Your new editor is a man with a long history in the news business, but who's been in sort of a quandary for years," Kincade replied. "But now he's ready to give it another try."

"So who is it?" a woman from the front row asked.

"Me," said Kincade. "*I'll* be taking over as editor-In-Chief."

In unison, the crowd stood and cheered the news. Kincade bowed gracefully as the cheering continued, a gracious ovation indeed, one he'd cherish in years to come. After a minute or so, he raised his arms to quiet the audience.

"There's much work to be done," he said. "You'll all be getting an information packet in the next few days outlining the changes we're going to attempt...and *achieve*. For now, you are all excused, with the exception of all reporters and columnists. I want to see you in the conference room in ten minutes."

Kincade looked at his watch as the crowd began to disperse. Kelly found Mary Jaggers as the two made their way to the conference room with the other reporters.

Everything had happened so suddenly; and now, Joel Kincade, the new Editor-In-Chief of *The Binghamton Bulletin,* would be conducting the first staff meeting in several months.

CHAPTER 16

Day five of the great dig had produced another six feet of depth for Marty and Brenna. They'd diligently charted their successes each day, writing down the precise depth achieved in Marty's loose-leaf notebook. His simple title, *The Hole To China*, was written neatly in black ink across the book's yellow cover.

The story written by Kelly Trapp a few days earlier had begun to draw ever-larger crowds to the dig site. Neighbors, passers-by and scores of curious outsiders had stopped to see for themselves what was occurring. The usually quiet neighborhood had taken on a new life.

Inside the hole one day, Marty began to worry for the first time. The soft earth they'd torn through the past four days had been covering a large section of jagged rocks. At the surface, most of the rocks were easily shoveled or chipped away, but below the outer edge of the smaller rocks lay larger ones. Marty and Brenna dug around some of the larger stones, then lifted them out one–by–one. Some were rather heavy, and required both children to crawl out of the hole, up the ever-steeper slope, and heave them onto the equally ever-growing pile of earth. This tired the kids quickly, taxing their strength and causing them to rest more often. This made their task not only more tiring but also very time consuming, and all of a sudden there seemed to be no end in sight to the obstacles now facing them.

A short pause for water allowed Marty to think things over. He was proud of what they'd accomplished so far. He'd actually dug a hole more than 30 feet deep, energized his neighborhood and sparked some interest among the residents. He knew the second phase of Kelly's story would be running in tomorrow's paper, and that it would probably stir up people's interest even more. His usually naive mind had begun sorting things out, thinking things through, and the rocks weren't the only obstacle concerning Marty. The books he'd borrowed from the library on China and the earth told him much more. He'd been reading and studying in his bed at night, and simply couldn't fathom what he learned. Estimates of the earth's depth from one point to its opposite point on the other side of the world were an alarming 4,000 miles. Temperatures at the earth's core were estimated to be over 5,000 degrees. The deepest hole ever dug had only descended about 10 miles. Marty wasn't quite sure how far 4,000 miles really was, or how hot 5,000 degrees could be, but he knew the numbers were way off the scale of his experience.

He thought back to a year ago, when the family had traveled to Buffalo to visit relatives. Marty recalled his father saying the trip had covered "about 200 miles." That same summer, a brief heat wave had scorched the area with several days of 100 degree weather. The local pool seemed the only relief from its clutches. Marty remembered learning in school about deserts, the hottest places on earth. He recounted Mrs. Paste's comments about "125 degree" heat. Marty grabbed his pen and paper from a drawer in his room, wrote down some numbers and calculated the best he could. But math wasn't Marty's favorite subject, and the results of his calculations seemed completely flubbed.

He estimated that, digging six feet per day, burrowing through to the other side of the earth would take him and Brenna some 10,000 years.

He checked his math a second, then a third time, then crumpled up his paper and tossed it into the waste basket at the side of his bed. He assumed the numbers were wrong—thought they had to be ridiculous—somehow he must've placed too many zeroes somewhere in the equation.

He shut off the light in his room and let his mind wander deep into the hole he'd dug.

Sure, he knew his math was probably wrong, but what if it weren't? And even if he was wrong, how far off could he been in his calculations? *Maybe this crazy idea was a mistake after all*, he thought. In no way would he ever achieve his goal at such a sluggish pace. He'd be lucky to even hit a mile by the end of the summer. He tossed and turned in his bed and played with the notion of giving up now. *I should, really—this is so impossible.* But the people, *the people, they* wanted him to keep digging now. He'd read it in Kelly Trapp's story; and what was more, he'd read it on the faces of total strangers.

For the first time in his life he'd been feeling a great sense of being *wanted*, of being counted on, of being *the one* people were rooting for. He liked the feeling too much to quit – though little did he know that his calculations had indeed been exact: On the crumpled paper lying in his wastebasket, the scribbled *10,000 years*, was right on the mark. Nor did he realize that the physical workouts his body had endured were releasing powerful chemical reactions that were stimulating both his muscles and brain to work together in harmony.

"Let's keep on digging, Brenna," Marty said, imploring his companion, *"We can do this!"* Rocks or no rocks, 4,000 miles or 40 feet, 5,000 degrees or 50 below, they'd keep on their scheduled dig, give the people what they wanted, accomplish the goal.

Marty wasn't ready to share his true feelings about their mission's impossibility with Brenna. She didn't need to know right now. On the contrary, she needed him to be strong, so he must contradict everything the two had experienced together in their young lives.

Brenna had always been there for Marty; never once had Marty needed to be there for Brenna. He liked that responsible feeling, and it gave him strength. He *did not* want this amazing feeling to go away…

On the other hand, Patricia Kent was also beginning to worry. The Kelly Trapp story had yielded uncompromising public support. She'd enjoyed the initial reaction the first account had brought, but her uncertainties now fell right in line with Marty's. She'd sensed the people bonding, the excitement of their neighborhood being in the spotlight.

Another story would be running tomorrow, more support would be forthcoming, and the kids would be under enormous pressure to continue digging against the odds.

Gary Kaschak

But who knew at this point how much more rock was hidden below? Would Marty suddenly quit, causing embarrassment to the family, the neighborhood and to Kelly Trapp? If Marty did jump ship, would Patricia's husband continually remind her of what a bad idea it had been in the first place?

Across the street from the Kents, another boy watched the attention being showered upon Marty and Brenna. He'd heard about the story in the paper and gotten his hands on a copy to see for himself. But he couldn't understand for the life of him how Marty Kent could draw the attention of so many people over such a *stupid* cause. He'd been informed that the second part of Marty's story would appear in the next edition, and though he clearly despised both Marty and the consideration he'd received, he looked forward to the article. It wouldn't take much to set this boy off, and he figured one more *goody-good* story about Marty Kent would do the trick. He tucked the paper under his arm and slowly walked towards home, snickering aloud as a devious plan began to form in his twisted young mind...

CHAPTER 17

Any limited time Scott Gardner spent reading was usually with a comic book or an edgy teen magazine. His school-books rarely emerged from his desk, and he often ignored his required reading assignments completely. Despite it all, he managed to stumble his way through school his first 13 years of life. He somehow succeeded in accomplishing far less than the minimum required by the schools, yet he was reluctantly passed through the system he so reviled, year after year.

He'd already begun smoking cigarettes; he pilfered his father's beer from the refrigerator at home; and he simply enjoyed harassing both strangers and neighbors alike.

People watched out for themselves around Scott Gardner, the master of unexpected plunder, as he thought of himself. He seemed to enjoy making anyone's life that he could miserable, rather than taking any real solace in the spoils he gained. He prided himself upon being defiant, fearless and dangerous, a most unholy combination of the worst attributes imaginable for one person to possess. He was satisfied that no one could discover even one significantly good thing about him. Even the counselors at school had been unanimous in their assessments of him. Year after year they'd recommended more counseling, scribbled notes on the side of his file indicating that bigger trouble with this boy lay ahead. They'd even "held" him back in the first grade, and since conducted numerous meetings with his parents, but nothing seemed to work. His "parental figures" must have been as bad as he was, they concluded; that was the problem, for sure.

The less-heinous acts Scott committed in earlier years were just an appetizer for later disturbances. Early on he claimed sole responsibility for soaping neighbors' windows on Halloween and tossing toilet paper into the trees, among other childish antics. The unparalleled satisfaction he got from getting away with something bad filled him with a strong desire to continue doing wrong. And later on he forked the horns of cars, pulled the fire alarm at school and broke the windows of abandoned houses and factories with rocks. The great pleasure he took committing these acts hardened into an addiction born out of the horrible circumstances surrounding his misled life. He wanted more evil – he needed more.

The Carpenters and the Morgans, the closest neighbors to Scott's shack of a house, fell victim to the worst of what he called "pranks." He used the short pocketknife he carried with him at all times repeatedly to ruin the tires of his neighbors' automobiles. A great feeling of power overcame him each time he punctured one tire, then the next, until the air around him hissed with the slow, dying sounds of hot rubber. He'd even step back to get a better look at his handiwork, like a painter or sculpture admiring his or her finished project, and he liked what he saw.

Of course, he'd never been punished by the law. There were never any witnesses to pin the crime on him, only the "biased" opinions of the Carpenter's and Morgan's, and they alone couldn't do in Scott Gardner. His father, Mike, always provided an alibi, protecting Scott from possible trouble from the authorities. That was just the way that family conducted their business, the way it had always been. Scott's father, known for his fiery temper and anti-social attitude, had earned an even worse reputation than Scott's.

He'd shared a similar path in life, only he had landed in jail on more than one occasion. *Disorderly Conduct, Drunken Driving, Disturbing the Peace* – those were only a few of the charges leveled against him. His sentences had usually been very brief, 30 days or so in the Broome County Jail; then he'd be back, despite the judge's warnings not to make life miserable for other people and to tow the line with the law. He'd been forced to accept "psychological counseling," and he became quite adept at tricking his counselors into believing he'd been rehabilitated. But at the moment his five-year probation kept him in line, at least in the public eye. Despite the dire consequences he faced if he should happen to violate his probation, he maintained a foul attitude, and couldn't care less what his only child decided to do with his life. Yet even so, he defended his son's actions, providing alibis each and every time Scott was accused of some wrong-doing. Mike Gardner was the worst possible form of human being, and an even worse father to Scott.

Right now, Scott Gardner perused the first installment of Marty's story with more fervor than he had any comic book he'd ever read. He cut out the article and tacked it to the dirty wall in his small bedroom, and commenced to carefully toss darts at Marty's picture with the ferocious appetite of a boy possessed.

He'd read each word of the article carefully, many times over, but he just didn't understand what the big fuss was all about. *City Boy Makes His Mark,* the dramatic headline screamed at him, and his skewed mind saw the story as a much different thing than it had been intended to be. He read on about Horace Mann's impending destruction, and how Marty was leaving his mark behind with his great dig.

He turned to another section of the newspaper, *Letters to The Editor,* and felt disgusted to see *each* one glowing with support for the dig. And all these old people, *A bunch of losers,* he thought, were actually egging Marty on, and imploring him to *Dig until you can't dig any more.*

After stopping to read the article still once more, Scott rose from his sour smelling bed, pulled the six darts from the wall, and then resumed his position on his mattress, taking direct and careful aim at both Marty and Brenna. *Thud, thud, thud,* the darts hit their targets over and over, until he finally grew tired of this game and disgustedly left his room.

Scott skipped down the 12 creaky stairs from the second floor two at time, creating as much noise as he could. He entered the living area and headed past his old man, who was lounging back in his sofa-chair, a beer in one hand and a cigarette in the other. "Where you going, boy?" his father shouted, not moving an inch from his relaxed position.

No reply. "I said, where you going?"

"Out," Scott said sharply, slamming the screen door behind him in a huff.

"Your mom went grocery shopping," Gardner snorted after him. "You gonna be home for supper?"

Scott paused on one of the broken stairs leading to the sidewalk. He didn't want to come home for "supper," which would be just another lousy meal thrown together by a woman who cared even less about him than his old man did.

The boy made no hurry to respond to the man. He despised his father as much or more than he hated Marty, and everyone else in the world for that matter. For as long as he could remember, he'd never seen his old man move from that chair once he got home, unless he had to eat, grab a beer, or use the bathroom. His dad never really showed any strong emotion towards Scott, just kept to himself, his television, his cigarettes and his beer. So Scott knew that when his father had asked the question, it didn't really matter to the old man where Scott was going or who he'd be seeing. His old man just didn't care.

"Naw, I'll grab something with the guys," he retorted, and off he went. He'd walk over to Larry Murphy's house, grab something to eat, hang out for the night, and probably end up sleeping over. He was the only kid he knew allowed to pull such things without getting his parents' permission. As long as he eventually returned home, that was good enough for both of those losers parents. Scott made this behavior all part of his persona, contributing to his tough-guy image, what made people so afraid of him.

And rightly so. He wore his freedom proudly, took it all the way, thought he was the coolest Joe on the block. He'd do what he wanted to, when he wanted to, and with whom he wanted to, any time he pleased.

He turned the corner off Narwood, paused to light up a half-smoked cigarette he'd been carrying in his shirt pocket and tossed his long, greasy hair awkwardly. He crossed Dewitt Street in the direction of Larry Murphy's house, just a few blocks away from his, yet worlds apart in so many ways. The Murphys' brick-rancher, situated in a modest but well manicured neighborhood, was a huge step up from Scott's dilapidated shanty. Larry Murphy had a clean room and an older sister and parents who were involved in his life.

The Murphys claimed the dubious distinction of being the only people Scott Gardner remotely respected, even though they took caution when he was around their son. Scott Gardner couldn't have known the number of times they'd sat down with their young son to warn him about associating with bullies. He also didn't know the Murphy's felt very sorry for Scott and his situation, felt as though they'd somehow been commissioned to help him. So they reluctantly allowed their son to continue his relationship with Scott – under very strict conditions:

Larry Murphy wasn't allowed to go over to Scott Gardner's house—period. (Little did the Murphy's know that no other solitary child was allowed to set foot on Scott Gardner's property, either). But unbeknownst to his parents, Larry Murphy led a double life, as a lieutenant in Scott Gardner's little army of evil. Away from home he stayed by Scott's side come hell or high water, taking orders, doing the master's bidding. He played the role of bystander as Marty Kent endured being pushed around, and he laughed along with all the others in Scott's mob, at Marty's expense. Yet unbeknownst to Scott Gardner, Larry Murphy was beginning to tire of all this, though was just too afraid to admit it. He knew that if he 'fessed up to Scott Gardner, he'd become another of Scott's victims. But the choice was his to make, just as the others in Scott Gardner's ugly world had to decide: Simply be part of giving misery, or be part of receiving it.

Scott reached the door of the Murphy household and saw Larry's mother through the screen door puttering in the kitchen. "Hey, Mrs. Murphy," he called, "is Larry home?" The pretty woman, who was churning a bowl of batter in her hands, eyed Scott, her heart racing at the mere sight of him.

She said nothing at first, scrambling to think of some excuse to say her son couldn't come out. But Scott was too quick for her. "Whaddaya makin' there?" he asked, sniffing at the aroma wafting across two rooms from the bowl. "Smells pretty good."

"Cake," Mrs. Murphy said softly. "Vanilla cake. It's Larry's favorite."

"Mine too," said Scott. He was playing a game—a game he usually won. He was good at two things: making life miserable for selected individuals, and making other more vulnerable types feel sorry for him. He took a second whiff and smiled broadly.

Uneasily, Mrs. Murphy sighed, "Well, perhaps you could have a slice later on." And even more reluctantly she added, "Maybe you could stay for dinner."

She rebuked herself silently just then, alarmed at how easily she'd fallen victim to this ploy. But it was too late to take anything back. She'd offered, and she knew he'd accept it.

"That'd be great!" Scott said. "That is, as long as Larry boy wants me to stay."

Scott spotted Larry coming down the stairs from his bedroom. Larry opened the door and stepped outside. They greeted each other with their "secret" hand salutation and walked towards the street together. Mrs. Murphy spoke out to remind the boys that dinner would be in about an hour; then she turned back towards her kitchen chores, to prepare the meal.

"Your mom is really cool," said Scott. "She treats me kinda good."

Larry smiled at the comment. He hadn't recalled Scott Gardner even once paying anyone a compliment. He perked up at the notion that maybe Scott Gardner might have a good side and maybe it would begin to show more often.

"Yeah, she's pretty cool most of the time I guess," Larry said. "Whaddaya want to do until supper?"

Scott smiled deviously. He put his arm around Larry's shoulder and began to walk slowly down the street before letting him go.

Scott spat into the street and asked, "Have you been reading about Marty Kent in the papers?"

"Yeah, actually I have," Larry responded.

"Whaddaya think of all that garbage about him diggin' a hole to China? I always thought that kid was a bit off, but this is ridiculous."

Larry looked at Scott whose face had now contorted into a look of sheer hatred.

Sure, Larry'd read the article. The whole town was talking about it. His own parents had even written a letter to the editor, and they were planning on visiting the site to encourage Marty. They thought the story was cute, and looked forward to future updates.

They'd even asked their son what he'd though about "a classmate of his being in the papers."

Larry took a moment before answering Scott. "I guess it's kinda stupid. "I mean, nobody can dig a hole to China, do you think?"

Scott Gardner sensed his friend's hesitation. "Of course you can't dig a hole to China! If it could be done, it already would've been done. Nobody's ever done it and nobody ever will, especially not that fat kid, Marty Kent."

"I guess not," said Larry.

"Yeah, and to make sure he doesn't, I've got a *plan*," said Scott.

"A plan?"

"Yeah, a plan," Scott said quietly. He huddled close to Larry. "You, me, and the others—we're gonna see to it that he never makes it to China, or even goes another foot lower."

The bully resumed walking down the street, at a slow, methodical pace. He urged Larry to join him at his side; then with great animated motions, he began to verbalize to his friend the plan his devious mind had concocted.

CHAPTER 18

In the early hours of the next morning, Scott Gardner glanced at his watch and rose from the guest bed in Larry Murphy's room. He went across the room and shook Larry roughly. "It's 1:30," he announced quietly, "time to get moving."

Larry Murphy lay motionless for a moment, his hands clasped behind his head, his eyes staring blankly at the ceiling, exhausted, but alert. He just didn't share the zeal Scott Gardner seemed to possess at the moment. In fact, he'd been contemplating the situation over and over for the past few hours, knowing that every tick of the clock was drawing him closer to the time Scott Gardner had chosen to close down Marty Kent's newfound stardom.

"Hey, get up, lazy," Scott whispered, nudging Larry sharply on his left leg. "We've got to get going—*now*."

Larry rolled from his bed and gently placed his feet on the wood floor. He decided that the battle occupying his mind had to go into brief retreat for the time being. He fingered his long black hair into place, laced up his sneakers and gently eased open the window of his second floor bedroom. He motioned for Scott to go first through the opening; then he followed quietly and gracefully. He eased the window back into place, then took the same route Scott Gardner had just seconds earlier and silently jumped the final six feet onto safe ground.

The boys cautiously wedged against the house a small ladder they'd earlier removed from the garage, to ensure their return would be as successful as their departure. They made their way around the back of the house, choosing to cut through the neighboring woods so as not to draw suspicious glances from any curious neighbor. Their dark clothing served as perfect camouflage against the bright, full moon, their smooth motions blending in with the stillness brought on by the early morning hour. The boys headed towards a chosen spot in the woods where they'd earlier been. They removed a pile of branches they'd previously assembled, tossing twigs and boughs to either side.

When the short work was over, each boy reached down and retrieved a dark shovel lying amongst the leaves and dirt. Larry pulled a pair of brown garden gloves out from under the shovels, jamming them into his back pockets.

"What are those for?" asked Scott.

"What? The gloves?" replied Larry. "For my hands, I don't want to get any blisters, you know."

"What a wimp!" declared Scott.

The dirt path of the woods led directly to Schubert Street, where the other boys already waited within the safety of the woods. They looked up and noticed the two now approaching; simultaneously they rose from seats they'd chosen on a fallen old oak tree. All remained incredibly quiet; the circumstances called for that. They spoke a few brief words to each other, then turned in the direction of College Street, hugging the edge of the woods and staying well out of range of the street-lamps as they went.

Scott Gardner led the way, his shovel perched over his right shoulder like a soldier carrying his rifle. The five other boys mimicked him, and under the light of the moon resembled a small platoon on patrol. They briskly crossed through all the shortcuts they'd discovered over the years, and came out on the east side of Recreation Park. They whisked their way across the Horace Mann school playground, and climbed over a broken fence next to Marty Kent's house. From there, they spotted the huge mound of earth lying ominously still in the dark. They crept closer towards the pile for a better look, then together knelt a few feet away from the gaping hole in the earth.

"I had no idea it was this big," commented one of the boys. A few others shook their heads, equally astonished at the sight. The large mound of earth withdrawn from the 30 foot cavity was truly something to behold, and the hole's width appeared more than eight feet across. The hole's actual depth proved to be the only thing none of the boys knew for certain. They'd read in the papers about it descending at least 30 feet, but the darkness of the hour shrouded the fissure like a deep, dark secret.

"Hey Larry, toss a stone down there," Scott commanded. "Let's see how deep it is."

Larry Murphy did as bid, bending down to look at the large assortment of rocks within the great mound of earth beside him. He selected one that fit fairly well inside his hand and dropped it into the hole. The other boys gathered at the rim, their young ears tuned into any noise that might signal to them the approximate depth.

A faint, cushiony noise cut off the rock's descent a few seconds later. Larry grabbed a larger rock this time, needing two hands to lug it over to the rim, then rolled it down the side.

"That took about three seconds," said one of the boys. "That's pretty darn deep."

"Shut up!" responded Scott. "Just grab your shovels and start filling up that hole."

The boys immediately obeyed. They soon discovered this was a fairly simple task, at least in the beginning. After all, Scott reasoned, filling in a hole was certainly far easier than digging one out, and with six pairs of hands doing the work, the great mound of earth that Marty and Brenna had diligently struggled to remove from the ground would be replaced in the whole shortly.

But the job wasn't that easy after all. After nearly 90 minutes of tedious toil, Scott Gardner dropped to his knees, squinting his eyes against the backdrop of the full moon.

He could barely make anything out inside the deep hole, but he did manage to see the extent of their progress. By his estimates, they'd filled in only about a third of the giant pit, and would need roughly another three hours to complete the job. He glanced at his watch. *At this rate, won't finish until 6:30,* he thought angrily.

Amidst it all, Larry Murphy paused to look up at Marty Kent's bedroom window, the light out, the shade drawn. He removed his garden gloves, using them to wipe the sweat from his brow. He really had no quarrel with Marty, and had actually begun to feel a small amount of pity for him, despite having been actively involved in bullying Marty.

With every shovel of dirt he tossed into the hole, he felt more distanced, more removed from the real world. He truly couldn't believe he was participating in such a heinous deed, and as he looked into the faces of his buddies, he wondered if they, too, felt the same. But he was in too deep at this point, no turning back from what they were now executing, this horrible act against a good kid's dream. He took his eyes away from Marty's window, then tossed another shovel full of dirt into the ever-closing hole.

"We need to dig faster!" whispered Scott Gardner.

"We *can't* dig any faster!" replied one of the boys rather loudly.

"You're being too loud!" Scott exclaimed. "Someone might hear us! And you *can* dig faster – just do it!"

For the next half hour, the group of young boys continued at a much more furious, brisk pace, their young bodies somehow able to withstand the punishment brought on by the rigorous exercise. Then Scott Gardner took another look inside the hole, feeling slightly better. They'd gained perhaps another four or five feet in a short time. He then announced to the boys: "Another ten minutes oughta finish it for tonight!" And as his voice echoed softly to break the silence of the night, the first dog began to bark.

The boys froze in their tracks, startled. The lone dog continued to howl, and his incessant barking only served to set off a chain reaction amongst the neighborhood canines. One by one, the chorus of heavy baying and yelping rang throughout the area, followed by the front porch light of the Johnsons' house flicking on. The Johnson home, whose back yard contained the dog who'd first begun to bark, sat directly across the street from where the boys stood. And just then old man Johnson emerged from the house, with his old German Shepherd, *Spike,* preceding him.

The boys were quite familiar with *Spike,* "that old *blind dog*" they'd called him.

Though none of the boys knew Spike's actual age, they were well aware of his keen senses of sound and smell despite his loss of sight. They'd seen the old pooch stumble into things on occasion, and staring at the opaqueness of his cataracts could be quite spooky. They felt fairly secure in their position across the street that the old dog wouldn't be able to catch their scent, and that old man Johnson could do little to see, hear, or pursue them, either.

But when Ned Fairly, the neighbor to the exact left of the Johnsons', emerged from *his* house, the boys grew more apprehensive. They watched the two men exchange a few words, then carefully cross the street, as *Spike* pulled forward on his short leash.

Though the boys weren't altogether sure they'd been spotted, they panicked and scattered, like a flock of birds leaving a watering hole that was being spooked by a predator. They grabbed their shovels, ran as fast as they could towards the fence on the side of the house, slid their shovels underneath, and scaled the short fence, jumping to the safety of the other side. In the short time needed for the six boys' escape, Ned Fairly and old man Johnson and his dog had barely made it across the street, their eyes still adjusting to the darkness of the hour.

"Did you see 'em?" yelled the older man.

"No, no, not really," answered Ned Fairly. "It's too dark."

"What do you think they were doing in the Kents' backyard?" Johnson asked.

"Let's go find out," said Fairly.

They raised the latch of the metal fence that circled the Kents' house and strode toward the direction of the hole, snooping around as best they could. Neither man had thought to bring a flashlight along, and only the full moon provided illumination.

"Nothing seems out of order here," exclaimed the old man, taking one last look around him.

"Oh, yes it does," countered Fairly, spotting something awry. "Come look at this."

They walked the perimeter of the great hole and gasped in horror at the massive mound of dirt to its side – it was now only half its original height and width. They could see that the rest must have been dumped back into the hole.

"Who would do such a thing?" asked old man Johnson.

"Low lifes," said Fairly. "I understand the Kent boy gets picked on all the time at school. Probably something to do with that."

They shook their heads, disgusted at what they saw.

"Should we call the police?" asked Johnson.

103

"Probably should," Ned replied. He crouched at the side of the hole, reached down and retrieved something off the ground.

"What's that?" asked the old man.

"A garden glove," said Ned feeling the rough fabric in his hand. "And it's still warm..."

Back inside Recreation Park, the boys stopped for a few minutes, catching their collective breath. Here an exhausted Larry Murphy noticed for the first time that he was missing one of his garden gloves. He searched his pockets, acting as calm as possible around the others. He glanced back at the path he'd taken to this point, sure he'd probably dropped the glove along the way. An uneasy feeling about the whole ordeal crept over him. He'd really not enjoyed any part of this *sport* he and the other boys had participated in, and now he'd lost one of his gloves along the way.

His mind raced with all the bad possibilities he could muster. These were his father's garden gloves, the one and only pair he used just about every day of his life to tinker with some vegetable or weed on his perfectly maintained property. Larry thought he'd simply toss the other glove away, but his father would notice right away that it was missing, so that idea was out of the question. He could go down to the hardware store in the morning, buy a new pair and place them in the shed, but his dad would certainly discern that it was a fresh pair of gloves and wonder where they came from and why they'd appeared.

Hey, maybe someone would find the distinctive glove and give it to the police as evidence, easily implicating Larry with undeniable proof of his mischief. Maybe he'd get arrested, maybe *The Bulletin* would run a new story on what a bad guy *he* was, maybe he'd get punished *for life*. The only logical action he could think of would be to retrace his steps to the property in the morning, making sure to tell no one of his plan. Chances were pretty good he could recover the glove, but the chances that he'd dropped it all the way back at the hole scared him like before.

"What's the matter with you?" Scott asked Larry, slinging his arm around his buddy's shoulder. "You don't look too good."

"I'm fine, just a little stomach-ache," said Larry. "Probably something I ate. I think I should go home."

The other boys indicated they wanted to go home, too; they turned to their leader, who nodded his consent "Yeah, let's get going before somebody sees us," Scott said.

The boys precariously brushed off as much dirt as they could from their clothing, then gathered their shovels. From there, the four boys from the second group bid farewell to Scott and Larry, each promising the other they'd never tell a soul about the night's events.

Scott Gardner turned down the dirt path of the woods towards Larry Murphy's house.

"Wait!" said Larry. "I think I should go home alone. I'm really not feeling well."

Scott eyed his protégé. He didn't like what he was hearing; he wasn't used to any of his gang members telling *him* what to do. He tried to look into Larry's eyes, but Larry was clutching his stomach, nearly doubled-over and kneeling on the ground. Seconds later, Larry heaved long and hard, coughing and gagging, and then he heaved some more.

When he was finished, he rose from his feet, and wiped off the corners of his mouth with his dirty shirt.

Scott said, "Yeah, maybe you'd better go on without me." He sounded sincere, but he wasn't about to play nursemaid for anyone. His time was more valuable than that.

Instead, he'd go on home, climb the stairs to his bedroom, throw on his headphones, and listen to some rock music, no questions asked by either of his parents. His dad, of course, would be passed out on his lounge chair, his mother, would be still be asleep for hours, alone in her bedroom...

Larry Murphy was feeling no better as he rounded the final portion of the path leading to his house. He placed both shovels back into the tool shed, then climbed the short ladder to the garage roof, turned and carefully lifted the top of the ladder, and carried it around the other side of the roof. He pushed the ladder into a patch of soft earth, turned back towards his bedroom, then slowly lifted the window before climbing in. He closed the window, removed his dirty clothing, and slid into bed, his mind still troubling about that lost glove.

A few tears streamed down his face as the consequences of his actions began to take their toll. He'd taken part in the cruelest of jokes, and for that, he was truly sorry. His involvement, his role in it all, brought the ache back to his stomach. He couldn't go to sleep, he tossed and turned till full daylight, at times crying some more. He wondered, as he finally escaped into a fitful dream, if he'd be able to find his lost glove, and how Marty Kent would react to his filled-in hole.

CHAPTER 19

Kelly Trapp was up a few hours earlier than usual. The excitement of seeing her work in print brought her a childlike eagerness, a certain awe, an almost surreal feeling that at times required her to pinch herself to see if it truly was happening.

She'd arranged with a local paperboy a special delivery of the edition to her apartment. She'd explained to him who she was, and that she'd like to see the paper before heading off to work. She tipped him a few dollars, and that was that. Money talked at all levels.

By 8 a.m., she'd already downed three cups of coffee. At 8:10, she'd dressed and walked outside, looking up and down Clinton Street for any sign of the paperboy. At 8:15, she finally saw him turn the corner towards her, his heavy *Bulletin* sack weighing him down on one side.

"Morning Miss Trapp," he said alertly. "Got your paper, right here."

He pulled a copy from his ink-stained bag and handed it to her proudly, feeling special that he was the one delivering the paper to Kelly Trapp. He smiled as she opened to the section of her story.

"I read the story before I started out," he said, catching her off-guard. "I liked it a lot. I'm going over with some friends later on to see the hole. It's all pretty cool, you know."

Kelly thanked him as he breezed past her to continue delivering his route. She trotted down the narrow sidewalk to her front porch, then settled down onto a summer chair she'd earlier pulled out to sit on.

Her wide eyes told all. She scanned the story once, then twice, before setting it down on the table in front of her. She picked it up again, and read it more slowly, like the pace of the average reader. Her smile was not masked. In particular, she loved the title, *His Hole To China,* and the fact that very little of the original copy had been tampered with by the editors. Also quite favorable was the article's position in the *Community* section.

After all, this was a story about a local boy, and it belonged in *Community.* Kelly would need to take things one step at a time, she reminded herself. Her thoughts turned to Harry Whiting, and a shudder suddenly crept up her back.

She retreated into her small apartment, and placed the newspaper into the top drawer of a desk situated in her living room. She pulled out a file she'd started marked *China,* and frantically began writing more notes about her piece. Her zeal and personal interest in the events, even the appeal the locals had shown, would not be enough to sustain the story. Her instincts had not been dulled by the sudden stardom she'd received. The story needed a new twist to it, something more to keep the people interested. She brainstormed just then, searching for some small tidbit of information to send her into a new direction.

One thought after another crossed her active mind.

She began writing her ideas down on paper, then scribbled out the words before starting again. Nothing with any merit seemed to come to her. She dropped her pen down on the desk and watched it roll off the edge, its slow movement across the wood, its sudden and abrupt descent to the floor. She reached down to the carpet to retrieve it, when the ringing of the telephone on the desk startled her.

She placed her hands over her heart, allowing the phone to continue ringing. *Eight – forty five,* she thought to herself. *Probably someone from work.*

"Hello," she said calmly after picking up the receiver.

"Kelly, it's Patricia," the frantic voice brought the look of concern to Kelly's face. "So sorry to be bothering you so early in the morning."

Kelly quickly placed the voice. A hundred images quickly flashed through her mind-a hundred "what ifs." And the tone, that horrible sound associated with doom, this was apparent in Patricia Kent's quivering, high-pitched voice.

"Patricia, what's wrong?" asked Kelly. "Did something happen?"

"Kelly…I, I…" she stammered.

"Slow down," Kelly said. "Tell me what happened."

Kelly could hear sobbing on the other end. Patricia sniffled into the receiver, then blew her nose loudly. The few seconds of waiting to know the reason for the call were killing Kelly. She raised her voice a little louder this time.

"Patricia, is Marty OK?" she asked.

"Yes, yes, he's not hurt or anything like that, but he's certainly not O. K," Patricia said through sobs. "He's outside by the hole with Brenna."

Kelly was relieved Marty wasn't hurt, but Patricia had just said he wasn't OK. Her curiosity was piqued.

"Try to calm down and tell me what is wrong," Kelly said as composed as she could.

"It's the hole," Patricia said. "We just got back into town a few minutes ago, and the hole…"

"What about the hole?" asked Kelly.

"It's not a hole anymore," Patricia said. "It's all filled in, at least half of it. That's how they found it this morning."

"*What?*" Kelly said incredulously. "How could the hole be half filled–in? It was over thirty feet deep yesterday."

"I don't know," Patricia cried. "We're trying to sort that out right now."

"Who is?" asked Kelly.

"The police, a few neighbors, actually, the numbers keep growing. There's lots of people from the neighborhood here."

Kelly pictured Scott Gardner just then. She pictured the other boys the day they pushed Marty around in the Park. Her blood began to boil, and her breathing came faster.

She soon grew beyond perturbed.

"Well, what do you thing happened?" Kelly asked.

"I think a bunch of boys snuck into the yard last night sometime, and filled the hole up with dirt," Patricia replied. There's plenty of sneaker tracks all around the area."

"What's your husband think?"

"He's pretty angry about it. In fact, I can't remember a time when I've seen him so upset."

The conversation continued for a few moments, then Kelly agreed to meet Patricia at her house in 20 minutes. She hurriedly dressed for work, raced to her car and headed for the Kents', all the while dreading what she'd soon be seeing first hand. She had her third installment now, a no-brainer. She'd interview the Kents, have the *Bulletin* photographer take a new photo of the filled in hole, and share with the locals what had happened to *The Hole To China*.

Kelly sped well past the posted limits, nearly causing an accident along the way. She parked as close as she could to the Kents' house, then trotted several yards before reaching the property. The size of the crowd that met her—probably 60 or 70 people—was astonishing, and she pushed her way towards the hole, where all the buzzing between the police and the neighbors took place.

She hugged Patricia the moment they spotted each other, had a few words with her, then turned her attention to the hole. Although she'd shared in the heartbreak the Kents were feeling, her reporter's instincts told her this new set of circumstances would make a great follow-up story. There'd be time for her to interview the police—get some sort of statement from them, to find out if there were any witnesses, and speak to them as well.

This was a golden opportunity, the perfect chance to take the story to the next level, a chance to make an even greater impression on the people of Binghamton.

"I'm Kelly Trapp of *The Bulletin*," she said to one of the two police officers. She pulled out her press pass, waved it in front of his face, then placed it back inside her wallet. "I'd like to ask a few questions, if you don't mind."

"O.K.," said the officer.

"Do you have any ideas as to who did this…this *cruel* act?" Kelly frowned.

"No, no we don't," said the officer matter-of-factly.

"Did anyone here see anything?" Kelly asked.

"A couple of the neighbors, Mr. Johnson and Mr. Fairly saw something early this morning," replied the officer. "And they found this glove near the hole."

He dangled the glove in front of her face, holding it by the tip of the thumb.

Kelly eyed the accessory with interest. "That's pretty strong evidence," she said. "Do you know whose glove it is?"

"No, we don't," said the officer. "We may never know."

"Why not?" asked Kelly.

"Mr. Kent here doesn't want to blow this thing out of proportion. He's not interested in any more publicity."

Kelly thanked the officer, looked around for Donald Kent, and finally found him having some laughs with a few of his buddies.

"Is it true?" she said, interrupting his conversation.

"Is what true?" he asked, a bit surprised at her intervention.

"That you have no interest in who the owner of that glove is?"

"That's right," he said.

"Why not?" Kelly yelled.

"Look," he said sternly. "Up until now, I was happy just letting Marty dig his hole, see how far he'd get. This changes everything now."

"Why's that?" she asked.

"I know my son, know him better than anyone," said Donald. "Sooner or later he'd give up on this thing, he'd quit digging in a few more days. This just speeds up the process of ending the thing."

"I can't believe you're saying that," Kelly retorted. She thought back to the librarian, Mrs. Springer, scolding her on her closed-minded attitude toward Marty digging to China.

"Why don't you let him give up on his own terms?" Kelly offered.

Donald Kent didn't particularly like being challenged, and Kelly Trapp had gone too far with her badgering now. He excused himself from his friends, took her by the arm and walked her several feet away from the others.

"Miss Kent, let me lay the facts out for you, the real simple facts," he started.

"Number one, Marty has never finished anything worthwhile, period. He's quit Little League, Pee-Wee football, basketball, swimming, you name it, he's quit it. Number two, he wants to dig a

111

hole to China—*a hole to China*, can you believe it? And you, you and the others are actually encouraging him, *encouraging him* to complete the most far-fetched fairy-tale of them all."

"Number three," he went on, "we're leaving here in a matter of weeks. All this publicity and attention, none of it matters when you get right down to it, because when the dust clears and all your stories are written, we'll be out of here, gone, gone for good, and who will care about Marty then?"

Patricia had paid complete attention to all her husband had just said. She'd noted the intolerable tone, the attitude, the disgrace. She couldn't believe he'd felt this way towards his son—*his only child*, she thought. She watched as he folded his arms and stuck out his chest in a proud display. Why? Couldn't he see the injustice he was doing to Marty, the incredible lack of parenting and nurturing and emotional distress he was causing? Why didn't he have the desire to chase down these criminals, physical evidence and all?

"Mr. Kent," Kelly began. "You may think you know Marty, and you may think you know what's best for him, and you may turn away from this impossible quest to dig a hole to China, and you may simply stop fighting the fight because you feel sorry for yourself, but let's get one thing straight here.

"Look around you, Mr. Kent. You have neighbors who care, despite the fact your home will soon be gone. You have a son, who by all accounts, has endured several years at the hands of these bullies, who has found something he's truly interested in, who in his youthful exuberance has touched a nerve in the community. And now you want to take it all away, simply because you think you already know the outcome. Let me tell you something, Mr. Kent. You never know what's going to happen, you never know how things will turn out, you never know even when you think you do. You want to rob Marty of this little slice of fame. Fine. As for me, I'm getting into this story, taking it all the way. I'll find out who these people were who filled in the hole, but we all know who they are, don't we, Mr. Kent?"

She stormed off just then, returning to the police to ask a few more questions. Donald Kent remained behind, and though he appeared cool on the outside, he contemplated all Kelly Trapp had just told him, all the bittersweet truths about his relationship with his

---

The Hole To China

son. He'd never been spoken to in such a manner before, never been challenged and told those things. He was angry with Kelly, but he admired her for the raw gumption she'd just displayed.

He walked across the yard to rejoin his neighbors, carefully hiding his feelings beneath the rough exterior he so carefully managed to maintain. He watched as Kelly made her way from person to person, eager to find out more of what had happened here.

A pit in his stomach formed just then, *a feeling of guilt,* he thought. *That peculiar physical response to an emotional episode.* He pursed his lips, rubbed his hand across his chin, peered at the people around him. He wasn't sure, but he felt a bit different than he had before. The coldness of his attitude towards Marty seemed slightly thawing out, confusing him, and he began to question himself with the challenge brought on by Kelly Trapp's onslaught.

Perhaps I've been too rough on the boy, he thought. *Perhaps I should be more supportive of him in his ridiculous dig to China.*

113

114

CHAPTER 20

The next morning a thunderstorm ripped through the area, pelting the earth with a relentless barrage of rain. Forecasters predicted only a short stay for the front, promising clear weather within 24 hours. Cool, dry weather would follow, and low humidity would prevail for several days thereafter. What *was to be* was exactly what had gone through Marty Kent's mind as he looked at the falling rain out his bedroom window. He could hardly believe his digging had ended so abruptly; and now, watching the water and the mud and the lightning, he simply wondered what awful thing would happen next in his miserable life.

He pushed himself away from the window and trudged downstairs, where a few neighbors sat visiting his mother. They'd seen first hand the nasty work of the intruders, and offered their assistance in any way possible. Marty saw that they were reading the newspaper, and his mother waved him over to the group.

"Look, dear, here's a copy of Kelly's latest story," she said. "It's very good. Maybe you'd like to read it."

"No, thanks, Mom," Marty said. "Maybe later."

His mother forced a smile, as did the other women at the table. Marty, feeling slightly antisocial, went back up to his room, closed the door, and started drawing pictures of holes.

"I'm worried about him," Patricia said. "He's always getting stepped on by the other kids. I don't know what to do."

"What we ought to do is find those boys who did this to him and make them dig the hole back out," said Cindy Fairly, Ned's wife.

"I second that," said Martha Davis," holding her coffee cup up in agreement.

Patricia smiled at her friends, appreciating their concern. *Only concern alone won't be enough*, she thought. Marty's fragile personality had been shattered, and her husband's decision to just let it all go without a fight was the biggest setback of them all. This was a decision the women at the table knew all too well, that Donald Kent was *The Man*, and what he said about anything was *final*.

"Maybe it's a good thing we'll be moving away," Patricia said rhetorically. "Maybe a change of scenery will do Marty some good."

The women looked at the article Kelly Trapp had written once more. *Vandals Ruin Boy's Dig* in large bold print, a photograph of the half-filled hole next to it, another photo of the one missing glove running alongside the first. Kelly Trapp had done an outstanding job on the piece, even indicated the Kents had no interest in "pursuing" the culprits, or filing any charges against the guilty once they'd been caught. But the story affected the community much differently. In fact, Patricia had received dozens of phone calls, some from friends and family, but most from total strangers. The people were upset, *very upset,* she thought. Most of them wanted a full-scale search to find those responsible, to find the owner of the missing glove. Each told Patricia how sorry they felt that Marty had lost his summer adventure. *This support will make it even more difficult to leave here,* Patricia thought.

Back at the factory where Donald Kent worked, the reaction of his colleagues paralleled what Patricia Kent had received at home. All day long, he'd heard pity in the people's voices, the anger and concern, and he was pleasantly surprised. In his mind, this digging of a hole to China was just a child's silly game; but the fact that all his co-workers had shown so much concern, and that he'd been so criticized by Kelly Trapp, set him to seriously pondering the whole ordeal. His fellow workers wanted the perpetrators caught, too, wanted them taught a lesson, even arrested.

More opinions and gossip abounded on the matter than on anything he could remember. Even his ever-tough boss, Carl Morris, had suggested some "time off, until the boy feels better." Of course,

Donald Kent refused such a ridiculous offer. He didn't feel his missing work would help his son cope with the problem any better. It was just another one of those "tests," one of those "setbacks of life," he thought. Marty would just have to handle it his own way.

The reaction at *The Binghamton Bulletin* was everything the Kents were experiencing at home and work, only on the grandest of scales. The switchboard operator couldn't keep up with the volume of phone calls. From early morning when the story first hit the homes, through the mid-afternoon hours, one angry call after the other came in. At first, Kelly was able to field the early calls, but reverted to hand-written messages by 11:00. By 4:00 p.m., more than a hundred messages were piled on her desk, and the calls were still coming in.

Joel Kincade had noticed the barrage of calls early on. He hadn't remembered anything quite like it before. *This is great for business,* he thought. He pondered how to keep the story alive, even for a while. Reactions like this were rare in the newspaper world, and they needed to keep the story going forward. He picked up the phone in his office and called the front desk.

"Carla," he said softly to one of the receptionists, "would you please send Kelly Trapp back to my office?"

"Certainly, sir, right away," the operator replied.

Kelly received the request a few minutes later. She dropped a pile of messages down on her desk, then picked them up once more. She'd want Joel Kincade to see first hand the number of responses pouring in. She stuffed them into an envelope and headed for his office.

"Kelly, please come in," Kincade said. "Have a seat."

"Have you seen what's going on today?" Kelly asked. She slipped the pile of notes out of her envelope and held them up for Kincade to see.

"Yes, I've heard the commotion today," Kincade answered. "That's why I called you in."

Kelly sat down across from Kincade. The feeling she'd always felt in his presence couldn't escape her now, only this time she felt more sure of herself. She'd always been confident in her abilities, but she'd finally had the chance to prove herself, and she'd passed that first significant test with flying colors.

"This story in today's paper," Kincade began, "it's gotten the people in a tizzy.

They're all angry at what's happened. You've struck a real strong emotion here. It's a pity the story couldn't continue on its original course. All the way to China, I might add."

The two chuckled for a moment, then Kincade continued.

"That's where the difference between good writing and good reporting comes in," he said firmly. "The course of this story has definitely taken a turn—a big turn I might add."

"What are you suggesting I do?" asked Kelly.

"I'm suggesting you follow what it provides you," Kincade suggested. "By the looks of things, this story is over. Oh, the people are upset and all, they want justice, some closure. But the story, the actual *story* of the hole to China, has ended."

"If that's true, then what should I be looking for?" asked Kelly.

"Young lady, the first two parts of your story you mentioned eminent domain, did you not?"

"Yes, yes, I did mention it."

"Have you uncovered any additional information on the subject?"

"No, not yet," Kelly said, "I haven't really had the time to…"

He cut her off, raising his right hand in the air like a traffic cop. She knew right away she'd said something he didn't want to hear, and she wanted to take it all back. Instead, she sat quietly and listened intently as he dropped his hand and squinted his eyes at her.

"Follow the trail," he said through a faint smile. "You might be surprised at what you find."

"I'm not sure what you're trying to say, sir," Kelly said, confused. "Are you saying you want me to drop the *Hole To China* part of the story and get more information on Eminent Domain?"

"Something like that," Kincade deadpanned. "Now go find where the story takes you."

Kelly rose from her chair and thanked her boss for seeing her. She wanted to please him, but she couldn't understand how writing about Eminent domain would keep the *Hole to China* story alive, how the new twist could hold the interest of the people as well as the original story somehow had. She held out her hand, and as Kincade took it in his, he said, "Kelly, this story may not be over quite yet. I have a feeling in *my gut* that something big is still going to happen, is still going to keep it alive. But the more you dig and pry and ask questions, the more you'll discover how many directions a story can go. Even one that, from the outside looking in, appears to be over."

The big smile on Kelly's face said it all. She nearly sprinted to her desk to review the notes from the people, and scribbled a memo to herself: the words, *Eminent domain,* underlined three times.

CHAPTER 21

The pelting rain from the previous day had given way to what the forecast had promised. The sun rose slowly, like a giant ball of red into the sky, the instant penetration of light revealing the damage done by the earlier storm.

Donald Kent stared out his kitchen window at the hole. He noticed a few fallen tree branches strewn about the yard, but saw first the mud around the hole. The storm had produced one big globby mess, and would probably need a few good days of continuous sunshine to harden back up. He thought about the big mess, but knew there was no sense pondering such matters for long. In a matter of weeks, everything would be gone, all leveled for the new school. He raised his cup of coffee to his lips, sipping the hot liquid slowly. He stepped outside to gather the newspaper, sniffed the comfortable air around him, then decided to remain on the front porch and enjoy the quiet morning with his paper and his coffee.

Although this was Saturday, his day off, he'd risen earlier than usual. He'd tossed and turned the night before, his mind processing so many things at once. He'd thought of his athletic injury, his promising career, his son and wife, the *Hole to China*, and eminent domain. He thought about the reactions of the people at work, how they so wanted retribution for what had been done here, and how he didn't see things quite as they did.

He thought of the loneliness he felt sleeping unaccompanied, and wished he could just go back in time, back to that baseball field, back to that fateful *slide.*

Upstairs in the master bedroom, Patricia Kent spent the same kind of sleepless night as her husband. The same thoughts occupied her mind, yet she perceived them much differently. She and Donald had differing views on Marty, and it was he who had both kept them together, and at the same time kept them apart. Such was the irony of the times. Divorce was rare in the 60's, and society gave it little or no acceptance. Patricia and Donald Kent, though they tried their best to deny it, were on course for a long and unhappy marriage.

Early in the morning, Patricia crept over to Marty's room and cracked the door open.

He was fast asleep, his slight snoring bringing a smile to his mother's face. She slowly closed the door and headed to the kitchen, and was surprised to see the light on and a pot of coffee already brewed. She looked around for her husband, heard the rustling of newspapers on the front porch, and headed out to his location with coffee in hand.

"Morning," she said blandly.

"Morning," he replied, not looking up from his reading material.

"Beautiful day today," Patricia said.

"Looks that way," Donald muttered.

She pulled up a chair next to him and grabbed a section of the paper to read. Her eyes glanced from story to story, looking for anything at all to do with *The Hole.* She'd liked the attention the story had brought to Marty, and longed for it to continue. She knew, however, that the moment was nearly over, that the people would probably lose interest in a few days, and life would go back to being mundane for her.

"Can I see that section?" she asked her husband.

"Sure," he said, and handed her the front page.

Her eyes dropped to the bottom of page one, where the headline, *People Want Justice in Hole to China Crime, by Kelly Trapp,* jumped off the page at her. "Did you see this?" she asked her husband. "They've got a bunch of quotes from all these people." She opened to page four, where a half-dozen head shots of local people featured their corresponding anecdotes. People she'd never seen or heard of, a mix of young and old, black and white, rich and poor, all had been asked the same question: "What do you think should be done with the Hole to China?" Patricia studied the responses, and found them to be the same as the people who'd called the house the day before. All wanted to find and punish those responsible, and all supported a search for the owner of the missing glove. Reading these words amazed Patricia. This unending support from the community was unparalleled, and all over a little boy's fantasy of digging a hole to China.

Her husband reached for the front page, not having perused it yet. (He'd been studying the box scores of the major league baseball games in the sports section.) He began to read the quotes, then shared with his wife the reactions of the people at his work-place. This spurred a conversation about Marty and the bullies and the effect everything could have on him, and the numerous facets of the issue took them in many directions. For the first time in months, Donald was actually taking the time to speak to his wife about something important, and when she reached for his hand, he accepted it, and for one, brief moment, clutched it before letting it go.

She looked up at him as he rose from his chair, the entire moment seeming rather abrupt. One minute, he'd tenderly held her hand, the next, he'd quickly leapt out of his seat.

"What is it?" she asked, concerned.

Donald scanned the area towards Rec-Park, his hand shielding his eyes. "There's a group of people coming this way, looks to be about ten of them."

Patricia rose and looked in the direction her husband was watching. He was right, about ten people were heading in their direction: five men and five women. Each was carried something over their shoulders, but the distance was too great to make out what.

"What are those people carrying?" she asked.

"Those look like shovels to me," answered her husband.

Within 30 seconds, her husband's guess proved accurate, and as they curiously studied each person, the group kept on coming right towards them. The unlikely assembly was being led by an athletic looking man of about 60, who, despite his age, was very muscular, in superb physical shape. He approached the front gate of the Kents' home and simply said in a cheery, warm-hearted voice, "Good morning. My name's Tom Doyle, and these here are some friends of mine. We've come here to dig out a hole. We're here to help the boy."

Patricia and Don stood speechless. A group of total strangers was standing in front of their house, armed with shovels. The older man looked at his watch and said, "Let's get started, got a long day of digging ahead of us."

A smile crept across Donald Kent's face just then. He walked down the four stairs of the porch and opened up the gate to allow the group to enter, uttering a weak, "Thank you." He looked at his wife and said, "Don't you think we should be waking up Marty?"

"Yes!" she shouted. "And I'll make more coffee for everyone!"

She rushed into the house and up the stairs to Marty's room. She opened the door, then opened the shade on the window overlooking the back yard. She jostled her son, who still appeared to be in a deep sleep.

"Marty, Marty, wake up!" she called shrilly. "I want you to see something!"

Her son couldn't quite register any of what was going on, literally being pulled from a deep slumber his mind and body so desperately needed, and there was no time to make any sense of any of it. He fumbled for his glasses, looked at the clock and said, "Mom, it's only 7:00. Why are you waking me up?"

"Come over to the window, Marty," said his mother excitedly. "There's something I want you to see!"

She sounds much more excited than usual, Marty thought. *People don't get this excited at 7:00 in the morning for nothing.* He rolled from his bed and crept towards the window.

The sight before him blew him away. "Who are all those people?" he asked. "And why are they digging into the hole?"

"We don't know who they are," his mother shrugged. "They just showed up out of nowhere. They want to dig the hole back out for you."

His eyes widened at the sound of his mother's words. His heart pounded hard in his chest at the sight of these total strangers going out of their way for *him*. *Good things like this never happen to* me, he thought.

In record time, Marty dressed himself in his digging clothes. He rumbled down the stairs and ran into his father, standing at the bottom of the landing.

"Dad," he said, surprised.

"You've got company," his father said happily. "I suppose they'd consider it rude if you didn't join them."

The smile Donald displayed, this sliver of the fathering he so desperately craved, was all the assurance Marty needed. He whizzed by his father, who reached out his hand and shook Marty's hair in a reassuring gesture as the boy ran by. Marty returned the smile, then walked back and hugged his startled father, before dashing out the back door towards the strangers.

Standing on the stairs, Patricia Kent had witnessed the tender moment between father and son. Tears formed in her eyes as she stepped back away from view. She composed herself, then deliberately made some noise on the stairs, acting as though she hadn't seen a thing. She walked up to her husband and reached out to embrace him. He pulled her towards himself, a nice, tight hug. He kissed her on the cheek, and silently said, "Maybe we should join those strangers."

She shook her head against his chest, and it felt so good to her. She didn't want the moment to end just yet. But her instincts snapped her out of her reverie. The strangers needed their attention, too.

"I'm going to call Kelly," she said, a happy realization. "She won't believe what's happening here."

125

CHAPTER 22

News of the arrival of the volunteers spread throughout the neighborhood like wildfire. At first, the adjoining neighbors noticed the activity at the Kent's, and Patricia placed a few calls on her own as well. Soon neighbors called neighbors, friends called friends, one call after the other transpired like a local militia placed into active duty. By 9:30, more than 100 people with shovels had joined the swelling ranks of volunteers, and by 10:00, most of the original 30 feet Marty and Brenna had dug out were re-excavated.

Kelly Trapp and a photographer were an excited part of the assemblage. This sight absolutely amazed Kelly—these people all reaching out in the most incredible of ways.

She hadn't seen this side of Binghamton before, and she was touched by not only the support given to Marty, but from her growing number of fans who'd enjoyed her reporting. She'd been recognized by the people, and they'd accepted her—at last.

"Do you believe all these people?" asked Patricia to Kelly. "This is simply incredible."

Kelly looked around her. She watched Marty and Brenna near the hole and smiled at the way Marty had assumed control. He appeared to have lost some weight, she noticed, and seemed to be more confident than when she'd first met him; he carried himself with much more sureness. She was happy for him, and for what the people were doing. She'd be running a huge story in the next edition of the paper on just this subject. The humanity and caring of the people would be her obvious lead.

"Marty's looking pretty good to me," said Kelly. "Has he lost a few pounds?"

"I don't know," said Patricia, taking another look at her son. "I suppose he probably has. With all this exercise, who wouldn't?"

A large construction vehicle emblazoned with the logo, *City of Binghamton*, suddenly rumbled down the street and stopped directly in front of the Kents' house. To park the rig required some doing, but the driver appeared relaxed as he jumped from the vehicle and made his way through the maze of people. He held some work orders in his hands, and asked a few persons where Donald or Patricia Kent might be found. After pinpointing their location, he held out his right hand to Donald, then tipped his baseball cap to Patricia.

"Lovely day," he said. "Looks like there's quite a crowd here."

"Sure is," said Donald. "What can we do for you?"

Kelly Trapp eyed the man. His appearance here was undoubtedly official business.

Maybe the news he'd be sharing would contribute to her story.

"There's a few problems here," he said calmly. "This here hole you're all digging, if you decide to keep it up—and by the looks of things, it seems pretty serious to me—it's gonna require a permit from the city."

"A permit?" Donald asked incredulously. "Whatever for?"

"Mr. Kent, have you given any thought at all to this digging running into any kind of lines?" the construction worker asked. "You could easily sever a water pipe, or an electric line. I'm surprised you haven't hit anything yet, to be quite honest with you. Somebody could get killed here."

"Then why can't the city send their men over to just survey the area?" Donald asked.

"They can," quipped the man, "as soon as you get the appropriate permits."

The man began to grow uneasy as a good number of people flocked towards him.

He suddenly realized that making his pitch in front of this gang of people, a gang all supporting the very thing he'd come to temporarily halt, was probably not the best idea.

He wasn't even sure, observing the looks of anger in the crowd, that he'd escape without some kind of confrontation.

"O.K. then," said Donald Kent, who'd also noticed the crowd's annoyance. "How do we get the permits?"

"You have to apply for one down at City Hall," the man said.

"Fine," said Donald, "then that's what we'll do."

"It takes about six weeks to get approved," said the man. "You know, these things take time."

The man's final remark preceded angry shouts from the crowd. One by one, adults came forward, basically telling the man that their own children had expressed an interest in digging to China, that they hadn't gone to City Hall for a permit, and that they had no intention of doing so. The man felt anxious to vacate the premises as more angry comments flew his way. He carefully returned to his vehicle, all the while mindful of what could happen next. He crawled into his truck and left as quickly as he could, thankful he'd escaped without being physically hurt by the mob, and kicking himself for the poor judgment he'd just shown. His own 10-year-old son had even begun to dig in their back yard, caught up in the *Hole to China* phenomenon.

Several minutes passed before the workers calmed down, and Kelly chose that opportunity to take control. She promised to contact the mayor right away, assured everyone that they were friends, and that she was certain the problem could be overcome in no time. It was enough for now—it would have to be.

Another setback provided by the same people eager to destroy our house, thought Donald. Sure, he'd do his civic duty; he'd run down to City Hall and apply for the permit, but what would be the point? Surely by that time the support would drop to nothing. And only a few weeks remained before the wrecking ball would come. The city would recognize this and probably deny the permit. The only chance left was to have Kelly discuss the situation with the mayor.

The volunteers who had become so upset with the question on the permit decided to ignore the request for now. Working in shifts right from the start, they organized themselves successfully and without debate. The original man who'd introduced himself as Tom Doyle assumed control of the digging. He posted schedules and kept the feverish pace going forward, arranging 30-minute shifts, eight people at a time keeping the workers fresh.

By noon, the story had spread to the suburbs. One local radio station, WENE, received a call from a listener who broke the news to the receptionist. She handed a scribbled note to the host, "Big Mack Franklin," who'd been reading about the story in the papers. *Hundreds of people with shovels are at the Kent house,* the note read. *They've dug the hole back out. Man from the city wants to close them down.*

The veteran host of *Good Morning Binghamton* quickly wrote a note to his producer, asking to confirm the information he'd just received. His morning talk show had already been filled with callers wanting to talk about *The Hole to China,* and this new bit of news, if confirmed, would undoubtedly light up the switchboard for the rest of the show.

He listened to an angry call about what had happened to Marty Kent. All the while, he looked through the glass at his producer, who was talking to someone on the phone. His producer hung up the phone, flashed a quick thumbs-up to confirm the story, and jotted down a note, which he passed through the panel of the glass.

"I've just received some startling information about this *Hole to China* tragedy," Franklin spoke into the microphone. "We've just learned that early this morning a group of about 10 adults, armed with shovels, came to the Kent home on the west side, and volunteered to dig out, *that's right,* volunteered to *dig out* the hole that had been filled in a few days before by a group of hoods. Apparently, that number soon swelled to over 100 diggers, and the hole is now even deeper, that's right, *deeper* than Marty Kent had originally dug. We've confirmed this information with Kelly Trapp, the reporter for *The Bulletin,* who's been handling the story from the beginning."

He clicked off his microphone for a moment and instantly watched the eight phone lines light up. He took the next call, then the next and the next. As one flashing phone light on his control panel died, it was replaced by another. On and on the activity continued for the duration of his shift, spilling beyond the regularly scheduled four hour program into the early afternoon hour, creating a programming issue at the station.

The DJ had lived in Binghamton his entire 58 years. He'd hosted several talk-show formats, most at the station he currently worked for, for nearly 30 of those years. He consistently enjoyed ratings nearly always at the top of the local charts, and his audience of listeners middle-age and up never hesitated to support him. With several college degrees, in Sociology, Communication, French and English, he was known to locals as the "smartest man in Binghamton." He sat on the Mayor's Board of Directors, and was counted on and called upon by many of the past administrations for advice. He was the voice of both the common person and the elite. His opinion *mattered.*

His mind reached back in time, trying to remember if the community had ever come together over one subject as it now had. He could think of nothing in particular; not one event had struck a chord at such a degree as this. He read the clock on the wall and was amazed to see that he'd gone 90 minutes past the usual noon conclusion of his program, and the lights on the console were still lighting up. He'd end things now, however, wrap up the show with his usual closing monologue which had made him so famous in the area. He knew that his words would carry some weight on the subject, and carefully crafted a rough copy in his mind. To get it just right for the people, and for Marty, was of great importance.

"Ladies and gentlemen," he began, "today we have witnessed a most unusual display of public opinion and support, directed towards one 12-year-old boy and his desire to tunnel his way to China. I have been following the story in the papers myself, and, like so many of you, I remember the time as a young boy when my quest to dig to China failed to go beyond five feet. Digging a hole to China was a sort of rite of passage, you might say. We all tried it, and needless to say, we all failed."

He paused for a quick sip of water, then continued. "At a tender early age, the noble cause of reaching the other side of the world via your own back yard brought out enormous excitement. The exuberance of youthful naïveté never stood in the way of attempting to achieve the impossible, because it didn't seem impossible to me, or by the sounds of these many calls today, to you either.

"We all know digging all the way to China with simple shovels can never be accomplished, just as we also know the entire world will never be converted to Christianity, nor will a major league baseball team win all the games on their schedule.

Yet, there are those who will try and keep trying. People like these may be faced with the same impossible odds day after day, year after year; yet, they go on about their quests as if they *could* happen. They prepare their lives accordingly. A potential convert rebukes the valiant attempt by the preacher. A baseball team loses a game. Yet they refuse to bow to the setback created by the inevitable. You see, dear listener, it is the expectation that keeps them going...not the result. They simply continue to dig.

"Now, does that mean I believe a boy can indeed dig his way to China? Well, it's the 'Yes, Virginia, there is a Santa Claus,' syndrome, or 'Where there's a will, there's a way.'"

Franklin's producer flashed another "thumbs-up" through the window. He motioned with his hands to continue on, to ignore the clock and the scheduled commercials waiting to run. This was too important to allow programming to get in the way.

The DJ provided some information, just enough to entice the populace even more, about the city demanding that the Kent's get a permit. He was careful not to indict the mayor, but he didn't completely let her off the hook, either, choosing a more casual approach to this new issue. He knew it was probably a temporary glitch, knew Mayor Thomas would have to buckle under this public support for Marty, but he also knew it made for great radio, for great debate. He also knew his show would probably swell the crowd at the Kents' even more.

"In conclusion," he stated, "I commend the people of this great city and area for what they have done today. To galvanize a populace of this size over a matter of childhood fantasy is simply unfathomable. I'm asking all of you, in one way or another, to go out and see the site for yourselves, to support Marty Kent in his digging, and the family as they prepare to vacate their property at the end of the summer. Myself, I'm on my way to the Kents' at the conclusion of this program. Thank you for sharing today, dear listeners."

Across the city and suburbs, of course thousands of people had tuned into the show. Like the great wave of support generated earlier in the day by the people who'd collected at the Kents', the grapevine had helped expand the usual listening audience to nearly twice its normal strength.

"Big Mack" Franklin had no idea what he'd soon be experiencing at Marty Kent's house.

CHAPTER 23

Among the great listening audience to "Big Mack" Franklin's show were Larry Murphy's parents, Scott and Rene. They'd spent many Saturday mornings reading the paper, drinking coffee, and listening in to the broadcast. Such a tradition had become like a religion to them, a small cut of their week escaping into the radio world of opinion and innuendo. They'd enjoyed the two or three hours taken out of their busy week to kick back, relax, and keep up with local happenings.

They'd tuned in like so many others had this particular Saturday, and listened to all the comments and opinions on the matter of the *Hole to China*. They'd sat in stunned silence as Mack Franklin issued his first report of the volunteers helping Marty, then erupted in an emotional outburst upon hearing the good news. Rene Murphy, in particular, had taken Marty's story to heart, and now this new information tugged her heartstrings. She'd been extremely upset when she'd read in Kelly's story about the hole being covered up, and she'd voiced her displeasure to her husband and to Larry about how "wrong" the whole thing had been, and that "they should find those responsible and punish them all accordingly." She'd even asked Larry his opinion on the matter, and what his friends would think about such a crime being committed.

All these thoughts had weighed on his young mind. He stretched the lies he'd been covering up even further, disposing, after all, of the remaining glove following his unsuccessful attempt at retracing his

133

steps and finding the lost one. He'd prayed that his father wouldn't think too much about the missing gloves; he'd hoped beyond hope that his father wouldn't put two and two together once he discovered them missing. Yet, Larry also wanted to tell them the truth, but still, the fear in his young mind of the possible repercussions, kept pulling him the other way.

A great tug-of-war transpired in his mind, a raging battle of good vs. evil. He knew that sooner or later, the thinning rope would pull him one way or the other, or simply just snap. He was one scared boy.

Just then he heard his mother yell, "Larry, Larry, come downstairs this minute! Come listen in to this radio show with us."

Her son, still feeling the ill effects from his role in covering the hole, had let his appetite shrink to nothing, and he'd moped around the house for one full day. He'd spoken to the other boys in Scott Gardner's gang, and had discovered that all of them were equally nervous about the lost glove; but he'd assured them he'd take the fall completely if they found out the glove's owner. He tried to avoid Scott Gardner, but Scott had already contacted him, calling him names and threatening to "kick him out" of the gang for good. Scott's promise of physical torture unless Larry kept his "mouth shut" played on his troubled mind with equal fear as did being caught. But he'd sworn especially to Scott that he'd never tell a soul who had been involved.

"What is it, Mom?" Larry asked, half-heartedly responding to his mother's calls.

As he came down, his mother waved him over to the radio. She turned up the volume and listened to Mack Franklin discussing the events of the morning.

"What's this all about?" Larry inquired.

"A bunch of people went over to Marty's house early this morning, armed with shovels," Rene began excitedly. "Within just a few hours, they'd dug out the hole, all the way down and past where Marty had dug. They just announced that over 100 people were down at the site, all helping with the digging. Your father and I are going over to help, why don't you come with us and help your friend out? He'd probably like that, don't you think?"

Larry's dilemma now faced him straight on. He could just say yes and go through the motions for a few hours at Marty Kent's house; or, he could say no, using the excuse that his stomach still upset him. He thought about the consequences of either action, and neither seemed to fit. His parents would undoubtedly sense the rift between Marty and himself, and that could possibility tip them off, send his detective-like mother searching for a little more than he'd want her to know. On the other hand, if he refused to go, blaming his stomach disorder, his firm mother would ground him to the house for a few days, and would probably even recommend a visit to Dr. Caldwell. He didn't like the way that sounded to him, either. His dilemma clearly came down to choosing between the lesser of two evils.

His mother was puzzled. She'd expected him to quickly jump at the chance to help his classmate. "Larry," she said earnestly, "is it your stomach, dear? Maybe I should give Dr. Caldwell a call…"

"No, I'm feeling a little better," Larry said, rubbing his stomach. "I don't need to *see him.*"

His mother stood up, her decision made. "Well then, I think we should go, all of us, don't you, dear?"

Her tone had dropped to just below sweet, and just above bitter as she delivered the rhetorical question. It was at these times when Larry knew the answer he'd give her, the answer she'd be expecting. She stood waiting with her arms folded, staring at him with an uneasy facial expression bordering between a smile and a frown. His short pause in responding caused her to purse her lips, tighten her gaze at him.

He couldn't take this much longer, he thought. He had to give her the answer she'd expected. "Sure, Mom. I'll go." His heart sank as he uttered the words.

The distorted smile on his mother's face suddenly vanished and was replaced by the widest and loveliest of grins. Larry returned the gesture, but he felt his stomach start churning once more. The feeling he'd encountered the night he and the boys filled in the hole returned to him just then, and with a vengeance. He felt as if he'd lose his marbles again, right there, and he quickly excused himself to dress in more appropriate digging clothing.

"Very well," said his mother. "Meet me and your father downstairs in five minutes. We'd like to get going."

135

He rushed to the bathroom upstairs as quickly as he could, pulled up the lid of the toilet, dropped to his knees and vomited. His body shook violently now, and he held his stomach with both hands and let go once more. He stood and quickly began to run the water in the sink, hoping the sound would help drown out his dreadful retching noises.

He dropped to his knees once more, continued to hold his stomach tightly, then unleashed a torrent of fluids into the bowl. He flushed the toilet, but couldn't yet muster the energy to get off the floor.

At least five minutes had elapsed since he'd entered the bathroom, and now he was feeling uncommonly dizzy. The sudden loss of fluids had left him temporarily dehydrated, and the lack of food had sapped his energy. He wanted to curl up in a ball and lay there, untouched and unbothered, until it all went away.

The rapid knocking on the door returned him to reality. He knew his Mother stood outside, knew very well he'd be unable to hide this from her for long. She opened the door, which he'd failed to lock, slowly, then rushed to his doubled-over figure slumped on the bathroom floor.

"Oh, dear!" she exclaimed. "I'm calling Dr. Caldwell, right away!"

Larry accepted her embrace. She quickly put a hand to his forehead to check for a fever, and found nothing to be out of the ordinary. She rushed to the linen closet, then quickly dampened a wash cloth with cool water. She pressed it onto his forehead, and instructed him to hold the cloth in place.

"You stay right here, young man," she instructed with fervor. "I'm going to call the doctor."

Larry held up his hand to stop her. She paused at the door and looked his way, then suddenly walked away towards her bedroom to make the phone call.

"*Mom!*" he shrieked. "*Please don't call! I'm O.K.!*"

His mother had already dialed a few numbers when the startled cry reached her. She placed the telephone down on her nightstand, and returned to the bathroom to face her son, who was still balled up near the toilet.

"Mom, don't call Dr. Caldwell," he said, feeling suddenly strong. "I have something to tell you."

CHAPTER 24

By mid-afternoon, several of the surrounding streets near the Kents' house were overrun with automobiles. People had parked their cars blocks away from the house, creating a traffic jam unlike any that neighborhood had seen before. Several men already at the site had noticed this, taken control of the streets and directed the logjam of cars to open parking areas. People eagerly walked up to a half-mile just to reach the Kents' house.

The numbers soon peaked at an estimated 300, with local celebrities creating a veritable "Who's Who," among those in the crowd. Mayor Thomas was the first of the celebrities to arrive, receiving a more lukewarm greeting than the gracious and warm salutations she'd been used to receiving over the years. But she'd expected just this. The Engineer from the city who'd earlier been chased off the property had informed her of his little visit to the site, and how his untimely comments had caused him to fear for his life.

The fact that he hadn't first discussed this issue with the mayor upset her, and she'd told him his "timing" had been more than a little "off." Though she'd thought of visiting the Kents to see for herself what was happening, she knew she'd be in troubled water there.

The fact remained that for all the decisions concerning the city, the buck stopped on her desk. These people from the Kents' community probably thought of her as the enemy now, the person who'd pulled the plug on their little neighborhood. Heck, she may as well have been driving the truck with the wrecking ball herself, so she knew she'd be taking a chance by showing her face to these people.

Kelly Trapp watched the mayor mingle with the masses, and thought to approach her, but then decided to wait a while, to give the mayor some time to get acquainted with her surroundings. Instead, Kelly turned her attention to local radio personality "Big Mack Franklin", who was shaking hands and signing autographs. She'd never met him before, only seen his giant caricature displayed on billboards along Route 17. His burly, six-feet four inches and 350 pounds was an easy target to fix upon. With a full gray beard, rimless glasses and impeccably maintained gray hair, there was no mistaking this man.

Kelly had listened to Franklin's show several times in the past, and she loved the way he communicated his thoughts and shared ideas with the people. She'd introduce herself to him as the person who'd been contacted by his producer earlier in the day, allowing for an easy segue into conversation. She watched him be hounded by loyal supporters and smiled at how wonderful such a thing would be, envisioning herself in that coveted position he so admirably held.

Then she spotted Joel Kincade entering the back yard, his magnificent figure equally unique, yet contrasting with the fuller bulk of Mack Franklin. Though Kincade didn't draw the crowds in the numbers the mayor and Mack Franklin had, it was still an impressive sight, watching her boss shake hands and wave to well wishers. He made his way slowly through the crowd, then spotted Kelly, who'd maintained her position near the hole.

"Afternoon Mr. Kincade," she said.

"Afternoon to you, Kelly," he stated. "Got quite a crowd on your hands, I see."

"Yes, sir. It started out early this morning and hasn't stopped."

"I know," Kincade declared. "I was listening in to the Franklin show, had to come over for a look. This sure is something."

"Let me introduce you to Marty's parents," said Kelly. "I've told them a lot about you."

"That would be nice," said Kincade. "I'd like to meet them."

Kelly raised her voice and called for Patricia, then waved as she caught her eye.

Patricia excused herself from a group of people she'd been mingling with, wiped her hands on an apron she'd wrapped around her waist, and extended her hand towards Joel Kincade.

"Patricia, I'd like you to meet my boss, Joel Kincade," said Kelly animatedly. "This is Patricia Kent."

"Very nice to meet you," Kincade said warmly. "I'll bet you had no idea this sort of thing would come from a hole being innocently dug in your yard?"

"You have no idea," said Patricia, laughing. "We had no clue the people would show us so much support. It's just beyond belief, really."

"Is your husband around?" Kincade asked.

"Oh, he's here somewhere," Patricia replied. "I'll go look for him if you'd like. Should take just a few minutes."

"Don't trouble yourself," said Kincade. "I'm sure I'll run into him soon enough."

"It's no trouble at all," Patricia said. "I'll be right back."

She scampered off towards the house, searching for her husband, then disappeared around the corner.

"You know, Kelly," said Kincade, "Donald Kent was *The Man* around these parts years ago. He was quite an athlete."

"Yes, I'd heard the stories before," said Kelly. She paused, then said, "You know, he's really had a hard time adjusting to all this stuff with the hole and Marty. The two of them don't get along very well. It's sad, really. He expects his son to be just like he was, the star athlete and all."

"Oh?" said Kincade. "I take it this boy isn't as gifted as his dad was?"

"You've seen his photo," Kelly reminded him. "Unfortunately for him, he's not athletic at all."

"I see," said Kincade. "Speaking of Marty, I'd like to meet him, too."

"He's down in the hole," said Kelly, pointing.

"Let's go have a look, shall we?" Kincade offered.

The short trip to the hole provided Kelly with just enough time to inform her boss of what had happened earlier with the man from the city. For Kincade, this provided fodder for another story, something to keep it alive. He spotted the mayor and knew this little glitch would be rectified, probably by the end of the day. In no way would she allow any delays in the dig, especially one requiring a six week wait for a permit. This situation at the Kents' would provide the perfect forum for her to apologize and set things right.

Inside the hole, Marty, Brenna and six others busily dug. The volunteers had earlier placed makeshift rope ladders along two sides of the hole, for climbing in and out. The slight angle that had been produced from the hole to the ground reduced the chances of a climber accidentally falling into the ever-growing pit, and large tray-like apparatuses had been fastened to cables on the opposite sides of the ladders. These were lowered into the hole, and filled up with dirt for the diggers, then hoisted back up with pulleys. Kincade studied the artful way in which this crude form of excavation had been set in motion. He peered into the hole, amazed at how far down the workers seemed to be. He suggested to Kelly that she write a separate story on the ingenious rigging of the equipment and its devisers. Then Kincade stepped away from the hole. "Remarkable!" he exclaimed with a grin. "With equipment like this, and all this help, the boy may very well reach China after all!"

"Maybe you can meet Marty later," Kelly said. "Looks like he's a little busy at the moment."

He agreed, then spotted Patricia Kent and her husband walking towards them. He knew right then the man was Donald Kent. He looked the same now as he had back in his glory days. He still had that well-chiseled, athletic body, and the ravages of time had been outwardly kind to him. They were introduced to each other, the steel grip of Donald Kent's mighty handshake surprising Kincade some.

"You must be very proud of your son," Kincade remarked.

"Well, I suppose I am, a little," said Donald.

Kent's lukewarm response caught Kincade off guard. He pressed on, loudly: "A *little*! Well, if it weren't for your son, I don't think any of these people would be here today!"

"No, I suppose not," said Donald, looking down and tracing his toe on the ground.

"Oh, it is wonderful, what's happening here today, that's for sure. But now we need a permit. So it's all but over now."

"So I've heard," said Kincade.

Donald continued. "But my real fear is, what is Marty going to do when it's all over? He doesn't know about the permit yet."

The hurt in Kent's voice was clear. Kincade had known the details of the Kents' plight, and he'd earlier discovered the unhealthy relationship between Donald and his son. Kincade was a wise man in these situations. Life's experiences had taught him so much about people.

"You know," he said, "I've been in the newspaper business my whole life. My father was as well. I kind of followed in his footsteps, you might say."

"That's nice," said Donald. "That's sorta what I was hoping would happen to Marty, but the kid can't even throw a ball right. He'll never be any good in sports."

Kincade eyed him. *Lonely*, he thought. *And bitter*. "I have three boys," he said after a moment.

"Really?" said Donald.

"Yep, proud of all three of them, even though none of them ever went into journalism."

"Why didn't they?" asked Donald.

"They just don't have the interest," shrugged Kincade. "Oh, I always wanted them to get into it, but not once did any of 'em ever give it a try. They all had other ambitions. Hard to believe that a Kincade wouldn't want to be involved in news."

"That must have been hard to take," said Donald.

"Yes, and no," Kincade said. "It was a little hard to see them choose other vocations – but it was a wonderful feeling to see them all succeed so admirably at what they chose to do.

"Funny thing about it, I've got a grandson going to college now, Journalism major. He'd been writing for his local newspaper since early high school. Loves the news game, really. I find the irony in it all very intriguing."

"Why's that?" asked Donald.

"Oh, I don't know," said Kincade. "Just the way nature skipped over a special skill in the family and placed it into the next generation. Things like this happen all the time."

Kincade turned to face Donald Kent, looked him squarely in the eye and said, "With kids, you've got to learn to just take what they give you."

It was the most profound statement of fact Donald Kent had ever heard, this simple sentence spoken by a man he'd never met until today. The words affected him deeply as he watched his son emerge from the hole to the gracious applause of those near him.

Donald turned to Kincade and said, "Thank you for that, Mr. Kincade. I appreciate what you've just shared with me. Now, if you'll excuse me, I'd like to go over and have a chat with my son."

Kincade, pleased with what he'd just heard from Donald Kent, felt genuinely good to have imparted some wisdom—wisdom Donald would hopefully share with Marty. He'd half expected Donald to ignore his statements, to maintain the stiffness of his character.

He watched as father and son posed together for a photograph, and hoped their relationship would blossom and flourish, not fall back to the way it had been.

He spotted Mayor Thomas and Kelly across the yard. He cut a short path between the crowd and gave the mayor a welcoming hug. They'd always been good friends, even back in her earlier days as a reporter for *The Bulletin*, and he'd prided himself on having been there to see her rise through the local political ranks. Come to think of it, he knew they were both proud of each another for the place they'd carved out for themselves in the world.

"I knew you'd be here," said the mayor.

"And I knew you'd be, too," Kincade smiled at her.

"It's truly an amazing phenomenon," Mayor Thomas declared. "All these people trying to do the right thing. Makes one proud to be a Binghamtonian."

"Yes, yes it does," he agreed. "I suppose there's nothing better to be proud of than that." He paused, then said, "I'm assuming you're going to reverse the city's stand on the need for a permit here."

"Well, yes and no," the mayor said thoughtfully. "I've already talked it over with Kelly. We still need to go through certain protocol here, certain permits need to be issued. We do need to take steps to protect the citizens. There really does exist the possibility of someone striking some sort of pipe or wire.

"But I also see what else is happening here. We'll push the permit out to them and send our surveyors over. I'll announce that decision to this crowd before I leave today."

She scanned the area and said, "It's so very sad for them that this place is soon to be leveled. It's a tragedy really, to be displaced from your home. And this old school, it has such character, it's such a magnificent structure, really. Just look at how beautifully it was built."

Kelly took a good gander at the old edifice. *It's true*, she thought, taking note of the dark red bricks, concrete gutters, an old metallic black–kettle-looking structure that was used as a fire escape. Asphalt playgrounds on both sides of the school, with tiered columns of concrete in each corner of the building, resembled lookout towers for a fortress. Twelve wide stairs led up to the main entrance, all surrounded by towering oak trees.

"I'd never taken a gook look at it before," said Kelly. "Are there any other buildings like it here?"

The mayor thought for a moment. "Only the ones downtown in the historic section," she replied. "They were all built over 100 years ago."

"Have they been preserved?" asked Kelly.

"Oh, yes, they have," she said. "They've all been converted into little museums. Most of them are right on Front Street."

"Who converted them into museums?" Kelly was intrigued by the direction this chat was taking.

"Well, the Historical Society did," replied the mayor. She paused to consider the question again, then looked at Kelly, who seemed to be in deep thought.

"Why do you ask?" she wanted to know.

"Oh, no reason, really," said Kelly. "It's just that if the Historical Society can save a few buildings downtown, why can't they come to the rescue of the old school, too?"

Her question now piqued the interest of both the mayor and Joel Kincade. Mayor Thomas smiled at Kelly, and said, "Yes, but eminent domain is a very specific law. If it's in the interest of the public good to knock down an old building in order to modernize a school, for example, then that's just the way it is. Plus, there was a vote on it last year, and it's what the taxpayers in the area wanted."

At that moment, Kelly realized she'd need to study up on the law of eminent domain.

She didn't like having to ask questions about it, yet she felt enormously helpless at her lack of knowledge of the subject. She looked at Joel Kincade, and remembered how he'd strongly suggested she follow the trail of eminent domain for her story, and now she'd wished she had done so. The time to explore this facet of the story had come.

"You know, Kelly," said the mayor, "there's someone here who could help you with some of your questions."

"Who's that?" Kelly asked anxiously.

"Mack Franklin, the radio personality," Mayor Thomas answered. "It just so happens he sits on the board of the Historical Society."

"Really?" asked Kelly, her face brightening.

"Really," said the mayor. "He's truly an authority on just about everything historical in these parts. I've often leaned on him for help in local matters myself."

Joel Kincade had listened intently to the conversation between the two. He'd carefully watched Kelly play the reporter, and he liked her style. He could sense the juices flowing in her veins, the pure feeling that comes with a rich idea. He picked up on her energy, watching as she gathered her information.

"You two continue your conversation," said Kincade. "I'll go find Mack."

Minutes later, Kincade returned, Mack Franklin at his side. He introduced himself to Kelly who admitted she was a diehard fan. Despite his popularity, he still appreciated hearing such words, as he'd never grown tired of receiving admiring comments from his listeners. He bowed his head graciously to her and said, "Your articles on *The Hole to China* have been fascinating. I look forward to reading more such stories by you."

Kelly blushed like a schoolgirl, feeling a bit uncomfortable standing toe-to-toe with the city officials and now with a celebrity. She pushed the feeling aside for the moment, tossed back her hair against the slight breeze, put on her reporter's face and decided to waste no time going after the information she coveted.

"Miss Trapp here is interested in the Historical Society," Mayor Thomas said to Franklin.

"Yes, I am," said Kelly. "Would you mind if I asked you a few questions?"

"Not at all," Franklin replied. "What would you like to know about us?"

"For starters," Kelly began, "I'd like to know how a particular building becomes listed as a historical site by a Historical Society?"

The DJ inhaled deeply and said: "Usually, if a building is 100 years or older, we'd be interested in preserving it. But, there are so many factors involved. It's complex, to say the least."

"How so?" Kelly asked.

"Well, there're some very specific guidelines to follow," he said. "Why, do you have a specific property in mind?"

"Yes," she said. She pointed to the old building that was to be leveled. "This one, the Horace Mann School. It's got to be 100 years old at least."

"Sorry to say, it's only 76," said Franklin. "It was built in 1890."

"Oh, I didn't know that," Kelly said, deflated.

"Why are you so interested in this building?" Franklin inquired.

"I was hoping the Historical Society could step in and save it from the wrecking ball. Guess that's out of the question now."

"I'm afraid the Historical Society would serve no useful purpose in this case," said Franklin. "They'd be going up against the federal government. The only thing they'd stand to gain would be more time. There's just not enough money to battle the issue in the courts. Most of the Historical Society's money comes in the form of donations from people and businesses. I'm sorry, Kelly."

"Well, maybe there's another way," Kelly pondered, her chin in her hand.

"I sincerely doubt it," said Franklin.

The mayor agreed. "He's right, Kelly. All the contracts have been awarded, for both the demolition and the reconstruction. It would be a nightmare to try and change things now. There would have to be a *very good reason* to stop it all at this point."

But during the pause that followed, Mayor Thomas's mind began to churn out ideas, as she tried to figure out Kelly's line of thinking and put herself in Kelly's place as a reporter. She looked at Kincade, then at Franklin, and finally back at Kelly. "Would you gentlemen excuse us for a moment? I'd like to talk to Kelly in private, please."

The two men excused themselves, only to be quickly cornered by adoring fans. Mayor Thomas turned to Kelly and asked, "Are you onto something here?"

"Maybe, maybe not," said Kelly, shrugging. "It's just a silly idea."

"Silly or not, I'd like to hear it," said the mayor.

"Well," began Kelly, "you know how you've been asking the people for ideas to draw people to Binghamton?" She pointed to the Hole. "Perhaps we've got it, right here."

"What, this *Hole to China*?" said the mayor.

"I know it sounds corny and all," Kelly started, "but look at how many people are here today. Maybe we could keep the interest alive, get the word out to the other New York media, maybe even the entire national media."

The mayor shook her head. "I'm afraid you're right – it just might be too corny. Remember, I didn't want to be remembered by anything too fantasy-like, and although this is great fun right now, it *is* pure Fantasy, of course. Plus, it wouldn't be permanent. I'm looking for something that is…well, something that will *draw* people to us to stay. I mean, how long are people going to come to watch folks dig a two-hundred foot hole?"

"I know," Kelly shrugged. "We'd need something more."

"A great deal more, I'm afraid to say," said the mayor. "The last thing I'd want is to become the laughing stock of the country. In fact, we need to be careful around here that this doesn't generate too much more publicity. I don't want us Binghamtonians looking like a bunch of idiots!"

Kelly's face lit up. "But Mayor, with what we're seeing here today, we're going to have a hard time *keeping* the rest of the country's media away. This is a small town for news, and this is about as big news as a small town like this can get. Look at all those people digging – you think you can keep a lid on that? The TV stations are probably sniffing it out already; they'll be coming, and then everyone will know."

The mayor pondered Kelly's statement and knew she was right. Once the local TV stations put the story on the news – and how could they not, now that Big Mack had done it for radio—it would soon plummet out of control, it would burst this town's boundaries.

And, if Marty continued digging, the piece would only *keep* building. If the story continued to build, undoubtedly criticism would arise, pointing back to her office for encouraging the dig, only to have the same office move to destroy it and drive people from their homes? She closed her eyes and sagged her shoulders. She last thing she'd ever figured on was someone in the neighborhood trying to dig a hole to China...

"You've got a point," she said. "Guess I'm stuck between the proverbial rock and a hard place. That's what I get for trying to show some empathy."

"I know the fix you're in, and I also know you mean well," said Kelly. "Anything I write about you will be positive, I promise."

"Thank you, dear, but that may not be enough to bail me out," Mayor Thomas remarked. "The national media is a whole other ball game. I'm afraid if we stop this digging and then level Marty's house they'll make us look like the big, bad wolf."

They shared a light laugh, then rejoined the others near the hole. For the first time all day, the diggers had called for a work stoppage, providing the perfect opportunity for Mayor Thomas to make her announcement about the permit. Predictably, her surprise statement was accepted by the diggers with fervor and excitement. There was still hope here, hope for this 12 year-old boy and his journey.

With the majority of the people still listening to the mayor around the perimeter of the hole, one man threw a tape measure down into the cavernous pit. A second man caught the other end of it, and pulled it tightly to the ground. He shouted, "*Sixty-four feet!*" Then he scaled a ladder to the top of the dirt heap. Hooting and hollering arose in plenty from the onlookers. Kelly wrote down the depth and the time of day, and got the appropriate names of key workers for her story. She looked around at the characters, and thought of the numerous little sub-plots to this story she'd discovered along the way. She planned out the next day's account, and felt she had enough now to write even several more. She had a full plate, and her mind almost burst with information.

The day's events, however, weren't to end on this note. Kelly turned in the vicinity of the street, and noticed a young boy and two adults walking briskly towards the group.

The boy trudged along with his head down, and the woman seemed agitated. Kelly looked closer at the child and recognized him as one of the boys who'd been bullying Marty. Kelly turned her eyes toward Marty, but he'd already noticed the new arrival.

Marty elbowed Brenna Nelson, who looked up at him, then turned to see what he'd been looking at. Brenna's shoulders went straight back, like the back of a dog prepping for a fight. Her eyes glared and she clenched her fists. *This is too good*, thought Kelly, as the trio of figures closed the gap between them.

Patricia Kent stopped and recognized Rene Murphy from PTA meetings at the school.

Her wide smile welcomed Rene, and the two women embraced for a brief moment. Then Patricia spoke. "Well, it's nice to see one of Marty's classmates come down here today. It's Larry, isn't it?" she asked, glancing at the boy.

"Yes, Ma'am," Larry mumbled politely, still not looking up.

Patricia turned to her son and noticed the angry expression on both his and Brenna's faces. She said, "Marty, isn't it nice of Larry to come today?"

Before Marty had a chance to respond, Rene Murphy announced in a loud, trembling voice, "Mrs. Kent, Larry here has something he'd like to tell you. Something he'd like to tell all of you." Tears began welling up in her blue eyes.

"What is it?" Patricia asked the boy sympathetically. "What would you like to tell us?"

Larry's mother commanded him to look up and talk so he could be heard. She crossed her arms, and her husband pushed his son forward, away from them.

Larry looked into Marty's eyes, then into Brenna's. He glanced back at his parents, who both nodded at him to begin speaking.

He began: "That glove that was f-found here the other d-day—uh, that glove was mine. I'm the one who filled in your hole, Marty. I didn't want to hurt anyone, I just thought it would be fun. I'm sorry, Marty."

A great hush rippled through the crowd as Patricia Kent grabbed her husband's arm, bit her lip and began to cry. The sound of so many voices that had filled the yard all day long were now reduced to an eerie silence.

Marty looked at Brenna, then at his parents, at Larry Murphy's parents, then at the hole. His eyes scanned all the people who'd helped him out. He took one step towards Larry and said, "You did it all by yourself?"

The young boy looked up. This was hard enough already. He didn't want to drag the other boys into it, especially Scott Gardner. He sheepishly nodded, and softly said, "Yes."

Marty knew this couldn't be true. He'd spent the better part of a week digging, and he knew it couldn't be possible that one person had filled in the hole overnight. He looked at his sometime tormentor, looked back at the hole and wondered what he was thinking.

Marty felt the grip of the people around him, felt the deep tension this moment held.

He thought back to all the bullying he'd endured at the hands of Larry Murphy. Sure, Scott Gardner had to have done the lion's share of the work, but Larry Murphy was no saint. He'd pushed and poked and punched Marty far too many times. He'd helped humiliate Marty in front of other classmates, he'd called him names and tortured him for years. And now here he was, standing before the jury, pleading guilty to all those things Marty was painfully replaying in his mind's eye. No doubt, Scott Gardner was involved here, and now Marty could clearly see that Larry Murphy was taking the full blame to protect himself from the worst person he'd ever known.

Marty looked up at his mother and could see the hurt coming from her. He looked at his father, hoping something in his eyes would guide him now. He looked at Kelly, whose heart beat wildly inside her chest, and turned once more to Brenna, who'd been waiting patiently for him to respond.

He felt a tinge of satisfaction, watching Larry Murphy now, cringing and so vulnerable before all these people. But the years of torment were not as strong as the rage he felt toward Larry Murphy now, after the endless nights of dreading the next morning because of him and the others. This was Marty's opportunity for revenge, a golden moment provided to him on a silver platter. He had total control of the situation, and though he felt just as uneasy as Larry Murphy must feel, it was Marty who manned the ship now.

Then Marty thought: *Maybe there's an even better way to get revenge on Scott – to take from him something – no, some one – he stole with his bullying.* Before he could change his mind, Marty grabbed a shovel leaning against a lawn chair, then quickly held it out toward Larry. The boy lifted his head and cautiously took hold of the shovel along with Marty. Then Marty reached out his free hand, and Larry took it, and Marty shook it as if he was greeting his best friend. Then Marty said, for all to hear, "Larry, would you like to help us dig?"

Larry Murphy was shocked. He hadn't expected this from Marty. He'd planned on getting back the same kind of humiliation and degradation he'd dished out; but now, in the midst of all these people, he was being forgiven! He looked at his mother, whose hands were crossed over her heart, then to his father, who stood proudly, despite the circumstances. He let go of Marty's hand, and took the shovel in both his hands. Marty let the shovel go, and Larry simply said, "Yeah – yeah, Marty, I would!"

The silence that had fallen across the lawn was quickly shattered by wild whooping and cheering by adults and children of all ages...

Kelly made mental notes of all she'd just witnessed. It had been quite a day already, and now, such an amazing ending was almost beyond belief. She watched Marty, Brenna and Larry disappear into the hole together, and wondered how she'd find words that could even begin to share with her readers what she'd experienced this unforgettable day.

CHAPTER 25

By the following Monday, the three local TV stations began covering the story, led by the self-proclaimed "News-Leader," Channel 12. The first station aired the story of *The Hole to China* that evening at 6:00, and by Wednesday, the two other stations had followed suit. With the continuing coverage in *The Bulletin* and Mack Franklin's talk show, not a single soul in the triple-cities area hadn't heard of what had taken place, and the story soon spread throughout the rest of New York state and northern Pennsylvania.

Not only was the public roundly informed of the story, they also continued to respond to it. By the hundreds they came, some armed with shovels, others with gifts, and most just out of curiosity. Visitors from other cities and counties were now arriving, hotels were beginning to fill up, restaurants were experiencing busier than usual bookings, and vendors seized the opportunity to make a quick buck. Hot dog stands, ice cream stands, lemonade stands, and four portable toilets all had been set up in the vacant Horace Mann School playground. Shirts imprinted with *The Hole to China* on the front side were quickly printed and sold by the hundreds. The usually quiet neighborhood had taken on the look of a busy inner city market area.

As promised, Mayor Thomas pushed the application for a permit to the top of the list. Engineers and surveyors found no obstacles in the way, at least none that could be seen as yet. Though the mayor showed some support for the dig, she expressed with emphasis the dangers associated with the undertaking. Engineers were interviewed by members of the press, charts and diagrams illustrating the dangers in digging as deep as Marty and company had planned. The biggest fear was now the safety of the diggers. Walls of dirt could collapse, corrosion could occur, someone could fall in and be *killed*. These were real dangers, so it was decided that two adults must be present at all times during digging, and an engineer would be sent out twice a week to note any structural damage to the hole.

The mayor was literally forced to announce a temporary hold on all permits for hole digging, as local children became swept up in the craze. Classes were even held at several schools in the area, outlining the do's and dont's of proper hole digging.

Amidst all the hoopla, the hole continued to get deeper. Workers rotated in shifts, and 12-hour days became the norm. By the end of that first full week of digging, a depth of 122 feet had been attained, and Marty himself never left the hole for more than a short break, save the one day his new wire-rimmed eyeglasses arrived, just in time for the cameras from Channel 12. His confidence soared along with his spirits, his bulging waistline was shrinking, his soft hands had become callused and tough, and the outline of muscles had begun to show when he lifted shovels full of dirt.

The transformation in Marty trickled down to his old nemesis, Larry Murphy. The forgiveness Marty had shown Larry brought out the goodness in him that had once been dormant. Larry was one of the first on the scene every morning, and usually one of the last to leave. Together with Marty and Brenna, the trio became inseparable, in the hole and out. They made a pact that at all times one of them *must* be in the hole digging, and keeping this pact became of utmost importance to Marty. Though he was pleased with the overall support of the people, he wanted to keep the original idea, the original concept, intact. This was *his hole.*

Marty's father was the third person to take on a major personality change. The conversation he'd had with Joel Kincade helped him see things in a new light, opening up a door that had so long been closed. He softened his approach toward his son and began looking at him admiringly. He even began to leave work early, so he could spend every minute he could with Marty in the hole. The father/son relationship that had so eluded them in the first 12 years of Marty's life was all washed away. Equally important, Donald Kent moved back into the master bedroom, abandoning the guest room for the last time.

By the beginning of the second week of digging, the local story had been fed by the three TV stations to their affiliate stations in New York City. Reporters were dispatched to the Kent household, and Marty answered questions at the side of the hole. Though the original intent had been a "human-interest" story, the national response was immediate.

All around the country, grade-school children were digging holes, books on China and the earth were being checked out of public libraries at a rapid pace, and a nation caught up in the social change of the mid '60s had wrapped itself as one around the story.

Newspapers around the country wrote opinion columns on the subject, some regarding the quest as utter nonsense, dismissing it as nothing more than "child's play," even criticizing Binghamton for encouraging the "ultimate of impossibilities." Others roundly hailed Marty for his courage, yet wrote with caution of the ultimate failure he'd soon be facing. Writers and editors wrote about Asia, comparing the conflict in Vietnam to Marty's *Hole to China*. *An Inch at a Time,* read one banner piece in *The Washington Post,* so vividly written and so profoundly worded that even the *President* of the United States took time from a busy schedule to read it. A country torn apart by war halfway around the world was learning now about *China.*

The surprises in store for Marty didn't end with all the publicity. At the end of an exhausting day of digging in the third week, the four remaining boys from Scott Gardner's gang showed up at Marty's house, each of them, as it had been for Larry Murphy weeks earlier, with stone-faced parents at their side. Donald Kent could see by the expressions on their faces that this was a serious matter. He'd known all along that Larry Murphy couldn't have filled in the hole by himself, yet he'd been aware of the rules on the street, about snitching on friends.

Marty, too, had known all along that those responsible were still at large. He hadn't asked or cared to know from Larry who else had been involved. He only cared to go forward at this point, didn't see the need to dwell on the negative. He wanted only to dig, and with every shovel of dirt, he threw the past behind him.

153

The boys approached Marty, Brenna, Larry and Marty's parents just as Larry Murphy had, heads down, body language indicating guilt. The ensuing greetings came from the adults, the apologies from each boy, the forgiveness from Marty. Things had repeated once more, the agony and pain and suffering from years past seemingly just melting away, as the likes of Jerry Turner, Peter Floyd, Roger Doyle and Greg Gibson broke down before Marty. The gang of six that had so haunted and hunted Marty had now joined him for something positive, now seeing a strong, mature Marty instead of a weak, powerless little boy. Of course, the one character still missing from the group hadn't been expected to take this route. There was still something terribly wrong with Scott Gardner, and Marty knew deep down, that no matter who else had come forward to confess his crime, the picture would not be complete without Scott, and Marty knew he wouldn't be safe until that cold day in hell came. But for now, safety in numbers would rule. Scott Gardner's little empire had come crumbling down around him, and now all the traitors were Marty's friends. The tables had been turned.

By the end of the third week, though, problems began to arise. The hole was becoming increasingly difficult to dig out. Larger rocks meant more obstacles for the crews.

Digging became more intense, better equipment was needed to chip away the rocks.

Despite the securing of the walls and the inspections by the city, erosion began to occur, and frequent slides sent more and more dirt back into the hole.

Proper lighting inside the hole was needed now; the angle of the sun kept light from reaching the diggers at the bottom of the hole. The 200-foot depth also meant a big drop in temperature, sometimes it was 30 degrees cooler at the bottom than it was above.

Removal of dirt had slowed down as the workers scrambled to provide additional ladder-rungs to scale the walls. Gradually, onlooker attendance began to drop; so did the numbers of volunteers. After a while, sometimes only the seven youths and Marty's father undertook any of the digging; at other times, hours passed before another foot of ground could be managed. Marty noticed these things, and began thinking about the future of the hole.

It was during this same point in time that Donald Kent came to understand more about the extended abuse his son had endured at the hands of Scott Gardner. He'd been climbing out of the hole, only 20 feet from the top, when he'd overheard the boys and Brenna talking to Marty about Scott. He hadn't really paid close attention to any of the talk in the past, but clinging to a ladder rung on the side of that hole, he learned the painful and horrible truth of Scott's constant bullying of Marty.

"I heard Scott's gonna try and get you real good," warned one of the boys.

"I heard that, too," said another.

"Let him try!" said a third. "We'll protect you."

The group let out a small cheer in response. Marty smiled, but not re-assuredly.

Marty said, "Why does he always want to get me? What did I ever do to him?"

"He just likes to pick on you, that's all," said Larry. "I don't think you have so much to worry about with us around to protect you. Plus, you'll be moving far away from him soon. You'll never see him again."

"I know," said Marty, needing no reminders of his impending removal from the property. "But I don't want to move anymore. I like it here. And I'm tired of being afraid, I'm tired of running away."

Brenna smiled as Marty looked her way. She'd been smiling more at him lately, he thought. He smiled back.

One of the boys asked, "Well, what are you gonna do if he corners you someday when you're not alone? He's sneaky. He'll try to find you all by yourself one day."

"I guess I'll just have to hope that doesn't happen," said Marty. "He's so much bigger and stronger than me."

"He's not bigger and stronger than all of us," said Brenna. "If he does anything to you, we'll find *him* alone someday and do the same to him. We need to send him a message before that day gets here."

Donald Kent sank back against the wall, trying to hide himself from view. He'd heard enough now. All the years of abuse his son had taken needed to come to an end. His earlier stance, of not getting involved, of letting Marty handle his own problems, would be a thing of the past. *Brenna Nelson is right,* he thought. Scott Gardner needed a message sent. It was time for Donald to step up and defend his son.

CHAPTER 26

Donald Kent was more than familiar with Scott Gardner's neighborhood. In his youth, he'd delivered newspapers to the very street the Gardner's lived on. With a customer base of over 100 homes divided over six long streets, he'd committed to memory many of the addresses and names of the residents he'd delivered to for three years. He remembered the barking dogs along Adams Avenue, the four old homes at the end of Martin Avenue, the elderly tenants on Dewitt Street, and the gentle residing slope of Peterson Street, the final turn on his 90 minute daily routine.

He hadn't been to the area lately, though his own home stood only a few miles away.

Narwood Street, where Scott Gardner lived, was in the opposite direction to most things from the Kents' home. Schools, shopping, the hospital, downtown, anything and everything else he needed was a considerable distance from his old stomping grounds. Years had passed since he'd been near the place, and he looked forward to seeing many of the old homes once again.

But the true nature of his re-visit wouldn't call for much nostalgia gathering. His stop would undoubtedly be a very private one. He had no intention of mentioning his trip to a single soul, and when his wife asked him before he left exactly where he was going, he simply replied, "Out to run a few errands." *It was a good enough excuse*, he thought, as he pulled the car out from the parking spot in front of his house, and drove towards his destination.

Gary Kaschak

He decided to drive up and down the streets of his old paper route, surveying the old, crumbling homes around him. He slowed to a crawl on Peterson, turned onto Davis, then made his way to Martin. *Not much has changed,* he thought. Only the properties appeared much smaller than he remembered. He began reciting the names of the people in his mind: *Johnson, Shaffer, Dooling, Cahill, Rivers, Cannon.* He'd remembered them all, just as he'd remembered entire baseball teams from the same era. *Fenstermacher, Jones, Calhoun, Parker, Weinstein,* all riveted for good in the back of his mind.

He turned down Adams, where the Davis's dogs had barked repeatedly every day he'd walked by their fenced-in yard. He'd never understood how the three German Shepherds had never grown accustomed to him over a three year period, how they never seemed to recognize or even become comfortable with him being around. He paused just then, listening for any sign of dogs on the old property. *Nothing,* he thought, and continued driving towards the Gardners'.

The first pass he made was a bit faster than he'd gone on the previous streets. He wanted no suspicious eyes spying on him now. He took a quick glance at the Gardners' house. *It's the old Hewitt place,* he thought. He continued on past the remainder of old homes on the street, then turned around and drove past the Gardners' once more, only this time, he drove at the posted speed of 20 miles per hour.

No activity seemed to be occurring around the Gardner's house, and for that Donald was grateful. He'd played out the scene in his mind several times on the way over, the possibility of a physical encounter with Scott Gardner's father in the forefront. On one hand, he welcomed the chance to take a poke at him, to redirect all the pent-up emotions inside his son that had now crossed over to him. In that he had no fear. On the other hand, he welcomed the notion of a peaceful truce, an honorable exchange between two civilized adults. But his knowledge of Scott Gardner gave him little hope that the latter would occur. Scott Gardner couldn't be the bad apple he was were there not a problem at the top of the tree. Donald was prepared now for a physical confrontation.

But his approach would be an honorable one. He'd introduce himself, try to make some small talk, then get down to business. Perhaps Mr. Gardner would take to his approach, be agreeable and

158

inviting. Perhaps he'd do his best to avoid a confrontation, perhaps he'd be the mature, responsible adult Donald hoped for.

Kent drove his car around the corner, then found a parking spot at the end of Davis.

Generally, no cars were parked at the end of the street, and he found it to be a comfortable place to leave his car. He shut off the ignition, locked the doors, and began walking towards the Gardners'.

It was only 8:30 a.m., and only now were people beginning to stir on this Saturday morning. Donald Kent walked briskly down the sidewalk of Davis, head down, eyes straight ahead. He kept thinking about the possible confrontation with Mr. Gardner. He focused on the words he'd choose to open the meeting, and his blood coursed through his veins with the thought of an impending fight. He turned the corner of Davis, entered Narwood Street, then finally looked up as the Gardners' pig-sty of a house caught his eye.

In the driveway to the right of the house lay an old, abandoned pick-up truck. The hood and trunk were open, a rusted out battery lay in front of one of the tires. The bald tires were nearly flat, and hub caps were missing or strewn about the backyard. In front of the wreck was a more current model, at least 20 years old, its condition rivaling that of the abandoned vehicle. Its inflated tires were nearly bald, just a hint of tread still visible to the eye. The passenger side rear window had been replaced with a makeshift one of plastic. Unruly patches of grass had pushed their way out of the many openings on the gravel driveway, and a hand-held lawn mower lay exposed to the elements, rusty and discolored, at the end of the driveway.

Donald studied the house for a moment, pondering how abandoned the place looked.

The old paint on the east side of the dwelling had lost any semblance of order. Though he knew the house had been white, it was hard to tell just what color it was from his angle.

More brown showed through than white, the obvious result of years of neglect. He spotted two of the upper windows of the second floor, broken, and heard the buzzing of a fan whizzing, then clicking, then whizzing some more. As he approached the front of the house, things seemed to worsen for his troubled eyes.

The small parcel of earth in the front yard held patches of bare ground mixed with unruly weeds and dandelions. Three of the four stairs leading up to the porch had been broken, and the porch itself was nothing more than rotting boards of wood. Nothing was level here; even the house itself seemed to be uneven. All the windows were filthy, and the screen door was torn; as if someone had ripped it apart, its dangling netting swayed at the slight breeze. To the left of the house, more car-parts and lawn tools were scattered about, along with an old barbecue grill missing three of its four legs.

Donald's heart began to pound in his chest as he carefully maneuvered up the four broken steps. It was now 8:45, and he knew the Gardner's might still be asleep. He pressed the rusty doorbell, but no sound came from inside. He knocked quietly on the door three times, then stepped back to wait for the answer. When nothing happened in the next 30 seconds, he knocked four times, a bit louder. He stepped back again, and, when nothing happened again, he walked over to the window and peered into the living room.

He experienced considerable difficulty focusing in on the dark room. The filthy windows and the glare forced him to cup his eyes and draw so close to the window that the tip of his nose touched the glass. He looked around the room, which seemed to be in more disarray than the outside. Magazines, bags of snacks, and newspapers were strewn about everywhere in sight. The television was on, but he didn't see anyone in the room.

But then he squinted his eyes and saw a figure of a man fast asleep on a lounge chair, his head cocked to one side, his feet up on the end of the chair.

Donald stepped back from the window, walked the few steps towards the door and drew back his hand in the knocking position. He held it for a moment, pausing to think things out more clearly. To wake the man would obviously be rude. After all, it was Saturday, and the possibility that the man was sleeping in on his day off crossed Donald's mind. Or maybe he'd been out late the night before. Other reasons came to him, but with each thought, his son's problems arose first and foremost in his mind.

He rapped on the door hard and fast. No response. He looked into the window again.

The man hadn't moved an inch. This time, Donald placed his hand around the doorknob, turned it to the right, and was surprised that the door opened, and squeaky sounds emanated from both the door and the knob. Donald pushed the door open and peered inside at the man, who moved ever so slightly in his chair.

"Excuse me!" whispered Donald. No reply. "Excuse me!" he said again, only this time with more volume and vigor.

The man finally threw open his eyes, rubbed them, scratched his stubbled face, and looked at Donald Kent. "Who are you?" he rasped. Then he checked the clock on top of his television set. "What are you doing in my house?"

The tone of his voice was exactly what Donald had expected. He knew he was trespassing, at least in the broad sense of the word. He hadn't exactly set foot in the house, but he had opened the door without the consent of the owner. He forced a smile at the man, who hadn't yet risen from his chair. At that moment, Donald realized why people had been so afraid of this man. The lack of upkeep on the property, the total disregard for others, his neglect of his own son, even his run-ins with the law, all made sense to Donald now as he sized Mike Gardner up. In a way, he too had been neglectful towards Marty, but in a much different sense. But either way, he'd ignored a need in his son, too, and his treatment was the same in kind, if not degree, as the neglect he could so easily note in this Gardner family. And the fact that he could find any similarities between himself and this man sent a chill down his spine.

"I'm Donald Kent," he said firmly. "I'm sorry to bother you so early on a Saturday, but I'd like to talk to you about something, man to man."

"Man to man?" said Gardner. "What's this all about?"

"I'd like to come in, if you don't mind," said Donald. "I'll only take a few minutes of your time."

Gardner rubbed his hand across his chin and tried to blink the sleep from his bloodshot eyes. He shoved a newspaper from his lap, pushed a button on the side of the chair which propelled him forward, and awkwardly rose from his chair.

"Who'd you say you were?" asked Gardner again.

"Donald Kent," Donald replied. "Our boys go to school together."

161

"Kent?" said Gardner sourly. "You're the father of that boy who's digging that hole, aren't you?"

"That'd be me," he said proudly.

"Most ridiculous thing I ever heard," said Gardner, eyeing Donald warily now, the cobwebs of the abrupt awakening being replaced by clearer thinking. He knew what he'd just said was an insult, but *this was his house*, and he could have his way with this stranger. He waited for Donald to respond, and when he didn't, Gardner said, "So what's your business with me?"

"I want to talk to you about your son," Donald said firmly.

"What about him?" growled Gardner.

"I'd like him to stop bullying my son, and probably, other kids, too."

Gardner stared at Donald's eyes, then looked up and down his athletic figure.

Then his serious gaze turned to a smile, he began laughing wildly, his uncontrolled chuckling breaking the earlier silence of the room. When he finally calmed down, he'd noticed no change in Donald Kent's calm expression. Gardner picked up a beer can from a tray alongside the chair, guzzled down the remainder of its contents, then boldly smashed the aluminum can against his forehead. He dropped the can on the floor and let out a huge belch in Donald Kent's direction.

Gardner hoped his rudeness would trigger Kent to do something physical. When nothing happened, he chuckled again and then said, "Now I know why your son's such a baby. His papa is just a big coward! Now, get out of my house, right now!"

He turned his back on Donald, intending to slump again into his chair, but he stopped short of it when Donald said, "I'm not leaving until we settle the issue between my son and yours."

Gardner pursed his lips, turned and walked towards Donald. Gardner was a heavy Man; his 260-pound frame outweighed Donald's by nearly 80 pounds. He'd figured at first that he could easily have his way with Donald, but now Gardner felt as if he was the one being pushed around.

Gardner said, "Hey—I thought I told you to leave. And I still see you standing there. What's your problem, boy?"

"I believe the problem is you," Donald said slowly and clearly.

"Oh, I'm your problem, am I?" said Gardner. "And what's an old softy like you gonna do about it?" Gardner began to poke Donald in the chest, forcing him back with each thrust of his thick index finger. He repeated, "What are you gonna do about it?" with each thrust.

On the fourth poke, Donald grabbed the man's finger with his right hand, then pulled it and the remaining fingers on his hand so hard, the bigger man dropped to his knees and began wailing like a baby. Donald had learned this move, an immobilizing stunt that could bring down the largest of foes, from police friends. He'd never had to use this move before, but he wasn't surprised at the results. His friends had demonstrated it on him, and he'd found the initial pain so severe, it had nearly rendered him helpless. He'd never forgotten the feeling, but more importantly, he hadn't forgotten the technique, either.

The air in Gardner's lungs seemed to stall, as his brain's commands couldn't respond to orders. Donald maintained his grip, watching Gardner's face contort and his bulging eyes plead for mercy. Donald asked Gardner if he was ready to talk, and when he didn't respond quickly enough, he tightened his grip around the man's fingers.

Gardner finally nodded, and then Donald began to loosen his grip. He slowly backed off the pressure, then released Gardner's hand altogether. Gardner drew back his hand, shaking it and grimacing in pain. The air in his lungs finally responded and he breathed out a long blast. He began to suck in more and more air, beads of sweat dripping down his face. He still didn't rise from his knees, and his pain hadn't subsided much at all.

Donald looked down at the man and said, "As I was saying, I'd like to *talk* to you about your boy bullying mine."

Gardner finally dragged himself up, then plopped into his easy chair. He grabbed a greasy napkin from the tray and wiped his brow. Then he said, "O.K., I'm listening."

"Good," said Donald confidently, and he took a seat on the adjacent couch. "It's my understanding that your son, Scott, along with other kids Scott has rounded up, have been picking on Marty for some time now," said Donald. "I believe it's been *several years*, in fact."

Gardner knew this was true, but he acted surprised to hear it. "So what," he deadpanned. "Kids are always getting picked on. I'm sure Scott gets picked on, too."

"Oh, I highly doubt that," said Donald. "On the contrary, I believe your son instigates just about every problem there is at the school, doesn't he?"

In response, Gardner threw up his hands in mock ignorance. Donald rose from the couch and approached him. "Look," Donald said, "from this point on, I don't want your son causing any more problems with Marty. In fact, I don't want him even *coming around* Marty. Do I make myself clear, Gardner?"

"Are you threatening me?" said Gardner.

"Oh, no, that would be silly now, wouldn't it?" Donald smiled. "It's not in my nature to make *threats* at people."

"Then what do you call it?" shouted Gardner. "You come barging into my house, you nearly break off my hand, and you ask me to tell my son to stop being a boy. If that's not a threat, then what is it?"

Donald looked at Gardner, who still appeared shaken. He said firmly, "As I just stated, it's not a threat, and it's not a warning. Let's just say, it's a *message*. That's right. It's just a message. It's entirely up to you now, however, the way you'd like to *interpret* the message. I only hope, that for the sake of my son and for your sake, that you *completely understand* the message I'm sending."

Donald reached out his right hand to Gardner. At first, Gardner didn't offer his, but then he slowly reached out to take it. Donald smiled once more, then fashioned a vice-like grip around Gardner's already sore hand. With adrenaline pumping through his veins, Donald Kent squeezed the hand like a boa constrictor squeezing the life out of a helpless victim.

Gardner slumped to his knees as he had before, the same helpless look that covered his face earlier returned, and just as before, he found himself both breathless and amazed at the power in Donald Kent's right hand.

"I just want to *make sure* you're getting the message," Donald said softly. He pulled his hand away from Gardner's, gave him a quick salute, and walked out the door and back towards his car.

Trembling, Gardner held his right hand with his left, in disbelief at how painful it felt.

In fact, his hand throbbed so hard, it seemed as though his heart had moved into it. He slumped against his chair, grabbed another nearly empty beer can with his free hand, and chugged its remnants down in a matter of seconds. He was still a few years short of completing his probation, knew that if he'd called the police they'd have no mercy on him, wouldn't believe his story, and probably would find cause to make him look like the guilty party in this situation. He knew he was in no position to draw in the authorities.

He'd bide his time, wait for an opportunity. Then, when that time came, he would take Donald Kent and his son down together...

Upstairs in Scott Gardner's room, the boy hadn't budged from his prone position on his bed. He hadn't heard a sound coming from the living room. He tossed and turned over a few times, but he never opened his eyes until the early hours of the afternoon, nearly four hours after Donald Kent had his way with his father.

CHAPTER 27

Kelly had been looking forward to this next meeting of *The Binghamton Historical Society*. The timing was perfect, really. She'd been thinking, often, of how she might save both Horace Mann School, and Marty's house and the others in the neighborhood, from being leveled. What better place for her to gain the information and knowledge she'd need than at tonight's meeting?

She drove up and down Robinson Street a few times, checking the address she'd been given against the few old stores on the strip that actually had numbers listed on their front windows. This was the oldest stretch of shops in Binghamton, mostly comprising Laundromats, pizzerias, barber shops and the like. At 7 p.m. on a Friday, the street was nearly empty, save for a few scattered cars parked along the curb. Kelly slowed to a crawl, then spotted a small sign, *The Binghamton Historical Society,* next door to *Able's Paint Store*. She found a spot about 50 feet ahead to park her car, then made her way to her destination.

Gingerly, she turned the door handle, then discovered some stairs leading to the second floor. She walked up the creaking 12 steps, noticing a definite lean to the right.

She found it both appropriate and ironic that this crumbling old building housed the *Historical Society*.

When she reached the top, she found the door already opened, a weathered chunk of wood holding it in place. Kelly noticed several voices coming from an area down the narrow hallway she'd spotted inside. No receptionist sat at the desk in the front room, so Kelly stepped inside and began to look around.

Aged photographs, some dating from around the turn of the century, lined the walls of the small space. Kelly studied the pictures one by one, finding some satisfaction in the fact that she was actually *enjoying* this. She'd never been particularly interested in nostalgia, or history for that matter, and she broke into a faint smile, thinking of the significance of the moment.

"Kelly, how long have you been here?" bellowed the familiar voice of Mack Franklin, who came through the open door behind her.

"Oh, only for a few minutes," she responded, turning to face the man. "I've been looking at these old photos of the area. Do they have any of Horace Mann?"

"Certainly," he replied, and walked over to a metal filing cabinet nearby. He pulled the handle open, thumbed through several manila folders, then produced a slim folder marked *Horace Mann School*.

"Here you are," he said proudly. "Have a look."

Kelly opened the file, briefly eyed a dozen or so photos of the old school, stopping at one particular picture of the ribbon-cutting ceremony welcoming the new school in 1890.

All the local dignitaries stood in place, and hundreds of people lined the sparsely populated streets surrounding the school. Even Recreation Park, situated across the street from the old school, was full of excited people, seemingly interested in getting a firsthand look at "the newest building in town."

"Look at all the people in this photo," said Kelly. "It's a shame they have to knock down such a beautiful old place."

"Yes," agreed Franklin. "And the irony of it all is that just as many people will probably be watching the demolition."

He placed the folder back into the file, extended his left arm out to Kelly, and said, "Why don't we go back with the others? The meeting should be starting in a few minutes."

She walked in front of him as he'd directed, headed to the end of a hallway and turned left. She followed his directions and entered a much larger room, where several people were seated around a large conference-type table.

"Attention, everyone," Franklin said loudly above the other voices, "I'd like you to meet Kelly Trapp from *The Bulletin*."

Introductions were made, lasting a few minutes. Kelly received compliments from the majority of the nine member board, congratulatory slaps on the back for her recent stories about *The Hole to China*. She'd enjoyed this attention, not yet quite realized that she was becoming a local celebrity in her own right.

One of the men pulled the seat next to his out for her, and she smiled and sat down as Mack Franklin announced the beginning of the meeting. "If you all don't mind, I thought we'd depart from our usual agenda for a few moments. With your permission, of course, I'd like to give the floor over to Miss Trapp, who'd like to discuss the pending matter of the demolition of Horace Mann School."

Many of the members nodded in agreement, and Franklin continued. "Very well. As you all know, Horace Mann is scheduled for demolition in early September of this year to make way for a new state–of-the-art facility. I'm sure that day will be bittersweet for many of us, but, as they say in the circus, the show must go on. We'll miss the beautiful architecture Horace Mann gave us, and the memories of the grade school, many of us in this room actually attended. But, as I've told Kelly before, the old building just doesn't meet the requirements for the Historical Society to stand in the way of its demolition. In fact, there is nothing we can satisfactorily check off on our list of 21 requirements to keep the place standing. On the surface, it's a lost cause. Nevertheless, Miss Trapp, if you would…"

Kelly stood to her feet. From the information Kelly had heard already, not to mention Big Mack's words just preceding, this certainly appeared, on the surface, to be a lost cause. But her background living in the inner city of Philadelphia wouldn't let her give up—just yet. She didn't like what she'd just heard, and she reminded herself how many times throughout her life she'd listened to the same thing, that familiar sound of giving up without a fight.

"It all sounds like a lost cause, I'll admit," said Kelly. "But there has to be a way we can save that building and the neighborhood it's near."

A throat near the rear of the room cleared loudly, and all eyes darted towards a handsome, middle-aged man seated at the end of the long table. He was perhaps in his mid '50s, smoking a pipe, whose long trail of vapors sifted the air aromatically. Kelly squinted her eyes as he turned to face them. His silver-streaked hair shone under

169

the light from the overhead fixture. Kelly noted dead silence a scant few seconds; then, without being asked, the man cleared his throat again and began to speak:

"My name is Bradford Davidson, Miss Trapp. I serve as attorney for *The Historical Society.* I'm afraid everything you've heard so far is quite true, young lady. Mr. Franklin has hit the nail right on the head. At this point, it'd be virtually impossible to halt the demolition of Horace Mann."

"You said, *virtually* impossible, " Kelly said.

"That's right, I did say that, young lady," Davidson replied. "I also said everything you've heard is true, which included what *you* also said."

"What did I say that's true?" asked Kelly.

"You said, *there has to be a way, "* he replied.

His comment raised surprised gasps around the table. Even Kelly hadn't really expected to hear words that supportive from the Society's lawyer. Davidson allowed a few seconds of conversation to pass; then he raised his non-pipe-holding hand to signal for quiet. "As an attorney, I have to believe what I'm believing *in,*" he said directly to Kelly. "Even the slightest glimmer of hope can sometimes be enough for a knowledgeable lawyer to allow a possibility to exist in his mind. But what it would take to overcome *eminent domain* – well, that's another story altogether. I'd say it's *this* close to impossible." He held his index finger about a sixteenth of an inch from his thumb.

Kelly winced at the gesture, then asked, "What exactly might it take?"

"Let's first examine the facts," Davidson said. "Mr. Franklin has already pointed out that none, I repeat, *none* of the 21 requirements can be met to make the school a historical site—even remotely met, I might add. Second, the city has already gone through the bidding process and awarded contracts to both the demolition company, and the construction company. We're talking big money, here, some of which has probably already been paid out by the city.

"Third," he added, "and most importantly, you're battling eminent domain."

"Why is that so difficult to do?" asked Kelly.

A large number of snickers and chuckles issued from the society members. The lawyer looked at Kelly and said, "Kelly, *Eminent domain* is big government – *big* government. And the law is very specifically spelled out: *Eminent domain* allows municipalities to take control of property in case like this one. I admire your spunk, Miss Trapp, but my advice to you, despite your eagerness, is to just let it go."

Kelly sat back down in her chair for a moment. The "facts" were clear, undeniably.

Nothing in what Davidson had just said should be giving her even a sliver of hope. But, as was her wont, she continued for a few more minutes to ask questions, until she hit on the right one: "Mr. Davidson, have you *ever* heard of eminent domain being defeated?"

Davidson took a long drag from his pipe and looked into the air as if in deep thought.

He exhaled the smoke he'd just puffed, then put his pipe down into the ash tray in front of him. "There is one case I do recall," he said.

"Really?" said Kelly. "Can you tell us about it?"

"It was out in Minnesota about 20 years ago. Similar circumstances, I recall, only it was an old high school, about 85 years old."

"Did they save it?" asked Kelly.

"Indeed they did," he said. "Let me tell you what happened."

Davidson took his time explaining what the people had done to preserve their little jewel of a school. They'd taken a little known law in eminent domain, and with amazingly strong support and pressure by the people, forced the government to reverse their decision.

"What the people did," he said, "was to find an unusual reason to preserve the building. No longer could it be used as a school; the law made that clear; but what they did was ingenious." He paused for a moment, then grinned, "I'm sure they had a very good lawyer."

A hearty laugh by the group followed, then Kelly said, "Well, exactly what did the people do?"

Davidson continued. "There's a clause in eminent domain—well hidden I might add – that basically says if the edifice can be preserved and maintained as a *museum* of some sort, then that, and only that, might save it. So the people banded together, raised money and made a museum of the building, which not only saved it, but actually drew people into it. They actually made money with it in the long run."

Kelly quickly asked, "Then what sort of museum could we possibly establish to save that building?"

"That's the question," said Davidson, "And that one's for you to figure out, my dear."

Kelly wondered aloud, "Then couldn't there be something we could do to at least postpone the demolition—until we can muster enough support for the idea?"

"Yes, I suppose there are some measures we could take," said Davidson. "But why bother, really? What on earth could the old school be used for that might promote any public interest? I'm sorry if I gave you any false hope; I simply pointed out the Minnesota story because you'd asked the question. The possibility of its happening here is so remote, so very remote, that it just wouldn't be worth the effort, in my opinion. It would take much more than public support to put a halt to things at this point. You'd need money—and *big* money—to battle the government."

"Maybe I could raise it from the people," said Kelly.

"Well, you do wield some power with the public now," said the lawyer. "But I think you need to think more with your head than your heart, young lady. The people here, sure, they're supporting the boy and his Hole to China right now, but when it comes down to money— and I'm not just talking about raising a little money here, I'm talking about big money that will need to grow as you go deeper into your battle – well, this community's people work hard for their money, and they've already voted for the demolition.

"Now keep in mind that in itself the demolition is costing the taxpayers. If you take this next step, you'll be affecting the lives many more taxpayers than just Marty Kent and a few of his neighbors. You'll be affecting the whole city's tax base."

This ended Kelly's portion of the meeting. She gathered her belongings, said polite good-byes, and headed down the stairs with Mack Franklin. They chatted for a few moments, then he bade her farewell, carefully watching as she made it safely to her car.

They waved to each other, then he disappeared behind the entrance door.

CHAPTER 28

Ample time had been provided for Marty and his comrades in the hole to do some serious soul-searching. The clean and clear path of 250 feet had now become a difficult obstacle course, a cruel twist of fate that left the diggers chipping at thick, unyielding stone, and gaining mere inches instead of feet in long periods of time. Things that hadn't even been mentioned just days earlier had begun to wear on the psyches of the youngsters. Boredom began to sink in, along with tired muscles and sore limbs. Talk of quitting altogether became more and more frequent as the chipping became tedious and mundane. With these factors came inevitable lack of desire; effort dropped off, and time spent in the hole digging was cut in half. The enthusiasm of youth that had so overcome them had now begun to wane.

Following two long days of nothing more done than chipping, the city engineer made his rounds. He'd heard the diggers had run into obstacles, that they'd hit a solid slab of rock. He'd brought with him the appropriate instruments to measure and calibrate the rock formation. He'd take his tests, and have them analyzed at the State University of New York campus in Vestal. He'd made the arrangements in advance, and promised the results of their findings would be ready that day between noon and 12:30.

At 11:50 a.m., Marty and Brenna were the lone figures inside the hole, though Kelly Trapp looked down on them from the rim – she wanted to get the scoop on the expert's report – and a handful of Marty's and Brenna's friends were there, too, shoveling dirt up top.

Marty knew how much Brenna's feistiness and tenacity had helped him continue on. Her determination was what he liked so much, what he admired in her so deeply. She was the scrappiest kid he'd ever seen; there were no obstacles she wouldn't try to overcome. She was tougher than any boy when it came to scrapes and cuts, and simply had no quit in her.

Right now she pounded on the rock as hard as she could, watching a few chips of stone fly past her. She reached into the soil all around the hole, looking for some soft earth, some opening, something to signal they'd reached the bottom of that formation.

But nothing but solid rock surrounded them. It seemed as though they stood on top of a huge boulder.

She said, "I think if we chip away for a few more hours, we're bound to break through. Rock formations can't be too deep, can they?"

Marty thought about what he'd learned from the books on the earth. He recalled reading about rock formations, and he knew they could be *unpredictable* at best. "Well, at this depth, those books said that rocks could be pretty deep," he countered. He sensed the eagerness in his friend, knew he needed to say something more encouraging just then.

He thought she was looking at him, well, *differently* than she had before, a more, *girly* look. And he said, "I think you're right, though. We've been pounding this rock for days, it's just a matter of time."

Brenna smiled reassuringly. She grabbed her shovel, and as she did, the voice of Donald Kent reached them from above: "He's here— the man from the city's here with the results. Come on up!"

The pair looked at one another excitedly, then dropped their tools and headed for the rungs. Marty held out his arm for Brenna to go first, and as he did, she turned impulsively to him and kissed him on the lips.

It wasn't a very long kiss. In fact, it was quite short. After all, this was a first kiss for both of them, so she lacked the passion an experienced kisser could provide, and the setting as the most unromantic of places. Marty was taken completely off-guard. *Hey, girls just don't kiss first*, he thought. In fact, he fell back against the damp wall of the hole to gather his composure as Brenna clambered up the ladder. He felt something in the pit of his stomach he'd never felt before. His heart thumped inside his chest, his breathing became shallow, but the feeling—the feeling of being kissed—and kissed by Brenna Nelson, was the best thing he'd ever felt in his young life. Yeah, he'd thought about this moment before, but his young mind had played it out so differently. He'd envisioned himself kissing Brenna several times, but he'd never given himself a realistic chance to do so. The thoughts, though frequent, had always remained very brief. Up until this point, his self-esteem had been so low it was nearly off the scale. But now, here in his hole, Brenna Nelson had kissed him, and she'd *meant it.*

"Hey, waddaya doin' down there?" Brenna yelled from the top of the hole. "Come on, they're all waitin' for us."

Marty scampered up the rungs, his thoughts returning to the man from the city and his report. But for each step he scaled, his thoughts mixed between what had just happened, and what was about to happen. He was excited, apprehensive and full of energy. He reached the top of the hole, spotted a group of people gathered at the picnic table to the left, and trotted over to Brenna Nelson's side.

The group of 11 people fixed their gaze on the man from the city. He carefully unrolled a rather large document from a cylindrical cardboard tube and flattened it out as best he could on the picnic table. All eyes fixed on the blueprint. It showed a series of uneven parallel lines, and though it was more technical than animated, Marty could clearly see that the densest lines on the graph were located just below the current location of the deepest part of the hole.

The man said, "What you're seeing here is a computed grid of the formations directly below the hole. These darker lines, here, just below the bottom of the hole, that represents a very dense rock formation. As you can see, here," he said, pointing a few inches below where the formation gave way to a long column of very thin blue lines, "once you get past this part, it looks pretty good. That's the good news."

"I'm afraid to ask," said Donald Kent, "but exactly how deep is this rock formation?"

"That would be the bad news," said the man. "Our estimate is, that solid rock formation is at least 30 feet deep, perhaps 40. It would

take weeks to dig through it, and that's *with* the proper equipment."
The man looked gently at Marty and the others and said, "I'm afraid
digging with shovels and hand tools would have little impact on that
rock. Based on this report, I'm afraid this is about as far as you'll get.
I'm sorry."

Kelly, never one to take *no* for an answer, piped up, "How
expensive is the equipment?"

"*Very*, I'm afraid," he said. "And would take weeks to deliver,
even *if* the money for it was available. The cold hard facts are that the
costs would be prohibitive, and we all know what the future of this
property is." He turned to Marty, looked at him with forlorn eyes and
said, "You should be proud of what you've done here, son. I think the
entire city is proud of you. It's a shame we can't help you any
further."

He rolled up his document, placed it back into the tube and slowly
walked out to his city vehicle. Both Donald Kent and Kelly Trapp
followed him, asking questions that seemed to have already been
answered. Marty stood near his friends, and Roger Doyle asked,
"What do we do now?"

Marty cleared his throat and waved everyone into a tight circle.
He wasn't the least bit surprised at the meeting's outcome; the books
on the earth had prepared him for such an occasion. In fact, he'd been
thinking things out for some time now, ever since they first
encountered that first small cluster of rocks. He'd known it was
probably at the fringe of a bigger, denser formation. Deep down, he'd
known it was only a matter of time before this day came, so he'd set
his mind to reading not only the books on the earth, but about *China*,
grasping for any bits of information that might help him make his
next decision.

He'd learned about some of the culture of China, the way the
government worked, and the size of the country in relation to his. He
knew how far away it was, knew something about the agriculture and
the climate. The more he'd read, the more he'd wanted to know.

"Let's all go back into the hole," said Marty. "I think we need
some privacy for what I'm going to say." He looked at Kelly and said,
"Sorry, ma'am, but we need to hash this out by ourselves."

In a short time, the seven youths present climbed down the rungs
and into the cold depth of the hole. Several flashlights sat inside, and

as each person leaned against the sides of the Hole, they snapped on lights, creating an eerie backdrop in the darkness.

Marty stood looking around at the disappointed faces of his new friends. He knew how they must feel; but for him, this seeming obstacle of all obstacles would only serve to send the Hole, his *Hole to China*, in a far different and more amazing direction than he or anyone else had imagined.

"I've been doing some thinking," Marty began. "It might sound corny and all, but I have a plan."

"A plan?" countered Roger. "What kind of plan?"

"Well, I've been doing a lot of reading about the earth," said Marty, "and about China, too."

Greg Gibson said, "My dad says China is one of those communist countries."

"That's true," said Marty.

"So what's your plan?" Gibson replied.

"OK," Marty said. He picked up a loose stone from the ground and said, "Did any of you know that the earth is about 4,000 miles deep, and it would take us 10,000 years to dig through it at the rate we're going?"

"No way!" said Greg.

"I couldn't believe it when I first found out, either," said Marty.

Peter Floyd said, "Why didn't you tell us before?"

"I don't know," said Marty, shrugging his shoulders. "We were having too much fun, and the people—the people were starting to believe we could do it. I didn't want to let anybody down. I figured we'd go as deep as we could until the school was torn down, and then that would be that. I guess I never thought we'd even get this far."

He paused for a moment, then said softly, "Plus, I made all these new friends. I didn't want any of you to leave."

"Don't worry about that," said Larry Murphy. "We've had a lot of fun doing this, too. Now tell us what your plan is!"

Marty said, "Can we all agree that we're never going to *dig a hole to China*?"

"Agreed," said the others.

"Then think about this: What if we *sent* China our hole?"

Brenna's eyes bugged out. "Send China our *hole*? How do you send anyone a hole?"

"Well, not the entire hole," said Marty, "just a *part* of it. We find a real nice box, and we fill it with some of the dirt from the hole. Then we send it to China."

Brenna said, "How do you do *that*?"

"Well," Marty went on, "I've done some reading on the United Nations. Its headquarters is in New York City, and China's one of the members, and they have a person who lives here half the time, and half the time lives in China. They call them ambassadors."

"Ambassadors," Roger said. "I've heard of them. We studied them in school this year."

The kids nodded, briefly remembering their teachers spending a few hours discussing the United Nations. They were a bit more interested now in what Marty had to say.

"O.K., so we get a box full of dirt," said Brenna. "How are kids like us going to send it to China?"

"We're not," said Marty. "Kelly Trapp is, only she doesn't know it yet."

"And how does Kelly get this box to China?" Brenna wanted to know.

"She works for a newspaper," Marty replied. "They probably have tons of ways to contact the Chinese Ambassador."

"When are you going to ask her?" said Roger.

Marty said, "I wanted to make sure you guys thought it was a good idea. If you do, we'll ask her when we're done talking about it – she's waiting right up top. So if we're agreed, why waste any more time thinking it over?"

Larry said, "O.K., hold it a minute! Let's just say Kelly gets the box to the right person. What do you want *them* to do with it?"

It was the best question so far, and one Marty had thought about before. His imagination carried the box to mainland China itself, where the Chairman himself would welcome the gift. Marty fashioned the notion that the Chairman would introduce the box to his people, an outpouring of love and affection would follow, and somehow, in Marty's wildest dreams, the world would be a better place to live.

"I don't know, they'd just keep it as a gift from us, I imagine," he said. "He could do what he wants with it. It'd be neat if he really did get it from us."

The others soon agreed with Marty's assessment – it was worth a try. Plus, they had nothing to lose by trying, and though it wouldn't be nearly as much fun as the digging had been, doing such an exciting thing would prolong their summer adventure.

Marty said, "Now let's go up top and talk to Kelly."

One by one, the group made the long journey to the top of the hole. It was a taxing, energy-zapper of a climb, and repeating the task daily had contributed greatly to Marty's sudden loss of weight. Though he hadn't hit the scales recently, last he looked he'd dropped close to 20 pounds, and the outer layer of fat that had so controlled his life was melting away like an ice cube in the hot sun. Marty waited for all his friends to go ahead of him, then asked Brenna to stay back a moment before scaling the wall.

"Brenna, what happened before, you know, the kiss," said Marty quietly. "Why did you do it?"

"Why?" she asked, perturbed. "Because you're one of the nicest boys I've ever been around, that's why." She clumsily walked over to him, gave him another surprise kiss on the lips, smiled and turned back to scale the rungs.

With this second kiss, the feeling he'd experienced from her first nearly doubled in power. He suddenly felt overwhelmingly giddy, happy, on top of the world. He wondered what life would be without Brenna, when the wrecking ball came in six weeks.

CHAPTER 29

Kelly stood with her arms crossed as Marty and his friends approached. She wondered how'd they react to the sudden, certainly unexpected decision made by the city engineer.

She herself was practically devastated at the news. This was the story, after all, that had energized her fledgling career as a reporter. It was her baby, her pride and joy. Kelly felt a peculiar knot in the pit of her stomach as she and Marty made eye contact.

"I'm so sorry about the news," Kelly began. "You should be proud of what you've accomplished here."

Marty didn't acknowledge her statement. In fact, he and his buddies formed a semi-circle around Kelly. She noticed the solemn, but not sad looks on all their young faces, and found this peculiar under the circumstances.

"You all look so serious," she said. "I thought you'd be angry or upset with the decision."

"We are *kinda* upset," said Marty. "But I knew something like this was gonna happen. China's just too far away for anyone to really dig a hole there."

Kelly was taken aback a bit by Marty's mature statement. All along she'd assumed he'd truly believed he could, and *would*, make it to China. Up to this point, she'd never given Marty credit for facing reality, and now, watching Marty and his buddies come to terms with reality, a most reassuring feeling overcame her.

Gary Kaschak

"That's surprising to hear from you," she said. "I thought that you thought it was possible to dig a hole to China."

"I know," Marty said sheepishly. "I think everyone thought that at the beginning."

"When did you know you truly couldn't?" asked Kelly.

"Oh, when I started reading all those books, back a while ago," Marty said, pausing.

"Then when we started digging, I just knew we'd never make it. It's just too far away."

He paused again, and Kelly sensed hesitation in him. "Is there something more going on here?" she asked, folding her arms.

Marty looked at the others, then back at Kelly. "We've been talking," he said. "We have a plan, and we need you to help us."

"Oh?" Kelly replied curiously. "What kind of a plan?"

"Well, now that we know it's impossible to tunnel through the earth, we were kinda hoping you could make a delivery for us."

"A delivery?" she asked, cocking her head. "What kind of delivery?"

Marty began: "We're going to get the finest box we can find, and fill it with some of the earth from our hole. Then we want you to see that it gets delivered…to China. To the Party Chairman himself."

Kelly began to laugh, but not disrespectfully; her laughter was directed more towards herself then to Marty. That Marty actually thought her connections were world wide she found rather comical, but as she calmed down, she noticed that none of the kids were laughing with her. Instead, they maintained the same serious looks on their faces as they'd had when Marty had popped his suggestion.

She cleared her throat and looked at Marty, this time, with the same kind of sincerity. "Let me get this straight," she said. "You're going to fill a box full of dirt, and you want me to get it into the hands of the Chinese Party Chairman?"

"Yes," Marty smiled. "That's right."

The initial comedy Kelly saw in the matter began to melt away as she realized the depth of the matter hadn't sunk in all the way. But these kids were serious indeed.

She hadn't yet had time to fully think out their plan; and admired the thinking and the initial idea. She was extremely pleased at Marty's maturity, and the kids' overall attitude:

182

Don't give up, redirect their plan, and take things in a far different direction than she would have imagined. These were her kind of people, the hard fighters of the world, like kids from the city, they were simple folks with courage and conviction.

"Marty," she had to ask, "what makes you think I have any connections to the Chinese Chairman? I'm just a local reporter, that's all."

"I know that," said Marty. "But someone else at the newspaper probably knows how we can do this. Maybe Mr. Kincade can help; plus, we don't want you to personally take it to the Chairman, just get it into the hands of the Chinese Ambassador to the U.N. He lives in New York City sometimes."

"He does?" she said knowingly. "How did you know that, Marty?"

"Like I said, I read all those books on China," Marty replied proudly.

The ease and conviction with which Marty responded, and the thinking that went behind the statement seemed so out of character to Kelly. This lost little 12-year-old boy she'd met only weeks earlier seemed so much more well adjusted and confident. She fashioned a faint smile his way, as his words seemed to melt the cold exterior she sometimes possessed.

"O. K.," she said, "let's say I make the contacts for you. Let's say the box of dirt ends up in the hands of the Chinese Ambassador. What makes you think he'd be interested at all in this unusual gift?"

Marty reached into his back pocket and pulled out a neatly folded document. He unfolded it before the others, then handed it to Kelly. "It's a letter to the Chairman," said Marty confidently. "I've explained the whole thing in there—go ahead and read it. I have an unfolded copy in my room; I don't want him thinking we're too sloppy or something."

Kelly took the one-page document from Marty and began skimming through the single-lined writing, printed rather neatly for a 12-year-old boy. She hadn't read it word for word just yet, but she found the contents to be appealing indeed. She folded the paper back up, placed it in her bag and asked, "Do your parents know about this letter?"

"No, not yet," Marty responded. "I want to show them after you tell me you'll do it."

This presented a most unique challenge, thought Kelly. She totally enjoyed being in the thick of things, and with this sudden change in the Hole's plans, she would be thrown smack-dab in the middle of it.

"I'll see what I can do," she said. "But I'm telling you now, I can't make any promises. China is a communist country; who knows if they'll even allow them to accept that dirt from you."

"They will!" cried Marty enthusiastically. "I *know* you can do it, Kelly!"

"All right then," she said. "Let me go back to the paper and see if I can make some contacts. I'll let you know something as soon I can."

Marty and the others surrounded Kelly, hugging her and cheering as if the amazing feat had already happened. She took it all in, watching their young faces and eager eyes, then looked at the Hole and thought of all the hard work and community spirit it had generated. She took a good long look at the Kents' home, a picture to keep in her mind.

The wrecking ball played heavily on her conscience as she pictured the crumbling houses and school in a blanket of rubble. She bit her lip, then walked briskly to her car, the children's yelling and screaming slowly subsiding as she drove away with all those horrific images flashing in her mind.

CHAPTER 30

Kelly had no time to waste as she approached Joel Kincade's office. She wondered what he'd think about this new twist in the plan. He'd been the one, after all, to believe in her before, and she hoped he'd have faith in what the kids were attempting here.

She rapped on his partially opened office door, pushed it slightly, and saw him angling his head to see who was on the other side.

"Kelly, come in," he said, waving her forward.

She did as directed, then sat down, as Kincade pointed, in the chair across from his.

"What brings you in today?" he asked. "How's the story of *The Hole* coming along?"

"Not too good, I'm afraid," Kelly replied. "The city got the results back on the depth of the rock formation. It's too deep and wide to crack with even the most expensive equipment. I'm sorry to say, but the digging is pretty much over for the boys."

"Oh, that's too bad," Kincade said. He paused. "I take it that will be your lead story for tomorrow's edition?"

"Yes, I suppose it will be," Kelly said in a low tone. "Only, I do believe there's more to this story. The kids aren't giving up. They have a follow-up plan."

Kincade perked up. "Go on."

"Remember when we first thought the story was over, when the bullies filled the hole in with dirt?" she asked.

"Yes," he said.

185

"Well, you said at the time to '*go find where the story takes you.*' I'll never forget it, sir."

"Yes, I did say that," Kincade agreed.

"Well," Kelly went on, "I followed this story in the direction of eminent domain. What I've found out about that is fascinating, indeed, and I'm working that out, too. But the story has taken a new twist, sir."

"Then let's hear what you've got," he said.

She handed him the letter Marty had written to the Chairman. Kincade placed his reading glasses on his face, and said to Kelly, "What's this?"

"It's a letter Marty wrote," she said. "It's to the *Chairman of the Communist Party of China.*"

Kincade chuckled for a moment, then began to read the letter. Kelly sat still, studying his face for any reaction. He seriously perused the letter, barely eliciting even the slightest of grins. When he finished, he folded his hands, looked at Kelly and said, "This is very good stuff, very good indeed."

"Marty wants me to get this to the Chinese Ambassador to the United Nations," said Kelly. "What do you think?

"I think it's marvelous, simply marvelous," Kincade repeated. "Ingenious, actually. That kid's got a decent way of thinking. I admire that."

Kelly felt relieved at Kincade's reaction to this matter. She said, "Do you have any ideas how we can get the box to the Ambassador?"

"Certainly," said Kincade. "But before we get into that, I want you to tell me what you've learned about eminent domain."

Kelly wondered why Kincade was switching gears right now, considering the circumstances of the Hole and Marty's letter. She wasn't sure how any of the information she'd learned from the Historical Society meeting she'd attended could serve a purpose at this moment, but she composed herself and explained as much as she could remember from the meeting.

When she finished, he raised his chin to her, and said, "We've got a whale of a story here, Kelly. From this point forward, I want you to count me in on anything and everything. I think I can see the direction this *could go* pretty clearly, and with the proper research and savvy reporting, I think we can help take this thing along all the way."

"All the way to where?" she asked.

"All the way *to China*," Kincade said without hesitation.

The reaction both startled and excited Kelly. Her heart raced, literally pounding against the wall of her chest. Kincade finally stood up and said, "Now, let me explain to you how I see this. Afterwards, I'm calling the mayor in for an emergency meeting."

"An emergency meeting with the mayor?" Kelly reiterated.

"I'll explain that to you when we go over everything," Kincade assured. "In the meantime, I'm sending you over to Collins."

"Collins? Who's Collins?" she asked.

"Collins?" said Kincade. "Why, he's a walking encyclopedia. The man's got more college degrees than anyone I've ever met. He works upstairs in the research department, I'm sure you've run into him a few times."

"Is his name Ray?" asked Kelly.

"Yes, yes it is," said Kincade. "See, you have met him then."

"Well, not directly," said Kelly. "He's kinda scary, always seems to be talking to himself. I try to avoid him as much as I can."

"He's as harmless as a pussycat," said Kincade. "The real smart ones, like Ray Collins, sometimes don't mix very well socially. Maybe it'd do him some good if you reach out to him, you know, try to be his friend. After all, you'll probably be seeing a lot of him now."

"I will?" asked Kelly.

"Oh, I suspect once you find out what a wealth of knowledge he is, you'll be the first in line at his desk every day."

"If he's so special, why haven't you told me about him before?" Kelly wondered.

"Because you didn't need him before," said Kincade, "and now you do."

"OK, I'll go see him," Kelly agreed. "But what specifically for?"

"The first thing I want Collins to do for you is to help you with the eminent domain issue," Kincade explained. "Tell him all you found out about converting the old school into a museum of sorts to save it. I guarantee he'll give you some information you need, something you hadn't seen before or thought of."

"What about the kids wanting to give the soil to China?" Kelly asked. "Should I write the story about that?"

Gary Kaschak

"I'll discuss that at the meeting with the mayor," said Kincade. "While you're meeting with Collins, I'll be making a few calls to some old friends of mine in New York and Washington, D.C. It's a very delicate matter. You concentrate on eminent domain. When Collins gives you what you need—and we need this by tomorrow night I should add – bring that information to the meeting. I'll be setting it up for 9:00 a.m., day after tomorrow. I'll make sure the mayor frees herself up from her busy schedule. We need to strike on this story before the people start forgetting about that Hole."

"That's not much time to get relevant information, is it?" Kelly speculated.

Kincade stood and raised his hand with finality. "Miss Trapp, we're in a business of deadlines. Time can never be our enemy. I'm fully expecting you to come to the table with something good. You go find Ray before you leave tonight, and I'll make sure he's in on what we need here."

Kelly returned to her desk, sorted through some things, and then heard her name paged. She picked up the blinking light on her phone, and settled back to hear the message.

"Miss Trapp, it's Carol, the receptionist."

"Hello, Carol," said Kelly. "What is it?"

"There's a gentleman waiting up here to see you. Says he has a message for you."

"Well, can't you just take the message?" she asked.

"That's just it," said the receptionist. "He insists on delivering it personally."

"Does he look familiar?" asked Kelly.

"No, I've never seen him before," said Carol.

"Then I'll be right up," said Kelly.

She quickly rose from her chair and briskly walked down the aisle of the newsroom towards the reception area in the front of the building. She opened the door and looked around the room. Several people sat there; this wasn't uncommon; prospective applicants, vendors, school-tours, among others consistently filled up the waiting room.

Kelly caught Carol's eye, and the receptionist quickly pointed out a middle-aged man dressed neatly in a shirt and tie sitting and patiently staring out the door onto the Vestal Parkway. Kelly noticed

188

his perfect posture, his polished shoes, his perfectly manicured hair. He held his hands together, neatly folded on top of a slim briefcase that was lying in his lap.

She walked towards him, the sound of her heels slapping against the tiled floor. He briefly smiled, rose from his chair, held out his hand and introduced himself. "Milo Decatur," he said. "Thank you for seeing me, Miss Trapp. I assure you this will only take a moment."

"No problem," Kelly said. "What can I do for you?"

He opened his briefcase and pulled out a manila folder with Kelly's name on it. He handed it to her and said, "This is from an admirer of yours. Good day, ma'am."

As he tipped his cap and began to walk away, Kelly shouted, "Hey, who is this from?"

The man continued sauntering away, only waving a little while opening the door with his other hand.

This is so odd, she thought, holding the folder, watching the man walk towards the visitors' parking lot.

She returned to her desk, grabbed a letter opener and sliced through the folder's seal.

She pulled out two pages, the first a short letter addressed to her, the second, a hand-drawn map. She put the map down and read the letter to herself:

Dear Ms. Trapp,

I have been admiring your work on The Hole to China *series in your newspaper. It has touched me and brought me to tears. I also understand you have entertained the thought of saving the Horace Mann School building and battling eminent domain. I would like to talk with you, in person, today at 2:00 p.m., at my home, about these issues. I assure you, it will be worth your while to meet with me.*

At the bottom the letter was simply signed, *Beatrice.* The envelope in which it had come indicated the lady's address.

CHAPTER 31

The hand-drawn map that accompanied the mysterious letter directed Kelly to the northern end of Binghamton, the hilly, curvy roads leading past *The Ross Park Zoo*.

She'd never had reason to traverse these roads before; she only knew that the woody properties were home to Binghamton's most affluent citizens. She carefully studied the magnificent structures she saw along the way, all the while following the composed directions, completely awestruck by the spectacular views offered up here, amazed at the sheer size of the homes and the spaciousness between them.

She turned on *Brooke Avenue*, the last turn she'd need to make according to the map, and folded it down the most winding road of all. She'd been paying attention to the numbers on the mailboxes, reciting the number *33* in her mind. The distance on this particular road was perhaps a half-mile, but it took her nearly two minutes to reach the end, where she spotted the number she'd memorized on a fairly modest mailbox, along with the name, *Talley-Whiting*.

She turned into the long driveway, whose shiny black coating gave off a freshly paved look. She detected no signs of activity in or around the house, no car in the vast parking area near the wide garage. She parked her car and walked to the edge of the driveway, where a small stream of water rolling down from the hills above moved at a mesmerizing pace, the gurgling sounds of rushing water soothing to both eyes and ears. She leaped over the narrow stream, no more than

Gary Kaschak

a foot wide, and walked to the edge of the property, where a slight incline, followed by a more severe one, met her gaze.

She looked out into the valley below, where everything looked so small, so miniature.

She could see many of the parts of town she'd come to know, and as she thought how wonderful a sight this was to behold, a strong female voice shouting, "I'm over here!" broke her concentration.

Kelly followed the sound of the voice to the back of the property. She spotted an elderly woman, perhaps 70, pruning and clipping one of the many plants, shrubs, bushes or flowers in the lovely garden. She wore a wide-rimmed hat, garden gloves and sunglasses, and appeared to be of average height and weight for a woman her age.

Kelly slowly moved to within a few yards of the woman, her back turned as she continued clipping one of the bushes.

"You're right on time," said the woman. "I appreciate punctuality."

She turned to Kelly, placed her shears down on the ground, removed her garden gloves and held out her hand. "Beatrice Talley-Whiting," she said.

"This is quite a place up here," said Kelly, taking the woman's hand and shaking it.

"Your garden is magnificent."

"Requires all my time," replied the woman. "But it's time well spent. I love it here, just nature and me. There's nothing like gardening. Do you garden, my dear?"

Gardening was the last thing Kelly had any time for, nor did she have the resources, having been an apartment dweller most of her adult life. Furthermore, she'd never been quite patient enough for things requiring such dedication and energy. In the city, gardens were a rarity, and indoor plants had never been a prominent feature of her childhood home. So, "No, never have," she answered truthfully.

"I suppose with the busy schedule you keep, it would practically be impossible to keep up on such things," the older woman said knowingly.

"Yes, that's exactly it," Kelly agreed. "I just don't have the time."

"Perhaps we should go over to the patio," said the woman. "It's much cooler there in the shade."

192

The garden patio was situated just outside the entrance to the back door of the house, a sprawling, split-level, cream-colored beauty. Kelly noticed a pitcher of lemonade with two glasses seated on a table, and she thanked the woman heartily as she poured them both a glass.

"I just love lemonade," said Kelly. "Reminds me of my childhood."

"You're from Philadelphia," the woman responded.

"Yes, how'd you know?" Kelly inquired.

"There's a lot I know about things in this city," said the woman, "especially at *The Bulletin*."

"Really?" said Kelly. "Why's that?"

"My son used to work there," she replied. "But it goes back much farther than that."

"Your son?" asked Kelly, remembering the name *Whiting* on the mailbox. "Your son isn't...Harry Whiting, is he?"

The woman rolled her eyes at the question, as if she'd known it would come sooner or later but dreaded it. She placed her lemonade down and looked Kelly straight in the eye.

"I'm afraid so," she sighed.

The exchange caught Kelly off-guard. She was confused, to say the least, puzzled by both the woman's response to the question, and wondered why she'd been invited here in the first place.

"Pardon me if I seem confused," said Kelly, "But I'd like to know why you invited me here. I didn't have a great relationship with your son, you know."

"Yes, my dear, that I was well aware of," Whiting's mother explained. "Harry complained quite often to me about you. You were a big pain in the neck to him."

"Then, why I am here?" Kelly asked again. "Do you want to scold me, too?"

The woman let out a huge chuckle that lasted several seconds. "Is *that* what you think?" she asked Kelly, then laughed some more. "Quite the contrary, my dear, I have no quarrel with you."

She quickly settled her laughter, and her face resolved into a deep frown. "I want to help you save that school," she said.

Kelly lurched backward in her seat; her eyes opened wide. She felt even the hair on the back of her neck stand up for a few seconds. *Did she really say what I think she said?* Kelly thought.

"Let me get this straight," said Kelly, "because I'm not sure I heard you right the first time. *You* are the mother of Harry Whiting, the same Harry Whiting I butted heads with every day of my life for the past two years, the man I helped remove from *The Bulletin*, and *you* want to help *me* to save Horace Mann School?"

"You heard me correctly the first time, dear," the woman replied. "And don't feel any remorse about Harry getting fired. He deserved exactly what he got from Mr. Kincade."

Kelly liked that statement. "I'm all ears," she smiled.

"Miss Trapp," said Mrs. Talley-Whiting, "I'm sure you sense some, well...*hostility* on my part towards my son. Trust me, young lady, he's earned every bit of it." She took another sip from her lemonade, then said, "I hope you've put aside enough time today for me. I'd like to share a good deal of information with you about several things. Off the record, of course. All this is strictly *confidential.*"

"Of course, uh...I'm flattered," said Kelly. "I have an hour or so..."

"My late husband, Benjamin," Mrs. Whiting proceeded, "was a difficult man to live with. I'm sorry to say that I stayed with him all those years only for the money, but there's much truth in that statement. I can't say there was ever any tenderness in our marriage, but money was always available. Nevertheless, I do have regrets now." She coughed, a hard, hacking cough, and reached for a small bottle of fluid in a medicine bottle on the table. She quickly sipped its contents, cleared her throat, and continued to speak. "Dreadful stuff," she said, tossing the empty bottle down on the table. "Hard to believe it's the only thing that brings me any relief."

"Are you ill?" asked Kelly.

"Quite," she replied. "I have cancer, and it'll be five months, maybe six at most before the Grim Reaper comes calling."

"I had no idea," said Kelly. "I'm sorry..."

"Oh, don't be sorry, young lady," Mrs. Whiting scolded. "It's all my fault. Those nasty cigarettes have turned my lungs to tar. This medicine is experimental, but I know the score. All it does is give me some comfort, buys me some little time, maybe."

Kelly squirmed in her seat. None of this made any sense to her. This woman wanted to help her, but she was dying. *Dying!* Why would she want to aid a cause that was certainly bordering on the impossible?

"I know what you're thinking," the woman said perceptively. "It really comes down to this, young lady: Before I die, I want to see something good come of all this – *this money.* I can think of nothing more worthwhile than saving that school, and that neighborhood, too, for that matter. Plus, I want that horrible son of mine to get as little of his inheritance as possible. And the plan I have is, I think, the only way to *properly* rid myself of all this filthy money. *"

"I see," said Kelly. "Obviously you've done much serious thinking about these matters. What's your game plan?"

"I have a few more things to tell you first; then we can discuss the plan."

The elderly woman spent the next half hour explaining to Kelly exactly why and how her son had climbed the ladder so quickly at *The Bulletin.* Kelly learned that *The Bulletin* had gone through hard times 10 years earlier, enduring a scandal that sent an accountant and *The Bulletin's* Assistant Editor to jail for participating in a scheme that barely left the old paper with any working capital.

Kelly was dumbfounded to learn next that Harry Whiting had been partially responsible for blowing the whistle on the pair; his keen eye for such things had enabled him to figure the whole thing out from his reporter's perch. Despite the pair's being caught, most of the money they'd filched was gone, and Joel Kincade was faced with having to borrow money at very high interest rates from the local banks to keep the paper afloat.

"But then Benjamin Whiting, my husband, offered to float a 10-year, interest free note to Kincade, and Kincade accepted his offer— but not without certain stipulations and having to promise some *personal favors* to Benjamin Whiting."

"What kind of 'favors'?" asked Kelly.

"My husband was a shrewd man," Mrs. Whiting said. "He always got his way, and he got his way once more in this affair. Joel Kincade's a proud man, but I'm afraid he signed his soul to the devil that day, and I'm certain he regretted it every day for the next 10 years."

"Why?" Kelly questioned. "What kind of favors did your son want in return?"

"It was very simple at first, and even Joel Kincade was satisfied with what he'd had to do," said the woman. "The first stipulation was to *promote* Harry to the suddenly vacant Assistant Editor's position. Joel Kincade had little problem with that; he'd been watching Harry's work, and he'd been pleased with him *in those early days*," she emphasized. "So Kincade made the announcement just a few days after securing the loan from my husband."

"Did anyone else know about this loan?" asked Kelly.

"No, dear, even I wasn't completely aware of the arrangement until my husband died and I began sorting through his personal effects. I'm quite sure not another soul knows any of this, with the exception of Harry, of course. May I remind you, dear, that all of this must remain *completely confidential*. No one else but you and me must know about this."

The woman had made the same request three times now, and Kelly would certainly respect her wishes. This was *too*-big news if anything, news she'd be very comfortable keeping to herself. In fact, some of the information she learned was making her downright *uncomfortable* the more Beatrice Talley-Whiting increased the size and scope of Kelly's knowledge.

"Yes ma'am," said Kelly. "I promise to keep it to myself."

"Very well then," said Mrs. Whiting, "I shall continue."

"The arrangement made between Joel Kincade and Benjamin Whiting called for semi-annual raises in pay, modest as to not draw too much attention, and a promotion to Editor at such time as the current editor, Scott Palmer, would retire. Benjamin Whiting was well aware that Scott Palmer was set to retire about five years after the loan was made, and that's exactly what happened. For Joel Kincade, things were moving along pretty smoothly, and the transition of appointing Harry Whiting as Editor was no surprise to anyone.

"Then, when my husband died, I saw this great transformation in Harry," said Mrs. Whiting. "It was as if all the bad parts of Benjamin simply entered into Harry. Oh, I'm not saying this as if I actually believe it to be something supernatural, but Harry most definitely took on an extraordinary resemblance to all of Benjamin's worst side."

"Why do you think that happened?" asked Kelly.

"Well, my theory is that Harry had never before truly came out from under his father's shadow. He'd always done everything for the old man; but now he felt free and clear to do whatever he felt like doing, and for some reason he felt best being rude and insensitive to others, just like his father had."

The woman grabbed a tissue, blew her nose and wiped her eyes.

"Can I get you something?" asked Kelly.

"No, thank you, dear," Mrs. Whiting said. "Just let me finish my story. It's getting late and you have other places to go. I won't be much longer."

"Let me ask you a question," said Kelly. "Why didn't Mr. Kincade just replace your son when things started going bad at the paper?"

"That's what I wanted to know," she replied. "And I found the answer amongst all those documents Benjamin left. You see, Kelly, Mr. Kincade's bank note to my husband was for a full ten years. There were specific clauses barring him from paying it off early, or taking his business to commercial banks. Mr. Kincade personally gave my husband his word on it."

"I know Mr. Kincade's a man of his word," said Kelly. "But conditions at work under your son were horrible, really. I just don't understand why he didn't make the change earlier."

"Miss Trapp, Mr. Kincade, despite getting trapped in this horrible promise to my husband, *is* a man of his word. He was seeing this thing all the way to the end."

"Then why did he recently fire your son?" asked Kelly.

"The ten-year agreement was up," she replied. "The promise Mr. Kincade gave to my husband was over. He was no longer responsible to keep Harry on."

"But Harry is an attorney," said Kelly. "Why didn't he use that to his advantage when he was fired?"

"Good question," Mrs. Whiting said. "Nowhere in the agreement were any provisions binding after the ten-year period. I'm afraid my crafty husband left out a very important part of the agreement that would have guaranteed Harry's permanent employment; Harry realized that and knew there was nothing he could do."

"What a bizarre story," said Kelly.

"Yes, I thought you'd say something like that," smiled the woman. "Now, I have something else very important to tell you before you leave."

"What could be more important than what you've just told me?" asked Kelly.

The woman pulled a business card from her pocket and handed it to Kelly.

"What's this?" asked Kelly.

"It's the name and address of the man I want you to visit next. He's my *personal* attorney."

Kelly scanned the card. "Bill *Running Bear*?" she laughed.

"Yes, *Bill Running Bear*," replied the woman. "And he's no laughing matter. He's my attorney, and an Onondaga Indian, a direct descendant of an Iroquois Chief."

"You must be kidding!" asked Kelly.

"I don't 'kid,' young lady," said the woman. "He'll be able to help us with the eminent domain issue. He happens to be the best real-estate attorney in the state, probably on the East Coast."

"Real-estate attorney..." Kelly mused.

"Oh, yes, the best there is." Mrs. Whiting chuckled. And she added, "He's very sensitive to issues dealing with the taking of land... I'm sure you know what I mean."

The remark mildly amused Kelly as she thought about the man's Native American roots.

"I can assure you," said the woman, "that once your mayor catches wind that Running Bear is taking this case, she'll know what she's up against."

Kelly looked at the card again. The attorney's office was on White Birch Lake in Windsor, which was some 30 miles north of Binghamton. "His office is on a lake?" asked Kelly.

"What would you expect of an Iroquois?" answered the woman.

Mrs. Talley-Whiting arose with dignity; clearly, the interview was over. She reached out and took Kelly's hand and walked Kelly to her car. Kelly opened the door and sat down, looking up at Mrs. Whiting against the afternoon sun.

The lady said, "Ah, I almost forgot to tell you one more bit of information. Did you know that my son recently secured a job at the law firm of *Anderson, Doyle and Finch?*"

"No, I didn't," said Kelly.

"Yes, he starts tomorrow," she said.

"Well, that's nice," said Kelly, "that he found a job so quickly, that is."

"Did you also know, Miss Trapp, that *Anderson, Doyle and Finch* represent *Ace Demolition?*"

"Ace Demolition?" asked Kelly. "Aren't they...?"

"Yes they are," said Mrs. Whiting. "Ace Demolition won the bid to demolish Horace Mann School, and Harry will be working directly on that case."

The lady said, "And I almost forgot to tell you the ... little information. But you know that my son ... security behind ... with her for Tim and Danforth, Davis and Kevin."

"No, I don't," he said Kelly.

"You go out stairs tomorrow?" she said.

"Well, that's nice," said Kelly, "but I wonder ... I am actually ... that far."

Kelly stood a long time. Mac Tigart had an inside. She heard Kelly repeat of the Danforth's.

"A ... Danforth?" asked Kelly. "Aren't they ..."

"Sure they are," said Abe Whipple. "Are Everything ... the old ... each morning ... Abe ... or ... four Danforth ... Kelly, all the ... dealing each ... in our case."

200

CHAPTER 32

Kelly's ride up to White Birch Lake on Route 17 was easy and quite pleasurable. The richness of upstate New York's woods surrounded her now, beautiful mountains and forests giving way to the tranquil Susquehanna and Chenango Rivers. Kelly thought of how things may have looked 200 years ago, when the Native Americans lived off the land, fishing and hunting and simply *surviving*.

She spotted a small sign for the turnoff to the Lake and rumbled down the old road, kicking up a cloud of dirt behind her. She first passed Lily Lake to her left; it had been aptly named for the sea of white lilies that covered the surface of this small body of water. She crept along slowly, trying her best to avoid the many bumps in the road. A half mile further, the view of White Birch Lake caught her eye from her vantage point above the entrance. She stopped for only a moment, examining this miniature haven in the middle of nowhere. Though it was only 30 miles from Binghamton, she'd never heard of the place before, and felt as if she'd escaped into the past.

The lake wasn't the biggest she'd ever seen, but it was of considerable size. It was easy for her to count the 38 cottages, most of them small retreats, vacation destinations for Binghamtonians, dotting the perimeter. She took a sharp curve to the right as her directions had indicated, still kicking up a cloud of dust behind her, and not long afterwards she spotted the cottage of William Running Bear.

He'd told her his place was the only one on the lake with a bona fide Indian teepee in the back of the property. He used this dwelling on occasion to "free his mind," and to "connect with the universe," he said. Though he'd explained this in full to Kelly, she'd had no idea what a real Indian teepee looked like. She pulled her car into the driveway and got out. She walked up the porch of the property, awestruck by the many Indian trinkets, blankets, hides, weapons and other various items spread along the perimeter. She studied the mounted heads of dear and bear and mountain lions high on the outer walls.

Then she was taken aback at a small sign, slanted and barely visible, cropped against the front door, that read, "Bill Running Bear, Attorney at Law."

She rapped on the door a few times, looked inside and saw no signs of life. She turned towards the lake, and as she did, she spotted a figure of a man carrying a stringer full of bass and perch approach her.

He wore the usual clothing one would expect of a fisherman; only the lone feather in his hair provided Kelly with his Indian identity. He made no indication that he'd spotted her, but she was well aware he had. He suddenly let out a shrill whistle, held out his free arm, and instantly, a beautiful hawk dove from the sky above and perched itself on his forearm.

He continued to walk towards her, fish in one hand, bird on the other. He walked with a grace Kelly had never seen before, a confident stride and a proud posture. He whistled once more, released the bird into the air, and dropped the fish on the lawn, no more than 30 feet from where she stood.

The man raised his hands to the heavens and began chanting an eerie song that Kelly swore she'd heard in the movies. No doubt he was giving thanks to one of his gods. The chant continued for a few minutes, then he picked up the fish and carried them up the stairs, opened the door and went inside, all the while saying nothing to the astonished young woman.

"Excuse me," she called after him. "I'm here to see William Running Bear. Is that you, sir?"

No noise came from inside, no response to her question. She asked again, only this time much louder.

"I am William Running Bear," he said, his voice startling her from behind. "There's no need to shout here. This is a place of harmony."

"I didn't mean to yell," said Kelly sheepishly, "I just wanted to get your attention."

The man studied Kelly carefully, examining her much as a predator might his prey.

She felt uneasy and raised her hands to her neck in a gesture implying vulnerability. He opened the screen door, nodded his head for her to enter, and followed behind her, closing the door behind him. "This way," he said. "We can talk in here."

Kelly followed him a short distance, through a small office at the back of the house.

She noted the modest conditions around her, the lack of modern amenities she was certain he could afford. A wood-burning stove sat in the living room; she'd noticed the large stack of firewood outside. No European-style pictures adorned the walls; they held only paintings of animals, Indian villages, even one of Geronimo, the old Apache war chief. The place seemed cozy enough, but Kelly was perplexed that the lawyer would be living in such conditions. She'd assumed he was a millionaire from his resume, that success would have affected him as it had many other wealthy people – especially *lawyers*, she'd thought a bit disgustedly. He led her into a small den and directed her to have a seat.

"Do you live here year 'round?" she asked him.

"Yes," he said softly.

"Do you hunt and fish for all your food?" she asked.

"Yes," he said. "I go into town for supplies now and then, but most of my needs are met right here."

She looked at his left hand, noticed he wasn't wearing a wedding ring. She knew herself to be pushy at times, but she had to know. "Forgive me for asking," she said, "but are you married?"

"No," he replied. "Marriage is not in my destiny." He paused, then said, "Perhaps we should get down to the matter at hand."

"Of course," she agreed.

She learned immediately how astute he was about matters of eminent domain and real estate law in general. He referred to specific cases he'd fought and won over the years, not to brag, but to educate Kelly at how difficult battling big government could be.

He explained that Beatrice Talley-Whiting had contacted him about the school and neighborhood, and that he'd be filing his motion with the courts tomorrow, to halt the progress of the demolition.

"On what grounds are you asking for a delay?" Kelly asked.

"I've followed this particular story since the people voted last year," Running Bear said. "I've had considerable time to prepare the case."

That was a peculiar comment, she thought.

"What do you mean?" asked Kelly. "I thought you were just contacted by Mrs. Whiting last week. Why would you have been preparing for a case you didn't even know you'd be part of?"

"But I *did* know," he said. "I had a vision of it."

"A vision?" she repeated.

"Yes."

Kelly felt a chill at the comment, the fact that this educated man would admit such a thing to her in the first place. But there was something very real about him, about his easy-going comments, his way of life, his fascinating record of achievement. She told herself to keep her mind open to him, despite the spooky feeling that had overcome her just then.

He sensed her concerns, her reluctance to truly believe what he'd just said. He'd grown accustomed to these kinds of responses and had learned to keep most of what he'd experienced to himself. But, unconcerned at her initial reaction, he knew from following her stories in the paper, and from the meditations he'd engaged in, that she was one he could afford to allow *in* to his world.

"You don't believe much in visions, do you?" he asked.

"Well, no, I…well, it's just, well, *different*, that's all," Kelly stammered. She knew that stumbling over her words, probably made her look foolish to the man. But who *was* the foolish one here anyway? *He*, not *she*, was living on game in the most modest of conditions.

"I understand," he said, smiling thinly. "You will become more comfortable with these things in due time."

As he went on to review with her more of his plan to save the school and neighborhood, she found his confidence in the matter more than reassuring. In fact, Kelly already felt as if they'd won the case; she couldn't doubt that things would turn out just fine. When he'd finished, Running Bear stood up and said, "There's much work still to be done."

He walked her to her car, and as she sat down in the driver's seat he crouched down to her level. He held out five small brown bags, each with some tribal symbols neatly tied at the tops.

"What are these?" she asked.

"This one, the blue writing, it is for you," he said. "Take this very soon, just before you sleep. Place this in hot tea, and drink all of it. It is important that you do this, soon."

"What for?" Kelly mused. "What is it?"

"Herbs," he said. "Things drawn from the earth. "Take this and you will experience your own vision."

"I'm not taking any drugs!" she said incredulously.

"These aren't 'drugs,'" said Running Bear. "They are strong herbs drawn from the earth. They are perfectly safe, and you'll experience no side effects from them."

She took the bag, examined the symbols.

"What do these symbols mean?" she asked.

He placed his finger on the talisman on one side and said, "This one signifies harmony, peace and tranquility."

"And this one?" Kelly pointed to another oddly shaped figure.

"Understanding," he said.

"I'm not sure I can take these," she said uneasily. "This is all a little weird for me."

"Take them soon," he said unwaveringly, "before the herbs begin to lose their potency."

It was all was *very weird* indeed, Kelly thought, but she certainly felt that something intriguing and, well *supernatural*, was reigning over this whole business. She may have been battling him outwardly, but she knew, deep down, that she'd take the chance, that she'd look forward to tonight, that she'd take his herbs and hope to experience those things he'd just promised her.

"What are those other bags for?" she asked.

He placed them into her hands and she studied the symbols, each showing different shades of white. "These are for Mrs. Whiting," he said. "To help her cancer."

"But she has lung cancer," Kelly snapped. "There's no cure for that."

"Tell her to take these over three consecutive days," the attorney said calmly.

"What's in these?" asked Kelly.

"Healing herbs," he said. "Herbs from these woods."

Silence fell between them from that point on. Running Bear simply turned and drifted away, vanishing from sight as he went inside. Kelly remained a moment in her car, staring at the herb bags and remembering all the man had just told her. She hadn't expected anything like this today; she'd just thought she'd be going to a simple informational meeting with an attorney. Instead, *all this* had happened, she thought...

CHAPTER 33

The impromptu meeting put together by Joel Kincade promised to be one of the most important in the history of the city. Kincade had easily convinced Mayor Thomas to change her schedule, his persuasive rhetoric cutting right to the heart of the matter. She came alone, though her presence was quickly noted by the other staffers inside the building. They also noticed Kelly Trapp and Ray Collins enter the room before Kincade closed the door.

When the four were seated, Kincade began: "I'd like to start by thanking Mayor Thomas for changing her busy schedule on such short notice. I do believe, however, that by the conclusion of this meeting we will all leave this room with a very clear understanding of how we can help alter the course of *The Hole to China* story."

Mayor Thomas acknowledged the greeting; then Kincade introduced Ray Collins. He seemed a rather shy, mostly disheveled and unkempt man. He wore a wrinkled white shirt and a blue tie that was too short and too wide. His stringy jet-black hair covered most of his eyebrows, and his long, skinny arms seemed too bony for his otherwise normal looking frame. He made brief eye contact with Mayor Thomas, then quickly looked down towards the floor. She wondered why such a seemingly out-of-place figure had been asked to attend such an important meeting.

Kincade said, "Now, I want to start by laying out the facts, to make sure all of us are up to speed on what's happening. Feel free to correct me any time the information I'm about to give seems even the least bit incorrect. Is that understood by everyone?"

The others nodded at Kincade, and he said, "Very well, then. Here are the facts as I know them. Let's start at the top, with the mayor's office…"

Kincade buzzed through the facts like a lawyer during a trial. He mentioned the city engineer notifying the Kents that the digging would stop due to both the report of the thickness of the impending rock formation, and the lack of proper equipment. Both cases Mayor Thomas acknowledged to be true. Kincade then proceeded to review each and every facet of the story, beginning with Kelly Trapp's first article, all the way to the present.

"We're all in agreement, then, with all that has happened," said Kincade. "Now, let's review a few more things, all of which, in my opinion, can be directly affected by this *Hole to China*."

Kincade passed around copies of Marty's letter and when all present held a copy he continued:

"As you all know, the boy, that is, Marty Kent, has written this letter to the Chairman of Red China. Now, I know it sounds far-fetched, almost like writing a letter to Santa Claus, but in this business, the news business, a story can be made of such things, and that's exactly what we are going to do."

A sudden silence overtook the room as the others eagerly waited for Kincade to continue.

"As I see it, we're all in a win-win situation here," he said. "Kelly's looking to expand her journalistic aspirations, and to save the school and Marty's house and neighborhood from demolition. Me? I'm looking for good stories, more reasons for people to buy and advertise with us. And Mayor Thomas, you're looking to draw people to Binghamton, to find a reason why people would go out of their way to visit our fine city. I believe we can all get what we want – and we can get it from this truly inspiring story."

"How so?" asked Mayor Thomas sharply.

"I was wondering who'd be the first to ask," Kincade said. "So I'd like Ray Collins to start by giving us his spin on the eminent domain issue."

The shy man cleared his throat, then began to speak in very technical terms. Now and then Kincade interrupted him, asking him kindly to reduce his explanation to laymen's terms. This was clearly quite difficult for Collins, but he honored Kincade's request and carefully began choosing more appropriate words for the setting:

"Miss Trapp asked me last night if there is any facet of eminent domain law that might save the school and surrounding homes at this juncture. Of course, I told her there is indeed. "But there's only one way," he continued. "And I'm sure this news will come as no surprise to anyone here. Simply put, the city, the mayor's office in particular, has the right to hold a second vote by the citizens—that is, if a 'just cause' warrants such a vote."

"Define *just cause*," droned the Mayor. "You are aware, I'm sure, that we've gone through a very long bidding process for both demolition and reconstruction. There's been big money spent already. If we decide to hold another vote, we'll be sued by all parties involved. *And*, may I remind you, as much as I've been touched by the boy's story, we all know it's still just a fantasy. We risk becoming a laughing-stock if we try to make his Hole To China our 'just cause.'"

"Yes, I agree, that would be risky," Collins said, barely above a whisper.

Kincade raised his hand. He thanked Ray Collins for the information he'd provided, then acknowledged he'd take over at this point. Kincade said, "Mayor Thomas, I believe, that far-fetched as this may sound at first, if we play this thing just right, the people of this city will actually *demand* that the school, and Marty's house and possibly the rest of the neighborhood, not even be touched by the bulldozers. And with enough public support, a second vote could provide the answer."

"Perhaps, in some dream world," said the mayor. "But what about all the other obstacles? Even if we could save the old building, we'd still need to find another site for the new school, and that would mean even more taxpayers' money spent…"

But Kelly broke in: "There *are* other available sites. They just weren't presented in the original list of possibilities before the first vote."

"And for very good reasons," the mayor interjected, "reasons that stand to save our taxpayers lots of money.

"I mean, do you people know that if we voted to build the new school on some other site, we'd probably still need to level that old school? Abandoned buildings have a way of attracting the *undesirables,* the less fortunate, you know. The property would still need to be maintained to keep rodents away, and the windows would need to be boarded up as well, creating an eyesore for the residents. All this costs money. The only logical thing to do with the building in any case would be to tear it down. The way we've planned things, the city only needs to spend money on one site, one property. It only makes fiscal *sense.*"

"Yes," said Kelly, "but what about the families who're being forced to move? It's not fair to them."

"Perhaps not," said the mayor, raising an eyebrow warily. "Where are you getting your information from, Miss Trapp?" she suddenly asked "From a lawyer by the name of William Running Bear," Kelly replied. "I met with him yesterday."

The mayor looked around the room at the others, who had begun chatting amongst themselves. "William Running Bear?" she asked. "What's he got to do with any of this?"

Kelly quickly explained the events of the past two days, including what she could of the meetings she'd had with both Beatrice Whiting and Running Bear. She ended by mentioning that it was Running Bear's opinion that a well-drawn motion to delay demolition would certainly succeed in court.

This news astonished Mayor Thomas; she certainly hadn't expected to hear of their involvement at this point. "Did you know about all this?" she asked Joel Kincade.

"Yes, we met this morning," Kincade replied happily. "I was as surprised as you are to hear it."

The mayor turned to Kelly. "I take it you know that Beatrice Talley Whiting is one of the richest people in the county."

"Yes, that's what I've heard," Kelly responded.

"And I take it you know who William Running Bear is as well?" asked the mayor.

"Up until yesterday, I'd never heard of him," said Kelly.

"Well then, Miss Trapp, let me tell you a couple of things about him that you may not know," Mayor Thomas said. "Number one: the man has never, I repeat, *never* lost a case in his life. Number two: the man has never taken on any case that, on the surface, looked possible to win. It's mind boggling that he's accumulated such an impressive record, considering the cases he's taken." She shrugged in disgust. If both he and Mrs. Talley-Whiting have joined forces, I'm quite sure you'll get your delay."

Kelly breathed easier. "I'm glad to hear that," She said. Then she went on to explain that the Historical Society had reviewed a list of 21 questions that needed to be asked before certain buildings could escape being razed. The fact that Horace Mann school did not meet one single criteria had initially frustrated her, nearly causing her to almost give up her fight. Then she explained how the Society had also mentioned the building could be saved if it could be converted into a museum that had at least some local significance.

"But," Kelly said, "at first I could find no worthwhile museum material that particular building might house. And of course, I'm quite sure the people of this city won't want to go back to the polls without good enough reason to support saving the building."

"You can say that again," the mayor cracked. "So what ideas do *you* have to make sure they do save it?"

Quickly Kelly said, "We could convert Horace Mann into a museum with not only local significance, but national significance as well."

"What national significance?" the mayor snorted.

Kelly looked at Joel Kincade and nodded for him to take the ball. Mayor Thomas turned towards Kincade, who said, "Now that we have all this information to digest, here's our plan. First, Kelly will run a story in tomorrow's edition citing the reasons the children need to stop digging our nationally-famous the Hole to China. Oh, I'm sure you'll receive some nasty calls to your office, Mayor, but we'll run the story, with all the facts, including graphs and pictures, whatever it takes. "The following day, when our readers think all seems lost, we'll run the story about Marty's letter to the Chinese Chairman—but we won't quote its contents. I guarantee you, that story will set off a frenzy in this town. At the same time, we'll run a story about William Running Bear's request for a delay. That'll set off the brass at *Ace Demolition*, who'll contact their lawyers, who'll contact us, who'll contact you, Mayor Thomas.

"Soon we'll be hearing from everyone, all at once, Mayor. The news will come fast and hard. Your office will be taking a lot of heat over the next few days. But if we play our cards right, it'll all be worthwhile, because following all this, I'll tap my contacts in New York City and Washington. I've got some old friends up at the *Washington Post* who would just love this story, and I'm sure the *Daily News* will lap it up greedily. Then I have no doubt it'll go national from that point."

"How so?" asked the mayor.

"Well," said Kincade, "it's not every day a 12-year-old American boy sends a gift to the Chairman of China. In fact, it's probably never happened before. The Washington and New York boys, they'll be calling on the Chinese Ambassador, that's for sure. And he won't be able to duck them. In fact, I'm sure the TV stations in Washington and New York will also love this story. I'll be calling them as well."

Kelly piped in, "What if the Ambassador ignores it all?"

"Oh, I thought of that, too," said Kincade, "and I'll get to it in a minute."

The excitement in the room was growing by the minute. Kincade pursed his lips and went on:

"By the time the Ambassador's been assaulted by a plethora of reporters, he'll have already read every single story from our paper, and Marty's letter as well. It's my educated guess he'll be a little confused by it all, and will have to contact the Chairman directly. Old Mao will be tuned in to the news from his high office, I can assure you of that."

"What if they still don't respond?" asked Kelly.

"He'll have to," said Kincade.

"Why's that?" asked the mayor.

"Because we won't be just sending this box of *dirt* to them," Kincade said, "we'll be delivering it *personally*."

"Splendid idea," Kelly exclaimed, "and I think I can already guess who'll be making the delivery…"

"Marty, of course!" said Kincade, pounding the conference table with a big fist. "We'll send *him* and his buddies. Savvy politician that she was, Mayor Thomas found herself warming somewhat to the plan, but she wasn't yet ready to give it her support. At the moment her mind was focused more on the logistical problems associated with organizing a second vote on demolition.

But, "It sounds like good public relations, at least," she said. "Do the Kent's know anything about this yet?"

"Well, the parents know some of it, just the parts they need to know," Kincade answered. "In fact, I spoke to them yesterday, gave them the short version. They're all quite excited about the whole thing."

"Does Marty know?" asked Kelly.

"Not yet," said Kincade. "He'll know in two days, when we run the second story. At that point, things will take a new and exciting course. Trust me, that Hole has a chance to become an important symbol. Maybe as important as the Statue of Liberty."

They all laughed at Kincade's final comment, but the mayor felt there was considerable public relations merit in Kincade's statement. She looked around the room and said, "You know, even if we proceed with this plan, it will still take time to arrange another vote. There's only a few weeks left before they start knocking down the school."

Kelly said, "I believe Mr. Running Bear will make sure we get all the time we need."

CHAPTER 34

Harry Whiting had read the news like everyone else in the city, but he'd not reacted like the general consensus. The inroads he'd already made at the law firm of *Anderson, Doyle, and Finch* seemed so trivial at the moment. He was stunned to discover his own mother, and that—that *Indian* were now right in the thick of things, though he couldn't for the life of him understand why they'd bothered to get involved.

For Harry, it was all about the money. Since the day his father died, he'd tried unsuccessfully to acquire his share of the inheritance, but a cut-and-dried will spelled out exactly when he'd receive *even a dime of it*. He wasn't surprised to learn he'd be next in line to inherit following the death of his mother; but he was anxious to get at least a part of it, *now*. He'd never been particularly patient, in fact he'd lived his whole life impatiently, by and large.

He'd phoned his mother following the breaking story, scolding her, calling her names, threatening to have her put away in a mental institution, all to no avail. His mother recalled the many empty threats he'd made to her before, and was not one bit afraid of him, her only child. On the contrary, he knew she felt disgusted with him and his ways, and she'd actually threatened *him*, saying she planned to distribute all the money to just such causes as this one. "You'll see not one penny of your inheritance before I die," she'd assured him.

So Harry Whiting stewed over the news for several hours while trying to ward off the angry owners of *Ace Demolition*. They weren't a happy camp at *Ace*; when they discovered that the *mother* of one of their attorneys had caused these new problems, they became livid, even threatened to "take their business elsewhere" if the problem wasn't resolved, and quickly.

Of course, this also didn't sit well with the partners of the firm. They hadn't been accustomed to embarrassments like this one, and they promised Ace the problem would be rectified in a matter of days. Then they heaved all of the pressure squarely onto Harry's shoulders.

But Harry was in a total quandary over the matter. His mother was perhaps the most stubborn person he'd ever known, and he'd just had the worst argument with her he could remember. He felt desperate, unsure of himself, angry and depressed. He tried to come up with one idea after the other that might smooth things out between them, put him back on even grounds with her; but deep down he knew very well that nothing would change the woman's mind now that she'd made a firm decision.

But then an incredible idea hit him. He picked up the phone and dialed his mother's number. When she picked up, he said, "Mother, it's Harry—please don't hang up, I want to talk to you."

"What is it?" Mrs. Whiting said coldly.

"I've been thinking about our conversation," Harry said. "I'm feeling like the whole thing was my fault, like I overreacted. I want to make it up to you."

His mother wasn't used to apologies from her son, and she was far too wary and tough to believe any of it now. He wanted something; she could tell it in his voice.

"So, the partners are putting some pressure on you, eh?" she asked sarcastically.

Harry bit his tongue, trying his best to maintain composure. "I know it may look like that, Mother, but I really feel badly about before. I wish it hadn't happened."

"Then why, Harry, did you speak to me like that?" she asked.

"It's just like you said, Mother. The partners, they're a little crazy right now. They don't like this kind of publicity."

"I'm sure they don't," she replied.

Noting just a hint of sympathy in her voice, he said, "Why don't I come over this afternoon? Perhaps we could talk things out."

"Come over?" she asked skeptically. "You haven't been here in months, Harry. Why would you want to come now?"

"Like I said," Harry began, "I'm feeling pretty guilty about what happened. I'd like to clean the slate, try and be a better son to you." He paused. "When's the last time you changed the filters in the house?"

"I don't know," his mother answered. "I don't know if I've changed them at all. Isn't that something the men from the HVAC do routinely?"

"Not really," replied Harry. "Why don't you let me come and take a look for myself? Better safe than sorry, you know. In fact, I'll check out the entire house while I'm there."

Mrs. Whiting wasn't convinced by any means of the sincerity of the promises he'd just made. But she thought she'd like to find out just what he was up to. She paused for a moment, then said, "This isn't like you, Harry, but very well, you can come over now. Pretty soon I'll need to take my medication and a quick nap. And oh, by the way, there'll be no talk about the school, my lawyer, the money, or anything related to all that. Do I make myself clear?"

"*Loud* and clear, Mother," Harry said. "I'll be over shortly."

He placed the receiver down, removed his glasses and put his hands over his eyes, keeping them closed as he reviewed the plan in his mind. A cold sweat began beading up on his forehead as he pondered how difficult his life had become without access to *the money*.

The first step in his plan directed him to his garage. He walked to one of the shelves on the far wall, reached around for a few seconds, and retrieved an unopened pair of gloves he'd purchased earlier in the year. He pulled them from the plastic, placed his hands inside, and walked across to the other side of the garage, where a storage closet stood against the bare wall.

He opened the door carefully, knowing that too much movement could send everything inside tumbling forward—the closet was packed with old trophies, awards, books, games, lots of items he'd kept from his youth.

But he wasn't interested in such trivialities now. There would be nothing nostalgic to dwell on this day. He moved a few items from the top shelf, then smiled as he spotted a small typewriter tucked against the corner. He gingerly removed the piece from its resting place and placed it down on the garage floor in front of him. He took a deep breath, then huffed an inch of dust from the old blue portable. The remnants of old dirt and powder filtered over him, causing him to cough several times. He huffed again, and still more dust flew, revealing a darker blue hue against the metal exterior of the old *Smith-Corona*.

A pile of tattered rags caught his eye. He grabbed a few and began to wipe away the crusted layer of filth clinging to the machine. He took the rags to a utility sink and ran some hot water over one of them, then swabbed the more stubborn stains even harder, then scraped away the bottom-most layer with the gloves.

He'd removed most of the stains from the exterior, but the spaces between the keys proved toughest to reach. He blew out as much trapped dust as he could, and when that didn't quite satisfy, he went upstairs and retrieved his vacuum cleaner, placing the smallest attachment onto the end of the long hose.

He was mindful not to get too close, or use too much power at first. He gave it a practice run against his hand, then a cautious short blast against the keys. He soon discovered this action worked rather well. Years of dust lifted from the narrow depths between the keys, and Harry patiently waited for the entire keyboard to come clean.

But he still needed the typewriter to look both clean *and* used. He got a bottle of rubbing alcohol, soaked several cotton balls with it, and patiently and carefully dabbed each key. Satisfied at last with the results, he swabbed the cartridge with alcohol, the bottom, the sides and the front, until the old typewriter looked close to new, and quite useable, in his opinion.

Now, if it'll only work, he thought.

He carried the vacuum cleaner up the stairs, placed the used rags and cotton balls into a plastic bag, then went back to the garage to get the typewriter. He brought it to his small study, laid it on a desk, grabbed one sheet of paper from a stack near the actual typewriter he used, placed it into the chamber, pulled down the paper into position, and began striking the keys.

At first, the slow movement of the daisy wheel barely reached the paper and left scarcely any ink traces behind. Harry started with the first row of letters, pressing the "Q", then a "P" on the other side of the board. He'd expected the arm of each letter to be somewhat immobile; after all, they hadn't moved for at least 15 years. But he kept at it for several strokes, watching both letters strike the paper harder, until finally each left a faint trace of ink, barely visible to the eye, on the paper. Harry rubbed his hand across his chin, concentrating on what he should do next.

Maybe there's another ribbon somewhere downstairs, he thought.

He returned to the garage, reopened the door where the typewriter had been, and pulled out a box full of odds and ends. Inside he found nails, buttons, ribbons, a spool of thread, tape, some old baseball cards, game pieces to Monopoly, toy soldiers, and an old address book. He fished about some more, moving the many items around and around as if he were searching a bowl of trail mix for the best treat.

He decided to empty the contents into another empty box alongside it, and as he did, not one, but two completely unopened typewriter ribbons plummeted into the second box. He grabbed the pair of ribbons, amazed that he'd not only found them, but found them *in this excellent condition,* he thought. He carefully placed the trinkets back into the original box, put them back where he'd found them, walked out and closed the door behind him.

"Beautiful!" he exclaimed aloud, walking towards the house, staring at the ribbons.

Upstairs, he removed the old ribbon from its cartridge, broke the seal on one of the unused ones, and, with little effort, edged it into place. Angling it in while wearing gloves proved a bit difficult, but he managed it in under a minute. He struck the "Q" and the "P" once more, and let out a huge sigh of relief as the ink settled onto the paper before him.

He couldn't believe that this dormant ribbon, maybe 15 years old, was working this well. *Now I need to see if the rest of the keys work,* he thought. He struck them one at a time, slowly working the rust out from underneath each key. He discovered most of the keys were in perfect working order, save for a few letters that contained slight flaws and struck the paper unevenly, creating words that didn't quite form straight lines. *It'll have to do,* he thought, and he removed his practice page, tore it into pieces and placed it into the same bag with the rags and the cotton.

To Harry, all this good fortune was a *sign*—a sign that what he was about to do had been sanctioned by some power or other, that it was O.K. for him to proceed. He took another blank sheet of paper and quickly rolled it into place.

The short letter he wrote seemed pretty convincing to him: His mother's pain and the suffering were just too much for her to handle now; nor could she deal with the grief of living alone; and the experimental medication she was taking really wasn't helping her cope with the hurt. He briefly mentioned "Harry," about how much she'd miss him, how she'd not been the best mother to him. He was careful to use the kind of language she'd always used; but he found this came "second nature," really—he knew her ways and her style well enough. There was no way a soul would ever believe *he'd* written the letter.

When he finished, he sealed it inside an envelope, and simply typed, "To whom it may concern" on the front. He then carefully retraced all his previous steps. He sealed the cotton balls, rags, typing paper and wrapping from the new ribbon inside a plastic bag.

He carried it to his back yard and placed it inside a barbeque grill. He doused the sack with lighter fluid, struck a match and tossed it into the grill, where flames instantly engulfed it, shrinking, then crumbling its contents to vapor like an ice cube in an oven.

When he was completely satisfied that the fire had done its job, he replaced the lid on the grill down and walked back inside.

All this had taken only half an hour, he noticed looking at his watch. He phoned his mother, told her he was a mite running late, got in his care and drove off.

On the way he reviewed the rest of his plan, which had worked so perfectly up to this point. He had it all figured out now, and it would all be almost *too perfect.* Harry envisioned himself on a Caribbean Island, surrounded by beautiful women catering to his every desire. He'd wanted it for years, even before his father died, and now, now *it will all be mine,* he thought.

As he drove within a few miles of the turn to *The Ross Park Zoo*, he went over the details again: He'd greet his mother, make some small talk at the door, she'd ask him inside. She'd wonder why he carried that old typewriter with him, and he'd tell her he'd cleaned it up and wanted her to have it. For some reason she'd always liked the old typewriter better than the new ones she'd had, he remembered, so she'd readily accept it from him. He'd prompt her to "try it out," and she would. He'd excuse himself for a moment, to check around the house to see if the filters needed changing, check the water heater, etc. While he'd be gone, she'd fool with the old typewriter, perhaps even begin writing a letter to someone—take ample time to *fill the keys with her fingerprints.*

He'd come back upstairs to check on her progress, making sure she was banging away at the keys. He'd excuse himself for a few more minutes, telling her he forgot to check the boiler and to "Keep typing, have some fun, I'll be back in a few minutes to talk."

Once he'd gone downstairs, he'd enter his father's old workroom, a setup similar to his own garage. He'd search for an old gas mask his father had purchased years ago from a catalog—a strange-looking device stashed away in the event of any "nuclear strikes close to home."

He hadn't been to that part of the house in a while, but he remembered the mask was still there after his father died. Once he found the mask, he'd place it in the garage, from which he'd be making his getaway. He'd return upstairs finding his mother still typing.

He'd share a laugh with her over how great the typewriter still performed; then he'd look at his watch and tell her she should be taking her medicine and her afternoon nap. He'd promise that when he returned from the hardware store with the appropriate filters and she woke up, they'd have time to talk, and that maybe he'd even take her to dinner at *Cortese's,* her favorite restaurant.

He'd gather up her medicine for her and fluff up a pillow or two on the couch in the living room. He knew she liked napping there, to the sounds of the television that contributed to a quick and easy drop-off to sleep. He'd sit for a few moments with her, watching and waiting till she slept. It wouldn't take long, really. The medication was both fast-acting for pain and sleep. She'd be out in 10 minutes, 15 minutes tops after taking a dose of it. Then he'd remember to check the windows in the house to make sure they were all closed. He'd check to make sure his mother was sleeping soundly. He'd then take the envelope from his pocket and place it next to the typewriter. He'd be sure to remove any paper she'd used for practice, wadding it up and placing it in his pockets where, he'd dispose of it on his grill later on. Then he'd go to the kitchen and remove her car keys from their holder there. He'd walk to the garage, open the door, then climb inside the car and turn on the ignition. He'd be wearing the same gloves he'd worn at home, being careful to leave none of his own fingerprints behind. He'd exit her car, close the door very slowly, grab the gas mask by the door, and pull the garage door down behind him.

The effects of carbon monoxide would be lethal, of course. Harry knew the toxic fumes would rise through the ceiling of the garage, sift through the floorboards above and fill the house slowly, silent killers that they were.

He figured an hour at most would be enough to kill his mother, at which point he'd return from his trip to the hardware store, where he'd have gone out of his way to say hello to people, especially to the employees of the establishment he'd come to know over the years. He'd tell them he'd purchased the filters for his mother's house, that he was being the good son, helping her with things. He'd deliberately look at his watch, announce the time, and head off back to his mother's home.

He wasn't afraid any visitors would come to her house while he was gone. She lived at the end of Brooke Avenue, far away from the other homes on the street. And the distance was too far for any neighbor who happened to be outside at the time to notice the fumes filling the garage. Passing cars presented no danger, since the property dead-ended near the woods beyond. He'd thought of everything – his scheme was fool-proof.

By the time he returned, he'd of course notice the fumes in the garage. He'd place the gas mask over his face, open the garage door and turn the car's ignition off. He'd make his way up the stairs, examine his mother's body, and when he found no signs of life, he'd drag her remains down the stairs, carefully lift her into place on the driver's seat, and re-start the car.

He'd then exit from the garage, close the door, toss a rock through a garage window, remove his mask, place it in his car and then burn it later, along with the few scrap pages of paper his mother had typed on.

Only one part of this plan he wasn't quite sure about: how good his *acting* skills would be when he'd come frantically knocking on the nearest neighbor's door, clear out of breath, telling them he had to use the phone, that his mother just killed herself in her car. He'd need to be pretty convincing, shed tears, tremble, the works.

They'd return to the house together, discover the broken window in the garage. Then ambulances, police, the press, all would barrage the house at once. Those would be small obstacles, no less; but after he'd be done with them, and the money—*all the money* – would be his for good!

CHAPTER 35

Kelly had never experienced such a vivid, realistic dream. She could only compare the sensation to the time she dreamed she would be falling forever, but suddenly awoke, happy to just be alive.

But this dream, this *amazing* dream, had seemed so real. *What separated it from all my previous dreams?* she pondered. The vivid details, the colors, and the fact that she remembered the *whole thing*, from start to finish.

She'd traveled down a long tunnel at a speed she couldn't describe. To her left she remembered seeing all the bad things in her life, the bad people, the bad things she did, the bad things others had done to her. The colors were so pale and gray, murky, sort of like a distorted photograph. She tried to look away, but couldn't. She watched in horror the day her cousin, Diana, was struck by a car as she played in the street. She saw Diana waving to her from a distance, smiling, happy, still nine years old.

Just a short span of time revealed these dream-images to her, but she was unable to give an accurate account to herself of exactly how long, in real time, the view had been.

Perhaps 30 seconds, maybe a minute. She couldn't know for sure. It was as if she'd taken a deck of playing cards and quickly thumbed through them all, too fast to see any one card clearly, but slowly enough to catch a glimpse of them all.

At the end of the dream, she was shown all the wonderful things in her life. She noticed the vibrant colors of her past, favorite moments of her life whiz by, times shared with family, friends and relatives, both dead and alive. She saw herself as a young girl being pushed high to the sky on a swing by her father. She remembered that day as having been very special between them, a day when the two had bonded and had so much fun together. Her eight-year-old mind couldn't fathom at the time that her father would be snatched away from her only a week later, dying of a massive heart attack at a young 35 years of age. In her dream she saw her little eight-year-old body hug her dad, and she could feel his love run through her heart, and it was *wonderful.*

But the super-fast dream speed she was enjoying slowed to a barely traceable pace. A beautiful golden gate opened before her, and as she entered it, her momentum increased a bit. She now entered a tunnel filled with tiny American flags along both sides, thousands of red, white and blue pennants blowing softly with a cool breeze. Now Kelly moved forward at breakneck speed, the blend of red, white and blue suddenly changed to all red, the deepest red she'd ever seen.

As the red began to fade, she spotted a woman ahead of her, dressed in white, beckoning for help, an older woman; and though Kelly couldn't quite see her face clearly, she was quite sure it was Beatrice Whiting, standing in a white fog. Kelly reached her hand forward, but immediately her direction began changing, reversing, going backwards. Kelly tried hard to change her direction; but the dream, not she, was in control; she could do nothing to help the woman, who now swiftly vanished from view.

Then a brown, four-door sedan whizzed by her, back and forth twice before it left her dream. Even then, Kelly felt confused by what she was seeing, and it was at this moment that she emerged from her deep sleep.

She felt disoriented at first; she held her hands to her chest, heaving and breathing wildly. She felt her hands; they were so clammy and hot. She turned on the lamp on her night-stand. She looked at her alarm clock. *It's only 1:00 a.m.,* she thought.

Kelly didn't sleep much the rest of the night; in fact, she kept the light on, tossing and turning, pondering the details of her dream. She'd never paid much attention to dreams before now, but this, *this* dream seemed so *real,* so *alive.* She tried to analyze everything she'd just seen, even took out a pad of paper to write it all down. She felt overwhelmingly confused for the most part; but then she remembered: William Running Bear had told her she'd not only remember this dream, it would reveal *her destiny.*

She finally fell back to sleep at around 7:00 a.m., and she woke again at 9:30, still wondering about all she had seen. She showered quickly, dressed and forced down a muffin. She stared at the telephone, picked it up once, placed it back down, picked it up again, began dialing a few numbers, but each time placed the phone down again. She felt foolish about what she had in mind now, calling Beatrice Whiting to warn her, but who else would know? How could she describe her dream to the woman, though, without Beatrice thinking she was crazy? Maybe she didn't even have to tell her why she was calling, she'd just casually say she was checking to see if everything was O.K.

No, she thought, she'd better make it an "official" call, from a reporter contacting a person who was suddenly in the news. *That'll be acceptable,* she thought, and she picked up the phone and dialed the number.

"Mrs. Whiting, hi!" Kelly said after hearing a soft hello. "I hope I'm not disturbing you."

"Why, not at all, dear," the old woman said. "Tell me, how did your meeting with William Running Bear go?"

"Amazing," said Kelly. "I'd like to tell you all about it soon. He's a very unusual man."

"Yes, he is," she agreed. "Listen, why don't you swing by here, tomorrow at around noon? I have so many more documents I'd like you to see, and we could talk things over for a bit."

"I'm not sure that's a good time for me," Kelly said. "Would today be an imposition on you?"

"Oh, today's not good," she said. "Harry is actually coming over in just a few minutes to fix a few things for me. He says he feels quite guilty about speaking to me so harshly yesterday. Funny thing is, he's never fixed a thing for me since Benjamin died."

"Really?" said Kelly. She felt uneasy about this bit of news. "He's probably looking to get as much information out of you about this case as possible."

"No need to worry, dear. I've already told Harry there'll be no discussion whatsoever about any of this. He promised he'd respect my wishes, and so it shall be."

After a few more words, Kelly hung up the phone reluctantly. None of this made any sense to her. No doubt Harry was up to something here, and the dream, *the dream* kept coming back to her, and especially the image of Mrs. Whiting beckoning for help.

She packed her things for work, then took her usual route, down Clinton to Main to Laurel and out Riverside Drive and onto the Johnson City Circle. All the while, though, thoughts of her dream kept haunting her, and now powerful feeling of dread overcame her. She checked the time as she merged onto the Vestal Parkway, headed west towards *The Bulletin*. She slowed down at the turn to the building's parking lot, but then she decided to keep on going and nearly caused an accident behind her. She waved at the driver who'd almost plowed into her, but he was in no mood to return her apologetic gesture. He sped by her, yelled something obscene, and weaved in and out of both lanes in an obvious display of who was boss of the road.

She'd been startled by the near accident, but her focus nevertheless remained: She had to reach Mrs. Whiting's house, and fast. She drove the last few miles of the parkway, spotted the signs announcing *The Ross Park Zoo,* and headed up the long road towards Mrs. Whiting's. She wasn't sure exactly what she'd say to the woman. Mrs. Whiting had just told Kelly her son was coming over, and for her to visit instead tomorrow. She needed a good reason to so suddenly and unexpectedly intrude. *Ah, the herbs from Running Bear!* she remembered. They were still in her back seat, waiting to be delivered.

That should work, she thought. She could apologize for having forgotten to deliver them sooner…

About halfway up the road, she spotted a familiar-looking vehicle coming towards her. As they passed each other, she noticed Harry Whiting driving his brown, four-door sedan, *the same car she'd seen in her dream.* This wasn't the car he'd usually drive to and from *The Bulletin,* thought Kelly; it was his second car that he took to company picnics and the like. Why was he driving it now? And why, if he'd come to fix things around his mother's house had his visit been so short? *Well, maybe he's gone to get some supplies,* she thought…

Harry hadn't noticed Kelly as they passed each other on the road; he was concentrating too hard on the things he still needed to do and worried about the things he'd just done. He'd calmly executed most of his sinister plan to this point, and that had surprised him. He had just performed the most despicable of acts, but he'd only hesitated for a moment, mildly taken with the thought of turning around and not following through.

But it had all played out so smoothly, so perfectly, just as he had planned it. In fact, it was as if the whole thing had been scripted and rehearsed beforehand. So he would proceed as planned, adding the one slight change he'd made—to drive to his house before the hardware store and burn the gas –mask and scratch paper, the way he'd disposed of the other evidence.

This would add about 20 minutes to his scheme, and that was all right with him.

Twenty minutes more for the carbon monoxide to take its toll, 20 minutes more to send her quietly "away." For that small fact he was thankful, that she'd go in her sleep, never wake up at all, never know or feel what had happened to her. In fact, he could see this deed as doing her a favor; after all, wasn't he simply saving her six months of anguish and torturous pain? In that light, this crime he'd committed was really no crime at all. *It's the right thing to do*, he thought. *Isn't it?*

When he got home, he first removed the few plastic buckles on the gas mask, then ground them up in his trash compactor. He then set the mask aflame in the same grill in which he'd burned the other evidence. The fumes billowed out with more fervor than the cotton balls and ribbon wrappers, the hard plastic and polycarbonate shield taking much longer to burn away. Harry sprayed more lighter fluid on the mask, and finally he watched most of it pulverize to a fine powder. He closed the lid and let the fire smother itself out, satisfied at the results.

Next he made his planned rounds at the local hardware store, and was certain he was seen and heard. If any suspicions of foul play rose concerning his mother's suicide, this would be his alibi. He was certain he wouldn't need an alibi, but who knew? It would be his ace in the hole, his insurance, you might say. He grabbed six air filters from one of the hardware store shelves, along with some duct tape and a few light bulbs. He really wanted this to look good, the loyal son taking good care of his widowed mother...

But as he drove up to his mother's house, Harry Whiting realized that this perfect crime, this fool-proof scheme that he'd taken all the way, may not have been so fool-proof after all. He saw something he hadn't bargained for: a police car and an ambulance in his mother's driveway, with the vehicles' familiar whirring red lights flashing. He hadn't expected to see curious neighbors along Brooke Avenue watching from the street, many now walking towards the crime scene. He wondered how this all had happened, how the authorities had been alerted, and so quickly. Most of all, he wondered if his mother was *dead or not.*

A cop stopped him as he entered the driveway. He rolled down his window and with feigned concern told the officer who he was, and demanded to know what had happened and why they were there.

"At this point, we're not sure what all happened, Mr. Whiting," said the officer. "It looks like an attempted suicide. Why don't you pull your vehicle over to the side?"

"Attempted suicide?" Harry asked with authentic concern. "What do you mean, attempted suicide?" Of course, he knew what it all meant. She must be alive—but was she *conscious*? Able to speak? Had the carbon monoxide affected her mind so she couldn't speak?

He parked his car on the street and followed the officer towards the house. He noticed that in addition to the garage door window, a window on the front door of the garage had also been broken; the glass shone, reflecting against the sun's rays. And the garage door had been opened, the car had been shut off, and all the windows in the house had been lifted open.

As they approached the house, he spotted his mother, sitting upright in the ambulance's gurney, receiving oxygen, looking disoriented. He grew tense and furious when he saw none other than Kelly Trapp, sitting alongside his mother, an oxygen mask attached to her face also. She turned and saw Harry as he briskly walked towards the pair.

"How is my mother?" he asked coldly. "And what are you doing here?"

A second policeman, who'd been snooping around in front of the vehicle, overheard the comment. He was the more experienced of the two officers, and it hadn't taken him long to realize that nothing about this whole business was quite adding up. He approached and said to Harry: "Mr. Whiting, it is my understanding that you were here, visiting your mother about 90 minutes ago. Is that true, sir?"

Harry didn't appreciate the man's tone of voice. At first he pretended he hadn't heard the question; he reached out to his mother to signal his concern and support; but when she angrily brushed away his gesture, the policeman grew even more suspicious.

Mrs. Whiting pulled the mask from her face, obviously displeasing the paramedic on duty. She pointed to her son and said, "How *could* you!"

Kelly removed her mask, reached into her pocket for a pen and ripped a sheet of paper from the startled paramedic's clipboard. Was this news, *big* news? She'd be very careful to capture as many accurate quotes as possible.

"What are you talking about?" Harry shouted at his mother.

"You know exactly what I'm talking about!" she snapped back. "You did it all, you set it all up—*you tried to* kill *me!"*

Harry had some quick thinking to do; and unless he did, he stood there naked to the world. "Set *what* up?" he asked in mock horror. "What exactly happened here, anyway?"

"You *louse!*" his mother yelled. "Trying to act the loving son to me—but I wasn't buying it. Before you left here earlier, you had it all set up. *You* started the car and you planned to put me in it!"

"What are you talking about?" he shrieked. "I haven't been to this house in months."

Harry pulled the police officer to the side and said softly, "You'll have to forgive her. Her mind isn't what it once was. She forgets things now, doesn't really have a good grasp on reality. I think it's her medication."

Harry didn't know that the officer had already taken statements from both women; that he'd learned that Kelly had discovered the old woman on the living room couch, and the entire first floor full of the car exhaust. He'd noted how Kelly had first broken the window of the garage door, then panicked when she found no signs of life, and

231

with clear thinking turned off the car. At once, Kelly found the whole thing to be an odd one, indeed.

Harry didn't know that she'd raced back towards the front of the house, looked inside, rung the doorbell, then broke the front window with a large rock nearby. He didn't know that Kelly, coughing and hacking at the odor in the room, had discovered Harry's mother on the couch, had dragged her limp body outside, and had begun to administer mouth-to-mouth resuscitation to her.

Harry didn't know that his mother had revived quickly. He didn't know that Kelly quickly ran inside, opened all the windows and called the authorities. He didn't know that they'd already been here for about 45 minutes—long enough to learn that he'd been there earlier, promised he'd return with some air filters, promised he'd take her to dinner when he finished fixing things.

"So you came to visit just now?" said the officer. "Your mother tells us that not only were you here earlier, you'd left, saying you'd be bringing back some air filters."

"No, no" chuckled Harry weakly.

"Then would you mind if we checked your car?" asked the officer politely.

"What for?" said Harry, beginning to panic. "Look, officer, I don't think all this is necessary..."

"Perhaps not," agreed the officer. "But let's have a look, shall we?"

All watched and listened intently now, neighbors, curious onlookers and Kelly and Mrs. Whiting, who'd overheard much of this interchange as it had grown from whispers to loud talk.

With as much authority as he could muster, Harry fumed, "May I remind you, officer, that I'm a lawyer in this town? Don't push it, son!"

The threat held no sway with the officer. He walked to Harry's car, whose keys remained in the ignition. He checked the back seat and found nothing out of line. Then he walked to the back and popped open the trunk and didn't need to look any further: Six blue air filters sat bundled together, a *Roy's Hardware* bag next to the package. The officer opened the bag, checked the date and time on the receipt, turned to Harry and said, "I think you'll be needing to come with us, sir."

CHAPTER 36

It was a beautiful summer day in the nation's capitol. Mid-80 degree temperatures accompanied by light cool breezes provided adequate comfort, even in the inner city.

Ping Kang looked out from a balcony connected to his bedroom at the Chinese Embassy on Connecticut Avenue. He took in the cool breezes of the city and enjoyed the old trees and the shade they provided to his home away from home. His thoughts strayed to many things just now.

Three weeks of grueling sessions had just concluded at United Nations headquarters in New York, and now China's U.N. Ambassador would be going home for the first time in three months. He longed to see his wife and four children; he missed them desperately whenever he had to go abroad for any extended time. Though he'd grown to appreciate the amenities of both New York and Washington, he could nearly taste the sweetness of his homeland. He pulled his airline boarding pass from his pocket and looked at it. *I'll be home in just four days*, he thought.

Meanwhile, he'd tie up all the loose ends needed to prepare himself for his journey.

He'd filled an array of suitcases with clothing and accessories, gifts for his family and the Chairman and a considerable number of important documents and notes. He knew he'd be passing through extremely strict security measures at Dulles Airport, even after a complete and thorough check at the Embassy. He'd have a full escort during his passage to the airport, and he knew security wouldn't miss a thing. Though he'd taken hundreds of photographs in both New York and Washington, he'd been aware that certain snapshots wouldn't be allowed out of the country on his person and would need to be spirited to his superiors "through channels."

Ping walked to his kitchenette and poured himself a cup of coffee. He carried it with him together with some of his mail, to read out on his balcony. He placed the pile on the middle of a round metal table and pulled up a chair. He took a few sips of his hot drink, then began sorting through the mail.

Most of it could wait, he thought, and what could, he arranged into neat little piles. He opened more-official-looking mail, read it, and filed it away for disposal during his trip home. A few pieces of "junk" mail he quickly tossed aside. Then he decided to address a large manila envelope and found it full of some unusual documents and papers. He noted the envelope's return address: *The Binghamton Bulletin*, Vestal, New York, and recalled hearing the town's name somewhere recently. He tore open the sealed top and pulled out a series of newspaper clippings, photographs and a letter addressed to Ping personally.

Missing, of course, were accounts of all the *new* news indirectly associated with the *Hole to China* information sent by Kincade. Headline news in Binghamton featured in-depth stories of the Harry Whiting arrest, side-bars with the ironic angle of Beatrice Talley-Whitings's efforts to at least delay the start of the demolition, and, the sudden appearance of legendary attorney William Running Bear into the mix. Additional stories told *Ace Demolition*'s take on things, and that the partners at the law firm Harry briefly worked had fired him. So much of this news abounded recently, Kincade had needed to assign three reporters just to cover these breaking stories; he put Kelly Trapp in charge of coordinating all the coverage.

Ping sipped his coffee and began reading the one-page letter. At first, what he read puzzled him. The document was signed by *Joel Kincade, Publisher*. Ping Kang read it a second time, placed it on the table and then began to thumb through the clippings and photographs that Kincade had laid out in chronological order.

The Hole to China, he thought. Then it hit him. He'd watched news reports weeks earlier describing a young boy in upstate New

York who'd been digging a hole in his back yard, trying to reach China. He'd scarcely imagined how and why this ridiculous story should galvanize an entire nation. Though Ping had, he admitted, become somewhat Americanized, at least in minor habits, he certainly didn't understand this mythical part of the "American Dream." He continued reading curiously, wondering to himself why the publisher of a mid-sized newspaper would be taking the time to send what now sat before him.

As Ping read the stories in order, he was touched by the accounts of the bullies filling the hole and the subsequent support for Marty of the townsfolk. He was particularly moved by a photo of the overweight Marty. He recalled his own childhood memories of being overweight, of the battles he'd endured over the years because of it. In his own unique way, this stranger from China began to identify with Marty Kent.

For some time he remained engrossed, reading and re-reading the articles, studying the photographs. When he felt he'd learned all he needed from this information, he turned back to the original letter from Joel Kincade.

Ping Kang focused his eyes towards the bottom of the page. One sentence indicated that this boy Marty Kent was interested in personally delivering a gift to the Ambassador, which in turn he wished the Ambassador to give to his leader, Chairman Mao Zedong. Kang decided he would indeed like to convey all this information to the Chairman, but Ping first wanted to know the nature of the gift. He also knew time would be a problem. He'd be leaving for China very shortly, and the usual response time from home to dispatches was slow, to say the least. But this case stirred something in Ping: A 12-year-old American boy wished to deliver a gift to the Chairman of the People's Republic of China. Perhaps given the potential public relations value of this gesture, Ping would get a more timely response from the Chairman.

At the end of his letter, Kincade mentioned that by the time this note had been read, all media outlets in Binghamton, Washington and the major television affiliates, would have been notified of its contents. *What a puzzling comment*, thought Kang. Kincade's letter had been obviously written with seriousness. Kang wondered why such a seemingly trivial request by the young Marty Kent would be deemed worthy of national news...

But Kincade had anticipated Kang's thinking on the matter. Included at the very bottom of the letter, in bold print, Kincade had included an entire paragraph about the possible seriousness of the issue. In veiled language, Kincade raised the possibility that China might lose face by rebuffing the well-meaning gesture of a little boy. Kang tried to see the issue in this light: this affair could very well lead to uncomfortable political jockeying between the two sides. And for a moment he applauded his astute political perceptiveness, that admirable trait that had proved the main reason he'd been selected for the Ambassadorship to America.

Kang stacked the documents neatly and placed them back into the envelope. He glanced at his watch and couldn't believe he'd been glued to this one project for so long.

He rose from his chair, headed back inside, and began dialing the international number to the Chairman's office, back home in China.

CHAPTER 37

Though no longer was anyone digging in the Hole, its *story* was moving along at breakneck speed. With the urging of Joel Kincade, every media source on the East Coast had taken to the story, and, as predicted, *Ace Demolition*, the law firm representing *Ace*, Beatrice Talley-Whiting and William Running Bear dominated news on the home front, while national newspapers, led by *The Washington Post*, had reported the new twists to the story—especially the juicy Harry Whiting attempted murder angle.

Soon even the tabloids got involved—*The National Enquirer* published a story about a man in the 1800's whom (they said) actually *did dig a hole to China*. Absurd as it may sound, Binghamton was now drawing the attention of the whole world. Other giants of the industry, *The New York Times, The Philadelphia Inquirer, The Boston Globe* and others placed the story on page one. Radio talk shows that had discussed *The Hole to China* in its early phases now resurrected it, some exploring the new twist in relation to the Cold War with China. Major TV networks dispatched reporting crews to Binghamton, setting up interviews with Marty, the Mayor, Kelly Trapp and others. *Time Magazine* ran a feature story with a photo of Marty standing next to his Hole, to grace their vaunted front cover. So in a very short span of time the nation came to know a boy named Marty Kent.

But the attention didn't end with the media. Marty received hundreds of cards and letters from strangers all across the country.

Kids reported their own successes in digging holes to China; many included photos, while others asked for Marty's autograph, plus free samples of the dirt from his hole.

Many of these notes came from young girls who looked up to Marty as a virtual Idol – especially since his chubby features from weeks earlier had now been replaced by a slimmed-down version of the "new" Marty Kent. Even the double chin he'd carried for the majority of his young life was fading away now, to reveal a handsome face that had been long-hidden under fat. The hot sun he'd toiled under for weeks had turned his skin to a golden brown and his hair to an almost bleach blonde. With his new wire-rimmed eyeglasses, Marty Kent's "outer package" had undergone a dramatic transformation.

Marty'd grown well aware of this alteration; he sneaked a peak at himself in the mirror more often than he ever had earlier, in his blubbery days. He was quite pleased with himself now, really liked the way he looked. But much more than this physical change pleased him, he thought: He'd never felt good about himself before all this happened; he hadn't liked the way he was treated, hadn't liked venturing out into the world too far, he'd feared both his father and those bullies who tormented him.

But now, things were different. Though he didn't quite realize it yet, he hadn't really changed inside, he'd only matured. He had always been a kind, obedient, friendly and helpful person; but now he was being appreciated for the kid he'd always been. He'd become quite aware that it didn't really matter how you looked on the outside, it was truly your inside that counted and what really was most important. And this thought he'd carry with him from this day forward.

Along with his own sudden stardom came the inevitable attention seekers to the Hole. So many people from near and far ventured to the site, the mayor proceeded to assign the Kents' house round-the-clock police support. Sometimes the numbers swelled to nearly uncontrollable, and people had begun filling bottles and cans with dirt from the hole. But very little could be done to stop them, short of closing the site to all outsiders, which the Kents refused to do. The mayor actually considered legal action that would enforce this option—until Donald and Patricia Kent phoned her office after they heard the rumors that she was pondering the decision.

"Mayor Thomas," began Donald Kent. "I understand you may be leaning toward closing down the Hole to visitors. I'd like to know if that rumor is true?"

She paused for a moment to gather her thoughts. The very last thing she'd wanted to do was to close down the hole, but the neighborhood was becoming like a circus, people trespassing on other's properties, and thoughts of looters and vandalism to adjacent Recreation Park and its treasured statues inspired the mayor's vigilance. "Well," she said, "the rumors you're hearing aren't *quite* true. If we were to do anything, it would be very temporary until we can come up with a plan to control the crowds. Those streets in your neighborhood weren't made to handle all this traffic; plus, there's reports that people are filling up bottles and cans with the soil. We don't need any kind of negative publicity about trespassing right now, with all the national attention…"

"I'm tempted to agree with you," Donald said. "But, the way I see it, something like this happens only once in a lifetime, and we're right in the middle of it. We are the ones being put out the most; it's still our property after all; but we've accepted the inconvenience. We know the crowds are getting out of hand and all, and there has to be a way to deal with 'em.

"But if you close the Hole to the public now, even temporarily, that may disappoint some family that may have traveled all day or even longer to get here. So we Kents don't want the hole closed down at all."

"Very well," said the Mayor. "Then perhaps you can organize your neighborhood to help out."

"You must have been reading my mind," Donald smiled.

"Oh, by the way," said the mayor, "My office has received an enormous number of calls about our trip to Washington. People are organizing their schedules to go with us. We believe several hundred cars will be following us down."

"Several *hundred*?" Donald said incredulously. "How can something like *that* be organized?"

"We're working on it," she said. "It's just a matter of time now. The Ambassador to China hasn't even responded to Joel Kincade's letter yet. I hope he does soon. Word is, the Ambassador is leaving for China in a few days."

"Do you think they'll actually invite Marty down there?" Donald asked.

"Well, if they don't, there'll be a lot of disappointed people in this country," she said.

"And that includes myself," said Donald.

For now, the mayor promised him, they'd keep the Hole open and dispatch more police officers to control the crowds bustling about the site.

CHAPTER 38

On the Chinese mainland, Chairman Mao had been watching American newscasts from satellite feeds tied in to just a few government television monitors. He'd been tipped off about Marty Kent and his Hole to China by Ping Kang, who forwarded any and all breaking news on the subject.

With local and world matters occupying most of his time, the Chairman ordinarily paid little attention to "local" American affairs. And he'd originally scoffed at the notion that a boy who'd obviously failed in an absurd effort to dig a hole to China should want to present the Chairman of the People's Republic of China with a gift.

But Kang kept insisting he was feeling extraordinary pressure from the American press. Incessant phone calls were pouring into the Embassy, and now badgering by colleagues *at* the Embassy was taking its toll on him. Kang had looked forward to enjoying his last few days in Washington in peace and quiet, but he now understood that such comfy wishes were not to come true – the Americans wouldn't let him rest about this affair. So Kang pressed the Chairman often for advice on what to do next.

One morning Kang found himself placed on hold by the Chairman's secretary, who told him that the Chairman was finishing up watching a newscast from America. Kang patiently waited for his Chairman to pick up the telephone, and moments later, the Chairman did.

Kang responded to his superior's greeting: "Chairman, it is good to hear your voice."

"Yes, and I to hear yours," the Chairman muttered with some impatience. "Tell me, what is up with this story of this Hole to China boy. I'm surprised the Americans are taking it so seriously."

"It is all true," Kang said. "It is part of an American folk myth, this idea of digging a hole to China. In itself, this is silly and nonsensical, of course. But this business has turned out to have serious international implications."

"Yes? How so?" the Chairman asked with annoyance.

"Mr. Chairman, for reasons I admit I cannot fathom, the American people have rallied in great numbers in support of the boy's wish to deliver a gift to you. In fact, I do not exaggerate in saying that it appears the entire vast country of America has taken a stand in this boy's favor."

"I see," said the Chairman. "So you are saying that, like it or not, we have been placed in a compromising position that may necessitate our doing something decisive about this matter."

"Yes, sir," said Kang. "And I would hope this matter may be addressed prior to my departure. I long for my homeland and would not like to return to China under the cloud of an unresolved international incident."

The Chairman sensed the loneliness in his Ambassador's voice and understood the Ambassador's – and his own—predicament. He'd grown fond of Kang over the years, had always felt true support from this devoted public servant. But if this matter was to be handled correctly, the Chairman must take more time to consider its delicacy before making a correct decision that would be advantageous to himself and his people.

"Very well, then," said the Chairman. "I can understand the loneliness a man can feel for his homeland, his wife and his children. I also understand the delicate diplomacy required in this matter of the young boy and his gift. It seems to me what is most important right now is to simply convey my willingness to accept this gift from the boy."

Kang was relieved. "Ah, that was my very thought on the matter, Mr. Chairman. I am delighted that we are in agreement on this," he said. "The question we must now consider is this: How do we handle the delivery of the gift? It is the boy's wish to bring it to me here in Washington, D.C., so that I may in turn deliver it to you personally. My present understanding is that if we accept this gift, people from the boy's hometown will be coming to us by the hundreds. And when the news that they plan to do so spreads, many more from other parts of the country may want to come to America's capitol city to witness the event."

"By the hundreds – and possibly even more?" marveled the Chairman. "Are you sure?"

"Yes, I am sure," said Kang. "This has been my understanding from a Mr. Kincade, the newspaper editor in the boy's hometown who contacted me about this plan."

The Chairman rubbed his chin and gazed at the ceiling for a few moments. At last he said, "Here is what we will do. First, we will prepare several statements for the press. You will first announce that we will indeed be receiving the gift; you will make the second statement when the gift is delivered."

"Yes, sir," said Kang. "And shall I then open the gift before the entire throng of people?"

"I think not," said the Chairman. "You must do so in private, with the boy alone. At that very time, you will inform me of the nature of this gift. Is that understood?"

"Certainly, sir," said Kang.

"Good. I will now seek the assistance of other members of our cabinet in framing an appropriate statement for you to make at this time."

"I shall at once contact those involved," said Kang.

The Chairman placed the receiver down, then rewound the newscast he'd just watched from America. He picked up the phone once more and issued a directive to the secretary on the other end to call in several of his aides at once.

CHAPTER 39

Nothing on earth excited Joel Kincade more than the thrill of the hunt, and nothing delighted him more than successfully completing a truly great story. This very passion had pulled him into the profession—the thought that on any given day something remarkable could happen, and that he might have some control over the results. The fact that he'd once made the difficult transition from beat reporter to sitting behind a desk had never changed those feelings. And it was *exactly* how he felt about this story of Marty Kent's Hole to China.

He possessed great satisfaction from the fact that this event had turned into the *small story of the century,* with more twists and turns than a Hollywood movie. *Truth really is stranger than fiction,* he thought.

Yet the biggest obstacle, which he'd foreseen from the start, was the current one. He'd anticipated a delay from the Chinese Ambassador, knew Ping would need to get instructions from his notoriously slow-moving government. Kincade had done his best to keep the thing moving along, especially in crafting and timing his letter to the Ambassador. He knew any prolonged delay would foil the flow of the plan and potentially ruin any international communication he envisioned, not to mention put the final nails in the coffins of Horace Mann School and the Kent home.

As he sat in his office glancing through the window at the activity in the newsroom, Kincade turned the pages of his desk calendar. *Two days,* he thought, and as he did, the red light on his phone lit up.

Kincade had instructed his secretary to notify him the moment any call from the Chinese Embassy came in. He'd received several other calls during the day, and though he'd hoped for the best each and every time the phone had rung, he'd come up empty so far.

"Yes Joyce," he said, "what is it?"

"It's *him*, sir!" she exclaimed. "Mr. Kang from the Chinese Embassy. He's on line three."

Kincade thanked her, then paused momentarily. He stared at the blinking light on line three and began to gather his thoughts. *Show time*, he thought, then confidently pushed the button to open the line. "Mr. Kang, this is Joel Kincade, thank you so much for getting back to me, sir. I know you're a very busy man."

"These are very busy times," said Kang, his accent but slightly Chinese. He'd clearly been chosen well for his post. "It is the nature of our business."

Kincade thanked Kang warmly again; the two men exchanged a few more pleasantries, and then Kang went right to the point. "Mr. Kincade, your letter was very inspiring, and the articles written on the boy, and I must say, this Hole to China matter piqued my interest. I was moved by this boy's spirit and heart."

"Yes," said Kincade. "Marty is a remarkable young man. I hope you'll get to meet him personally."

"In fact, Mr. Kincade I am pleased to tell you that this meeting has indeed been arranged," said Kang. "If it is at all possible, the Chairman himself has asked me to invite you to bring the young man to the Chinese Embassy in Washington, D.C., two days from now, at approximately this time of day."

Kincade was surprised that the Chairman had authorized such quick action, but he figured they could swing it. So, "I believe everything is in order for us to be there in two days," said Kincade. "I'm delighted to accept your invitation on behalf of Marty and our city. May I add, Mr. Kang, that you please convey profuse thanks to your Chairman from all of us here. This will be an important step for both our countries, in my opinion."

The men spoke for several more minutes, firming up the precise time and place to meet. Then, more casually, each man shared a few family stories, and some news about the weather and international sports competition. Nowhere in their brief conversation did they discuss politics or ideologies; both men knew very well that their meeting in two days might become a crucial crossroads in opening up communications between the two countries.

After he put the phone down, Kincade hurriedly contacted all the media outlets he'd originally alerted when the story went national. Local press was the first to know, of course; and soon afterwards the power of numbers helped work their magic, and all the media outlets had the scoop: *Marty Kent was going to Washington!*

The 36 or so hours between receiving the invitation and the actual trip proved to be quite hectic. Mayor Thomas decided to charter a city bus to carry Joel Kincade, Kelly Trapp, the Kents, Marty's closest friends and key members of the upstate New York media. Tucked safely away within the underbelly of the bus' luggage compartment would be Marty's gift to China. The mayor's office also announced through the media they'd be handing out tiny American flags, to be displayed on any vehicle joining them for the trip. This would make their convoy easily identifiable and create a fine impression for the watchful eye of the entire rest of the nation.

The Mayor had also decided to begin to organize the large additional contingent of vehicles' trip from the Catholic Central High School parking lot. The city's only Catholic high school was situated just east of the Kents' house, and north of Recreation Park. The parking lot would accommodate the vehicles and the press; it was also close to Marty's *Hole to China*. That the day of the trip fell on a Saturday, when rush hour wouldn't be an issue, would certainly work out well for traffic-flow maintenance.

The bus would pull into the parking lot at 7:30 a.m., but that would be long after the day's activities had begun. Residents going to D.C. with the convoy were asked to arrive at 6:00 a.m. or soon after, at which point they'd register and receive their flag. The local Chamber of Commerce would be on hand to issue coffee and donuts and to help arrange the cars in an orderly fashion. The police would place several officers at key points in the departure route, and the whole entourage would probably resemble an incredibly long, if much more colorful than usual, funeral procession.

The mayor had also contacted officials in all the cities and towns along the six-hour route from Binghamton. Municipalities quickly contacted local police and State Trooper barracks along the well traveled Route 81 through New York and Pennsylvania, and then along Route 95, the final leg of the journey into Washington, D.C.

Media warned motorists along the route to be cautious and allow easy passage to the huge number of cars in the procession. The organization and planning had come together so quickly, yet so perfectly – but how the event itself would go in Washington was anyone's guess.

When the journey itself actually transpired, all went beautifully. Hundreds of well-wishers lined the route out of town, most waving tiny American flags as the bus containing Marty and his entourage slowly rode by. Binghamton resembled, not a funeral, but more a Macy's Day Parade in downtown New York City, only these weren't tourists with some passing interest in a few floats and bands, these were residents, friends and family proud of what Marty had accomplished and proud of what they now were experiencing. This was history in the making, and Binghamton, *Binghamton, New York,* was for this day the center of the nation's attention.

But the event's notoriety didn't end with just the local residents. For six hours, huge throngs of people gathered on hillsides, parked alongside the road, did whatever it took to get a glimpse of the caravan. These many Americans also had been deeply moved by the story of the young boy from Binghamton. Flags waved as the bus rode by, cheers from thousands resounded, along one huge, continual thick line of people stretched over 300 miles.

Inside the bus, the kids enjoyed the attention immensely. Kelly Trapp sat alone just behind them, taking notes along the way. She watched Marty carefully now, fully enjoying the joy he'd so deserved. Of course, this whole story had amazed her, right from the beginning. She closed her eyes and envisioned it all again, including her visionary dream, in which she recalled seeing thousands of tiny American flags along the tunnel she'd raced through. She replayed the sequence of events over and over in her mind, feeling something she'd never experienced before in her life: that she'd been *blessed* to have been the one to produce this story.

But she also thought of the meeting back in Binghamton she'd be missing today, that would include the mayor (who, it turned out, couldn't make the trip due to this meeting), *Ace Demolition* and their attorneys at *Anderson, Doyle and Finch*, William Running Bear and

Beatrice Talley-Whiting. Kelly felt a bit upset to be missing such an important meeting, but they'd deemed it off-limits to reporters. But she'd be able to get the news after the meeting from the appropriate parties. *Why does everything have to happen in one day?* she thought. Then she crossed her fingers and said a silent prayer that the rest of the story would be as perfect as all that had happened so far.

CHAPTER 40

An extraordinary amount of tension seemed to vibrate in the conference room at *Anderson, Doyle and Finch.* Most of those present usually reserved their Saturday mornings for golfing or boating, or other such "rich folks" activities attorneys engaged in on weekends. The three men of the firm assigned to the Horace Mann School case were dressed casually; they'd even left sports coats and ties behind. They seemed to share an attitude of confidence verging on *arrogance* about the whole affair. Seated to their left was a more subdued Charles Quinn, owner of *Ace Demolition*, the company that had successfully bid to knock down the school.

None of this went unnoticed by William Running Bear, who'd dressed impeccably this day. His black, three-piece suit, white shirt and tie contrasted markedly with his pulled back, jet-black, pony-tail-tied hair. His legal adversaries glanced contemptuously at him now and then, as if he were some sort of misfit who didn't deserve to have earned a license to practice law. Though he knew the three attorneys on the opposite side of the conference table were well aware of Running Bear's past successes, he could see that none of them were letting themselves feel even slightly threatened by his presence.

Contributing to their smugness had been the appointment of the arbitrator for this case. Stanley Polen was a tough 60-year-old who always stuck to the facts ("period!") and had never been swayed by political affiliation, greed or public opinion. His choice had rendered the trio of lawyers representing *Ace* overconfident, Running Bear surmised.

They looked as if they had their facts in place and thought they'd researched the case well enough to induce Polen to dismiss it in a matter of minutes. They still couldn't fathom why Running Bear had decided to get involved, but they wondered mildly what he'd have up his sleeve and looked forward to being the first lawyers to pin a loss on William Running Bear's perfect record. Their victory, they figured, would serve both themselves and the firm they represented quite well.

Across the table from them, in low voices, Running Bear and Mrs. Whiting conferred, but not about the imminent meeting. She was talking with him about how the herbs he'd prescribed, and which she'd taken over the past three nights enabled her to fall asleep so quickly. And on waking up each morning she'd actually been feeling much better, she said, stronger, more energetic, more rested—plus, her appetite was beginning to revive.

She was now skipping her daily naps, taking frequent walks, and the pain—*the pain* – had become a mere dull annoyance. She was eager to make her next doctors' appointment in three weeks and sure he'd give her a new prognosis.

Mayor Thomas and her secretary sat next to Running Bear and Whiting. The Mayor looked a bit nervous. Her mind was split in two, *just as Kelly's must be right now,* she imagined. She was unhappy she'd had to miss the Washington trip, *But this is important city business*, she thought,. *just as important, if not more, as the trip.*

One of the law firm's attorneys checked his watch. Stanley Polen was running a few minutes late. He'd been re-reviewing for a last time the petition by William Running Bear and also studying the original Planning Commissions details on the plans to level Horace Mann School. He'd studied the procedures the City of Binghamton had followed in the matter and found no oversights whatsoever. He was, however, well aware of Running Bear's undefeated record, and since his own wife, children and grandchildren were pulling for Marty, he had to admit feeling hard-pressed not to root for them. But, he'd have to hear something most tangibly convincing here today to cause him to order another vote on the question.

He at last arrived, some 15 minutes late, and sat at the head of the table. He led the usual introductions; he'd met all the parties in the room except Running Bear. He spoke directly to this seeming "odd man out" as he officially began the meeting. "I have before me a petition to not only halt the demolition of Horace Mann Grade School, but also to authorize the citizens of Binghamton to go back to the polls to cast a new vote on the demolition issue, with which I'm sure you're all familiar. It is my understanding that Mr. Running Bear, representing Mrs. Talley-Whiting, is the petitioner to the state of New York in this matter. Is that true, Mr. Running Bear/"

"Yes, it is," Running Bear said confidently.

"Very well then. Let's get right to the heart of the matter, shall we?" said Polen. "On what grounds do you wish to enjoin the demolition of the old building and restrain the building of the new school to preserve the neighborhood that now designated as the new school's duly allotted, Mr. Running Bear?"

The pony-tailed attorney pulled out several copies of the original study done by the Mayor's Planning Commission and passed those to the three other attorneys, the Mayor and the Arbitrator. "If you'll notice," he said, "I've circled an entire particular paragraph in red and highlighted two other sentences in yellow. If you'll quickly scan your copies of the study, I'm sure you won't find these difficult to find."

Papers shuffled briefly; then one of Ace's attorneys looked up and smirked, "So what's the problem here?"

But Stanley Polen was deeply impressed by some of the wording of the designated clauses. He looked again at Running Bear. *He's good*, Polen thought. Aloud, he said, "Mr. Running Bear, would you like to answer the question just put?"

"Gladly, Mr. Polen," Running Bear replied. "Let me first read the designated excerpts, if I may."

Polen nodded, and Running Bear began, "'The Planning Commission, after an exhaustive search, has determined the following sites to be viable alternatives for the relocation of the Horace Mann grade School, should the initially appointed site prove for any reason less satisfactory.'"

Running Bear read the three sites' information mentioned in the document. Then he stood up, dropped the document onto the table and looked across at the three lawyers.

"So, is that it?" one of the three asked.

"No, there's more," said Running Bear. "I submit to you that a fourth site, one that is at present unmentioned in the Planning Commission's study, would actually be superior to the site presently designated *and* to the three alternatives now listed."

"So what?," quipped another attorney. "What's so special about that fourth site, anyway?"

Running Bear explained immediately: the fourth site he had in mind, though it might cost more initially to acquire, would be, long term, prove a more beneficial one to the city, even than demolishing and reconstructing Horace Mann School's current site. Plus, use of this site would allow the four families whose homes were now earmarked for demolition of the school to remain in their homes, saving the city a bundle on security of eminent domain.

Running Bear's primary concern, he went on to explain, was for the city to recognize that people were more important than buildings. He then argued that the 50-acre tract of land adjacent to the west side of Recreation Park would prove to be a more viable option than any previously suggested. This was city owned land, he explained, whose water tables and sewer hookup availability allowed for easy access. And the grade school children of the area who might attend a school on this site would be just as safe as those walking to the current school, a fact most voters had ignored when they cast their earlier votes.

Running Bear finished and waited for a response. *Ace's* lead attorney said, with pained condescension, "Uh, we appreciate your research on this, Mr. – uh – Running Bear. But what good is it to bring any of this up now?"

With outspread hands the attorney turned to the Arbitrator. "Mr. Polen, the voters have made their decision; my client has organized his men and machinery, purchased appropriate supplies and submitted all the appropriate paperwork. Is it not absurd, really, to ask at this juncture that the voters go back and with such scant justification vote again on this matter?"

"Yes, I'm inclined to concur," said the Arbitrator. "Perhaps the city didn't consider all the available options; but that doesn't mean its actions on this questions were illegal. Mr. Running Bear, I understand your desire to keep those four families intact, to not have to force them out, even to build this museum everyone's been talking about. But I'm afraid these attorneys are in the right, Mr. Running Bear – you just haven't given me enough reason to consider authorizing another vote."

Unfazed, Running Bear smiled and turned to *Ace's* owner, Charles Quinn. "Tell me, sir," said Running Bear, "is it not true that in addition to owning *Ace Demolition*, you also own *New Day Renovation Company?*"

"Yes, that's true," Quinn answered.

"Then it may interest you to know that I've taken the liberty of running some cost estimates on the possibility *restoring*, rather than demolishing, Horace Mann School*,"* Running Bear said.

Quinn leaned forward in his seat. "Go on."

Running Bear said, "My findings indicate that renovation of the property would be substantially more profitable to a restorer than would demolition to a wrecker. More than doubly profitable, in fact."

Running Bear handed out some papers containing his careful estimates. Quinn studied the numbers for a moment, nodding with interest. "Yes, these numbers look in line to me," he finally said.

"I assure you they are," said Running Bear. "I've even taken pains to have them reviewed by an independent accountancy firm."

Charles Quinn leaned over to the trio of attorneys. They whispered among each other for a few moments, and Quinn shrugged several times as they reviewed Running Bear's figures.

Ace's lead attorney looked up and said, "My client wants to know exactly how another vote might benefit his company. He would like to be sure, of course, that his company won't lose out in the long run if the course of action you may propose is taken."

The Arbitrator cleared his throat and raised his right hand to gain the room's full attention. "It seems to me that what Mr. Running Bear has reviewed with us would in no way negatively affect *Ace Demolition* or its sister company, *New Day Renovation*. Are they indeed both part of one and the same entity? If, as I'm certain they are, then any profit would simply revert from one side of the company to the other—that is, if we were to authorize another vote, and if the vote were to change the direction the city's already taken. *New Day Renovation* would submit a new proposal to the city, and I'm sure that, in light of the new information before us, the city would work out a deal that would prove fair and equitable for both sides of this controversy."

Mayor Thomas submitted, "I agree with that assessment."

"And you, Mr. Quinn?" asked the Arbitrator.

Quinn conferred briefly with his attorneys, and then addressed the table. "Considering what Mr. Running Bear has proposed, and the mayor's encouraging agreement, I must say I'd be foolish to not go forward with this plan instead of the one already in place."

"Very well then," smiled the Arbitrator. "Let it be known that with this agreement by the parties here today, as is in my power, I will order that the city conduct a second vote of the citizens on the matter of the new location of Horace Mann School."

Case closed, thought Running Bear, glancing at the Arbitrator with just a hint of a grin.

CHAPTER 41

Ping Kang was trying his best to describe to the Chairman the scene in front of the Chinese Embassy. He stood peering through the balcony curtain at the huge, gathering crowd outside. A telephone cradled against one ear, Kang pulled the curtain out a few more inches with his free hand. He glanced at his watch; the convoy from Binghamton must be within 30 minutes of the nation's capitol now. National TV crews had remained in contact with many local media crews set up along the parade route, and were now carrying the story live, from outside the Embassy.

Kang watched as extra horse-mounted police arrived. Police cars and armed officers and security personnel on foot in the close vicinity seemed numerous, and Kang estimated the crowd from his vantage point to easily number in the thousands. He'd expected large numbers, yet he was still surprised at the sea of humanity he was observing.

"Thousands of American citizens of all ages and hundreds of police and security have assembled outside," said Kang to his Chairman. "I've heard reports that this has also been the case all along the route the boy has taken since he began his journey from Binghamton."

"Are there protestors present?" asked the Chairman.

"I see a few, whom I understand are motivated by opposition to any possible 'thaw' in Sino-American relations that may result from this affair," Kang said. "But they are under control and, from what I understand, have pledged to express themselves non-violently. So I hold every expectation this even will ensue peacefully."

"Let us hope that's the case," said the Chairman. "Is your speech well-rehearsed?"

"Yes, Mr. Chairman," said Kang.

"You will be overrun afterwards by American reporters," said the Chairman, with a smile in his voice. "Do your best to avoid getting trampled."

"All these people—I had not expected this many," said Kang. "Are you certain I should open the boy's gift in private, as planned, or should I open it before the entire assemblage?"

The Chairman had pondered Kang's question carefully. He was certain the Americans would expect the gift to be opened in the sight of all – but he was concerned that it wasn't yet known publicly what the gift would be. He couldn't risk public embarrassment, and was thus unwilling to take any chances on a public revelation of the gift.

So he said, "I understand you feel pressure to open the box for all to see. Nevertheless, stick to our original plan: Bring the boy inside the embassy and open the gift there. You are to inform me of its nature at that time, and not before."

"Very well, Mr. Chairman. But what of the press? They will expect to come inside to film the presentation…"

"Again, let it be as we decided beforehand: Take only the Binghamton woman responsible for the story inside. Afterwards, she will have the privilege to report what she's witnessed to her counterparts."

"Very well," Kang replied. "What of Mr. Kincade, and the boy's parents? Shall I ask them, as planned, to join the boy and the reporter?"

"Yes," the Chairman replied. "There will not be a large contingent of people attending the gift presentation. "But I trust your good discretion to allow any additional participants entry into the Embassy."

"Thank you, Mr. Chairman, for your wise counsel," said Kang. "Now I must go outside to meet the press prior to the boy's arrival."

Kang hung up the phone, walked to the mirror, smoothed a forelock of his hair and adjusted his black tie. He went to take one last look out the window at the swelling crowds, then raised his head proudly and headed for the door. He briskly took the 12 stairs down to the Embassy's main floor, and noticed that a majority of embassy staff had gathered at windows to watch the crowds. He pushed open the main door and walked through it, to be immediately surrounded by media.

Kang remained poised and upright as a barrage of questions assaulted him. He answered as many as he could, revealing only the least bit of information. The Chinese way with the press was to keep the answers short, sharing little or nothing that might provide a sharp reporter with ammunition for an unfavorable story. The Chinese had been good at avoiding too-critical press attention for years, but this event was unlike any other Kang had witnessed in his days in the States.

Wanting badly to walk away from the ever-vigilant media, Kang at last received his wish when the attention of the reporters quickly turned to some growing noise in the crowd below. Something was happening, and hundreds of heads turned in the direction of the sounds. People began cheering, standing, all looking north, up the far end of closed-off Connecticut Avenue. A Binghamton city bus, followed by an unending trail of cars decorated with American flags, was turning the corner behind a police escort.

In a rush, the reporters grabbed their equipment and piled down the Embassy stairs towards the convoy. Several streets had been partitioned off to allow the hundreds of cars to park, and a special area, perhaps 100 yards from the Embassy, had been cleared for the bus to park in. They'd also cleared a large space in which the media could place their cameras and microphones, and it was at this particular place where the biggest crowd was thickening, hoping to catch a glimpse of Marty as he exited the bus.

For several minutes the big city bus sat in the reserved area, its idle engine sending a wave of heat across the great crowd. They'd agreed in the beginning to let nothing begin until all the cars from the Binghamton area had been parked and their occupants led into an area roped off just for them. The delay was expected to take about one hour, which could only add to the crowd's suspense, Kang thought.

Inside the bus, the kids looked excitedly out the windows, anxiously awaiting the word to proceed. The bus driver had earlier warned them that there'd be a delay, but all the preparation in the world couldn't keep them from fidgeting. Most of these kids had never been outside of New York State before, let alone to Washington, D.C. This was the greatest adventure of their young lives, and they couldn't wait to bust out of the bus and head towards the Chinese Embassy with their gift.

Marty looked out the window by his seat at all the people. He couldn't believe how many he'd already seen in just one day, and now this crowd was the biggest of them all.

And as he began rehearsing in his mind what he'd say to the Ambassador, he grew increasingly nervous. He knew he was representing his whole country now, and he didn't want to say anything wrong or even stumble over his words. But he had gone over in his mind countless times exactly what he'd be saying; now he needed only to concentrate on those and *only those* thoughts.

Just then the bus driver yelled, "They're ready for us, now!" He ten-foured the dispatcher and clicked off his radio. He looked around the bus to make sure everyone was ready. As he began to push forward the handle that would open the door, Kelly suddenly shouted, "Wait!"

She rushed towards the front of the bus, then eagerly said, "I think Marty Kent should get off first, then the other kids. It's only right."

Her logic provoked no argument. Marty deserved to lead the way, and he was whisked forward in record time by countless pats on the back. Marty looked at his friends, then said, "Guys, thanks for wanting me to go first, but with all that's happened to me, with so many new friends and people helping me, I'd rather not go first. I want to go last."

His mother felt a lump rise in her throat as she listened to her son speak. Her husband reached for her hand, looked at his son and said, "Marty, I'm proud of you for that. Come on back here with us."

His friends playfully swatted him on the back again as he joined his parents in the rear of the bus. The bus driver finally got a thumbs-up, and he pushed the handle forward, opening the door with a giant *whoosh*.

One by one, the small contingent of kids vacated the bus, adjusting their eyes to the blinding sun. The incredible noise of people cheering seemed almost unreal to Marty.

He'd never imagined people could make such a racket as he slowly followed his friends down the three stairs of the bus and towards the cordon of police officers that held back the waiting crowd.

But the decibel level Marty had just experienced paled compared with the greeting he received the instant he emerged from the bus. Marty watched dozens more policemen form an even firmer barrier between his group and the crowds. Yellow police tape hung everywhere, barricades loomed, there seemed so much to see, Marty couldn't keep his eyes on any one thing. But the deafening noise kept thundering in his ears as he walked towards the luggage compartment with the others in his little company.

Cameras clicked everywhere as the bus driver reached into the deepest part of the carrier and rolled out a red wagon, and box roughly two feet wide and four feet long. He carefully wheeled out the wagon, and put a burlap bag into the box in the wagon. Then the driver pulled out a somewhat larger wagon, while press crews lined the sidewalk just inside the barrier, TV cameras lined up to catch the action from the best viewpoints they could hold.

When Marty saw that everything was ready, he grabbed the handle of the wagon, and followed two policeman towards the Chinese Embassy, which Marty could see it in the distance, maybe 300 feet away. While he pulled the wagon with one hand, Marty returned the constant waves of the spectators with his free arm.

The box inside the wagon was beautifully decorated in all-American red, white and blue. Flanking the box were flags of both the United States and The People's Republic of China. Behind the first wagon, Brenna Nelson hauled the second, larger wagon, which was also draped in the American colors as well, and which appeared to carry a lighter load. Brenna, too, returned the many waves coming her way, while the other boys and adults trailed behind her and Marty.

Across the nation, most regular TV-radio programming had been temporarily interrupted to allow citizens everywhere to view this historic moment. Millions of Americans had literally dropped what they'd been doing to watch the events in Washington. Even an eager President Johnson was tuned in at the White House, watching carefully with several of his Cabinet members and family, while across the globe, Chairman Mao and his top aides did the same, via satellite transmission.

Normally, even the slowest of walkers would have only taken a few minutes to make it to the Embassy; but amid the seemingly never-ending attention of the crowds, Marty and his followers ambled along very slowly. The smooth, flat concrete of the sidewalk made pulling the heavy box of dirt in what was Marty's wagon relatively easy for him.

Marty looked behind and smiled at Brenna as police waved them forward to where the Chinese Ambassador waited patiently for them.

As the two approached the Ambassador, they pulled their wagons into a semi-circle around him; then Marty and his friends quickly assembled themselves around the wagons. A White House aide who'd been assigned to the meeting stepped to the battery of microphones before them and made introductions, ending with Marty Kent.

Now all the shouts and screams faded to utter silence as the people waited for Marty to speak. For an instant Marty felt overcome by awe and gratitude and just couldn't speak. Seeing his hesitation, Mr. Kang put an arm around Marty's shoulders and drew him to his side. "The Chairman of the People's Republic of China extends his hand to you, young Mr. Kent," Kang began. "He will gratefully receive the gift you have brought us, if you'll be pleased to bring it into the Embassy."

"Inside the Embassy?" interrupted Donald Kent. He extended both arms towards the vast crowds. "What about all these people – and the press? They came here to see this gift given."

"That is understood," said Kang. "But I must follow the orders my Chairman has given. Your reporter, Miss Trapp, has been chosen by our ruler to announce the nature of the gift to the people."

"What about all the other reporters?" asked Kelly. "They'll be wanting to come inside, too."

"Only your small group will attend the gift-giving," said Kang softly. "This is the way we have chosen to receive the honor."

Seeing that the Ambassador's wishes would not be altered, the small group awkwardly turned towards the Embassy, gathered the gifts and began pulling them up the broad expanse of steps. Behind them, the crowd started to stir and to shout mixed boos and cat-calls at the Ambassador. But a dozen or more police officers stood forward to shield the group from any interference as they entered the building. The instant the acceptable assemblage had all entered it, two burly Oriental men closed and locked the great Embassy doors behind them.

264

CHAPTER 42

Despite not being allowed to view the actual exchange of the gift from Marty to the Chinese Ambassador, the large crowd of people outside the Embassy remained there.

After the small entourage had entered the Embassy, the White House aide who'd introduced Marty and the Ambassador to the microphone had promised the crowd a short wait, no more than 45 minutes, before the American contingent would emerge from their meeting and return to announce to the people their gift to China.

Rumors and opinions flew throughout the crowds. Television crews interviewed people at random, asking their opinions about the nature of the gift. Most people guessed the gift to have something to do with the flags of both countries, somehow uniting the two countries in some new bond or other. Others guessed the gift would be a plaque, while still others felt something specifically from Binghamton would be presented.

Certainly, no shortage of opinions existed among the people. When the door of the Embassy opened a mere 30 minutes later, the assembled media scrambled toward Marty and Kelly as they emerged to more crowd cheers. Marty's face flashed a huge smile before more than a dozen cameras. He and Kelly Trapp were led to the small podium, to make their announcement to the people.

For several minutes, Kelly briefed the media prior to the main announcement. Meanwhile, Marty was drawing equal amounts of reporters' attention, and he had told Kelly as they exited the Embassy that he thought she should address the crowd before he did.

She hadn't planned on spending too much time speaking, perhaps only a few minutes. She'd give enough information out to provide the press a good story, especially considering what had been the Chinese Ambassador's reaction to the gift.

Kelly scanned the swelling crowd; she took in a deep breath and began: "My name is Kelly Trapp, and I'm a reporter for *The Binghamton Bulletin.* I'm the Journalist who first broke the story of *The Hole to China*, as it's come to be known, and Marty Kent has asked me to speak first about the meeting that we've just concluded with Mr. Kang, the Chinese Ambassador.

"As many of you have read, a few weeks ago, after Marty and his friends had been informed that it would no longer be possible to dig their Hole to China any further, they came to me with an idea: to send a gift to China. At first, I thought it to be a nearly impossible task for them to fulfill, considering the red tape involved, dealing with politics and all. But as Marty shared with me his idea, I found it so perfect, I just had to put aside my preconceived notions of how unlikely it seemed. I thought about how hard these kids had worked to dig this great hole. And suddenly, I knew it wasn't impossible. And sure enough with a little help from many friends, we – Marty, his buddies, my editor, Joel Kincade, Mr. Kang and Chairman Mao Zedong of the People's Republic of China – made it happen!"

As the crowd roared fresh applause, Kelly motioned Marty and the other kids forward to join her. Then as they waited, an awesome silence fell before she spoke again.

"I know," she said, "you all were disappointed earlier when the Ambassador asked us to go inside to present the gift. But I can assure you, he was courteous and gracious to all of us, and he was visibly touched by the gifts the children gave.

"You see, at first we had just one gift in mind to give to China. But then last night Marty came to us with an idea for a second gift, so we brought it with us, too. Both gifts were accepted honorably and with gratitude by the Ambassador. And now it's time we let you and our entire nation know what those gifts were."

A hush came across the great audience gathered. Kelly looked at Joel Kincade, who stood aside beaming with delight at how easily

Kelly was handling herself in front of the nation. She had, according to plan, built in just the right amount of melodrama to create this suspenseful moment.

Kelly went on: "Most of you probably saw the wagon Marty was wheeling in with a box draped in the American colors. Well, inside the box, Marty placed soil dug from the *deepest* part, the very bottom of the Hole. It was his idea that if he couldn't reach China through his digging, then at least maybe some of the *soil* he and his friends had dug could reach China instead. So that is what was in the first box, ladies and gentlemen – the soil from 253 feet down in the backyard of the Kents' home."

Enormous bursts of applause filled the air as the cameras continued clicking around the scene. Kelly held up her hand after a while to calm the crowd, but the cheering and clapping continued for another full minute.

When it stopped at last, Kelly said, "We thank you, very deeply for your support; we felt it every foot of the way down into the earth. But now I still need to describe the second gift to you.

"In token of the many hours of sweat and toil put in by not only Marty and his friends and neighbors, but also by many residents, old, middle-aged and young, of our fine town, we also presented the Ambassador and Chairman with the original shovel Marty used to begin his historic dig, and continued to dig with, till at last the digging stopped. This, Marty thought should be the second gift we presented to China."

Inside the Embassy, Ping Kang conversed via telephone with his Chairman as both witnessed the events from their respective locations. Kang rose from his chair, as still another deafening roar from outside the Embassy drew him like a magnet to the window.

For all his political sophistication he was utterly amazed at all that had happened and that was transpiring around him, and not the least by the incredible show of support by the American people for Marty Kent and his gifts. He walked away from the window as the cheering continued.

Kang said, "Mr. Chairman, the boy's presentation was most sincere. His were truly gifts from the heart."

"And most unusual gifts they are," said the Chairman. "I trust you'll bring them to me the moment you arrive here tomorrow."

CHAPTER 43

Marty's box of dirt and shovel was delivered, as the Chairman had requested, to his home. No "official" delivery of the goods such as had been witnessed in America earlier took place; no crowds had gathered at the airport when Ping Kang's flight arrived. In fact, the people of China were given no "official" public knowledge of the ceremony that had taken place in Washington, D.C.

The same night he received Marty Kent's gifts, the Chairman entered his bedroom, removed his bathrobe, placed it on a chair beside his bed and looked over into a corner of his sumptuous room, where sat a box full of American dirt and a rude, roughly-used shovel. His wife, Madame Mao, was reading as she lay in bed, and as her husband neared her, she looked at him knowingly. For three days his mind had mulled over these American gifts. He wasn't sure what to do with them, or even quite how to respond to them. He'd as yet sent no official acknowledgment to the United States, no letter of thanks to Marty, no official statement or announcement regarding the gifts. He hadn't yet asked the opinions of his staff about the matter; in truth he wondered if any of them even cared about it. He walked to the corner, picked up the shovel and turned to face his wise wife.

"What shall I do with these gifts?" he asked. "Are they anything more than the product of a child's fantasy? Should I merely discard them? Who besides you and me and perhaps Mr. Pang would know, and who would care that I'd done it?"

His wife looked over her reading glasses and watched as her husband began to pace restlessly about, his customary practice to help him clear his mind when he needed to make important decisions. She placed her book down on the bed, slipped out of the covers, came behind him, put her hands on his shoulders and gently rubbed them to help relieve some of his tension.

He accepted her gesture gratefully and at once. His head rolled from side to side as she seemed to hit all "the right spots." She kept at it for a few minutes, then pulled away. He thanked her reverently and kissed her on the forehead tenderly. She'd grown accustomed to his gentle manner, and she never grew tired that this man of great power still held her on high. She'd been his sounding board for years, and she knew he was struggling inside now, with this entire strange *Hole to China* situation. As in times past, perhaps her words of advice at this time would be received as gifts from her of the most intimate kind.

She said, "My husband and comrade, I wish you only peace of heart and mind. May I ask: Why are you so concerned about the gifts this boy has sent you?"

"I do not want to appear weak to the Americans." he said firmly. "I must respond in a manner befitting of a head of state. This is how it must be."

She asked, "Would I be correct in supposing that you have given considerable thought to what should be done with the boy's gifts?"

"Of course, but no response I imagine seems quite...appropriate."

She'd hoped he'd respond with some more concrete idea, but for some reason when it came to this issue, he wasn't seeing things as clearly and decisively as she'd seen in times past. She said, "You know the boy worked so very hard on his project. Perhaps it would be right for you to reciprocate his gift in some way."

"Yes, that I have thought of. But what sort of gift would be appropriate for a 12-year-old boy to receive from the head of state of the world's most populous nation?"

"Oh, I think the gift from you need not be anything lavish or extravagant. Perhaps, comrade husband, your gift to this boy should be one in kind with the gift he gave you."

"But he sent dirt and an old shovel," the Chairman grumbled. "Would a head of state give that kind of gift in return?"

"Why not?" his wife replied. "Would it not be the perfect sort of gift?"

She walked to a small chest of drawers near the gifts and pulled open a drawer. She reached in and pulled out the large folder Joel Kincade had given to Ping Kang containing all the stories and photos associated with the story. She thumbed through several pages, then held one up and said, "Here—this story describes the depth of the hole when the digging stopped."

She handed the paper to her husband, and his eyes opened wider as he reread the story. She looked at him as he perused the words for a few more moments. The feeling overcame her that he might again begin to see things as she had foreseen them...

"But of course!" he cried. "That is it! We shall deliver a fine load of Chinese soil to the boy. That would indeed be the most appropriate gift of all! This soil the boy sent symbolizes the sweat and toil of the American worker – and are we not a Workers' Republic? Therefore why should we not send this boy the gift of our workers' labor and soil in return?"

His conclusion was exactly what she'd hoped it would be, and she didn't mind in the least letting him feel the idea was his own. Nothing in the world pleased her more than to see her husband respond in such a way, in response to her honoring role in their marriage.

So, "Wonderful!" she cried. "It would be a most honorable gift to return to America."

"Yes, but we must do still more," he said. "The gift we give should be of greater significance somehow than the gift we received..."

"Yes, I believe that would be wise," she agreed. "Can you think what that something more significant might be?"

He picked up the article once again, then said, "The boy dug to 253 feet. We shall emulate his effort, and dig a hole to the exact depth of his. From there, we will excavate the soil and send it to America as our gift to him."

"Who shall perform the digging, and where will this hole be dug?" his wife asked.

"Our hole shall be dug in the very yard of this palace, dug by the children of China, united together in an effort equal to the

271

Americans'. When a plan for this dig has been finalized, and we are prepared to move forward with it, we shall contact the Americans and send them news film footage of our great effort."

"How long do you think such an effort will take?" she questioned.

"The boy from America had many assistants," the Chairman said. "We shall gather some of the Republic's strongest 12-year-old boys and work in long shifts around the clock. The great Chinese people should easily complete such a task in ten days, I would imagine."

"Ten days?" she asked, skeptical. "What if we run into the same obstacles the American boy did?"

"I will make sure we do not have that problem," her husband responded. "We shall also bring in our greatest geological scientists and have them run tests to find an area of ground that will offer our diggers the least resistance. So we shall be sure to reach our goal rapidly."

"Ah," she reminded him, "but there was one *girl* in America who also helped with the digging. Chinese girls also are very strong."

She felt uncomfortable now; she knew she was pushing things farther than perhaps she ought to. Would the Chairman allow females to work alongside males in this manner? It was unorthodox, she knew...

But her proud husband would not condone Chinese youth appearing weaker than the Americans. "Yes then, we shall have girls, too," he said firmly.

CHAPTER 44

When the news from China reached the States, informing Americans the Chinese were in fact digging a hole equal to the size of Marty's, a ripple effect tore across the nation.

Broadcast feeds from China were transmitted through American satellites, relaying the great progress the Chinese children were making. Consequently, the entire nation turned its collective attention to both China and the Hole in Binghamton, New York.

The fact that a return gift would accompany Pink Kang on his short return trip at the successful completion of the Chinese hole grabbed the attention of countries around the globe. The two countries had never really maintained a solid relationship in the past; moreover, they had never seen a thing eye to eye, politically, morally or economically.

Imports and exports were all the two great nations had in common. But the exciting fact that television feeds, albeit it very brief glimpses, were being sent from China to the United States, press around the globe noted as a significant step in establishing relations between the two countries.

All the commotion drew considerable attention from the White House, and they began communicating with the Chinese behind the scenes. Plans emerged to hold an official ceremony commemorating the Chinese presentation of the gift to Marty, and though neither nation's leader said a word to the other, their many underlings made the arrangements in exact accordance with instructions from the very top.

Beautiful weather in China and a near perfect plot of ground measured out by Chinese geologists resulted in the dig's lightning-quick results. Dozens of 12-year-old boys and girls worked round-the-clock shifts in an effort to dig 253 feet in 10 days or less. Each day of the dig, the results were measured and handed over to the Chinese press to broadcast throughout China. The first day of digging, 52 feet, was perceived by the Chinese as representing superior strength in numbers, and they proved to be more than accommodating by supplying the rest of the world with this information.

By the third day, they'd tunneled 140 feet, and by the fifth day, they'd reached a depth of 200 feet. Chinese children waved at cameras, posing with mounds of dirt around them.

They were having the best of fun, and knowing their images would be broadcast around the world was more than any could have ever imagined happening.

Midway through the seventh day, the great effort by the Chinese children reached its conclusion. Dozens of Chinese little ones stood proudly at the top of the hole as the last mound of earth was lifted out. Within minutes, the final feed transmitted around the globe.

The Chairman was on hand for this final portion of the great effort. He applauded his young followers and made a grand speech on Chinese superiority to America. He was proud of these children, and as he looked at the great mounds of earth, he could only think of China's greatness and the enormous pride he possessed in his country.

He quickly assembled his leaders together at the palace. They'd not met as a complete unit for some time now, and he felt the timing was just right. He wanted to make absolutely sure that all the final plans between America and China for the gift to Marty Kent would be in perfect accordance with his wishes.

"We have done well with this hole," he said, addressing his staff. "China has once again shown its superiority to the Americans."

"What shall be done with the hole now?" asked one of the men.

"We shall clean the area around the hole," the Chairman began, "then a great plaque shall be made and put in place to honor those who dug this great hole."

Another official asked, "What gift shall you send to the American boy?"

"The gift shall remain a secret until the day we present it to young Mr. Kent," the Chairman answered. "Ping Kang will have the honor of delivering the gift to the boy personally."

For a full hour, the Chairman laid out his plan to his staff. At the other end of the world, President Johnson held a similar meeting with his Secretary of State.

Said the President, "When this gift is presented, the entire world will be watching. And I believe the situation calls for my presence."

"Indeed it does," agreed the Secretary of State. "A wonderful opportunity to make an impression on the *entire world*."

President Johnson chuckled. "Who would have thought that a boy digging a hole to China would be the top story in the world? I know I sure wouldn't' have." The President looked his Secretary in the eye. "I believe the time has come to have a one-on-one with Chairman Mao. Could be historic."

"Yes," agreed the Secretary. "Have you given any thought as to where the meeting should be held?"

"The world will be expecting us to meet right here in Washington," said the President. "But I believe it would be much more appropriate to make a little trip to Binghamton."

"I was thinking the same thing," said the Secretary. "We hold the meeting at the site of the Hole. Plus, I have an idea that, if it's all coordinated just right with China, it could make a lasting impression upon the world – even change it, maybe."

"Let's nail it down, then," said the President.

They spent the better part of an hour discussing the American plan, and at its conclusion the President stood fully satisfied with every aspect and detail. "Let's get the staff moving on the arrangements," he instructed. "We've got a few calls to make – including mine to Chairman Mao."

276

CHAPTER 45

It wasn't every day the mayor of Binghamton, New York, received a call from the White House. Though she'd hoped that sooner or later a call from the President would come, Mayor Thomas couldn't help feeling that special sensation when her receptionist announced, "The President of the United States is on line one."

She'd had her fair share of special moments in her life; after all, she was one of only a handful of woman mayors in the country. She'd overcome great obstacles and prejudices in her political career. Politics, however, was still generally considered a man's world. She'd never conversed with a President before, never been invited to the White House.

In earlier days, she was fortunate enough to meet President Eisenhower and President Kennedy. But their exchanges had been brief, no more than handshakes and quick hellos; yet, both meetings had left indelible impressions on her.

"Hello," she said softly into the telephone. "This is Mayor Thomas."

"Lyndon Johnson." There was no mistaking the President's unique voice.

"I'm honored, sir," she said. "I've been hoping you'd call soon."

"Well, I'm glad to," he said. "You know, your boy Marty has sure caused quite a stir around the world."

"He certainly has," the mayor agreed. "He's a wonderful boy."

"He's why I'm calling, of course," President Johnson said.

277

Gary Kaschak

"Yes. Please go on, sir," Mayor Thomas urged.

"Keep this confidential, but we've been dealing behind the scenes with the Chinese for some time now," said the President, "firming up everything to do with the Chinese gift to Marty, and I'm happy to say we've just about nailed down all the details."

"That's wonderful!" the mayor exclaimed. "When will the meeting take place?"

"One week from today," said the President.

"Splendid! Will it be in Washington?"

"No," he said. "Ma'am, we'd like it to be up there in Binghamton. More specifically, we'd like to have the meeting at the site of the Hole."

Mayor Thomas was shocked—one week wouldn't be enough time to prepare the city for the floodgate of reporters and dignitaries. Throw in with the miraculously scheduled re-vote on the school issue just six days from now, with this out-of-the-blue request by the President—*It's simply too much,* she thought.

What if she showed reluctance to accept his offer? But she just couldn't refuse him; this was the President asking. But neither could she postpone the scheduled revote on the school; volunteers and locations were already scheduled for that day.

She took a deep breath and said, "Mr. President, this event could cause Binghamton some serious scheduling problems. We're holding an important referendum in six days…"

"Ah!" he broke in. "Are you talking about the Horace Mann School issue?"

"Why, yes, I am." She was utterly amazed. "You mean you're actually familiar with that little problem of ours?"

"Yes, I've been briefed on it," said the President. "We both need that vote to move things in a different direction. Mayor Thomas, I realize that these two events would be jammed real close together, and just now it may seem impossible for you to handle 'em both. But with what I've read and heard about Binghamton, I don't think y'all should have a great deal of trouble holding that vote *and* getting the support of the people to get the place ready for the ceremony at the Kents' around the same time. I just want to make sure before we get the message to the press that your up to speed on everything that's got to happen."

278

"What about security?" the mayor asked. "What about accommodations?"

"The FBI and the Secret Service'll work with your local police on all those matters. We'll be sending some special agents up there tomorrow to start planning, right alongside your people. Don't worry, I'll be well protected; we'll have all our gorillas and spooks and your 'finest' ready to handle any eventuality."

Mayor Thomas gasped. *"You're* coming, Mr. President?"

President Johnson laughed heartily. "I'm sorry, Mayor Thomas, I seemed to have forgotten telling you that little detail. Yes, I'll be making the speech following the Chinese Ambassador's gift presentation."

The mayor's mind was whirling now, not being able to fathom how she'd manage to prepare her town in such short notice. But she knew the President would accept no excuses. This was LBJ himself, and he was relying on her in a big way to make it all happen.

So the mayor said, "Mr. President, it will be our honor to host the event; just have your people tell us what you need done."

"Wonderful!" said the President. "Someone in my Cabinet will call you shortly and go over the entire itinerary with you. It should be one glorious day." He paused, and then added, "You know, if we play our cards right, and if the vote on the school's a positive one, we could even make sure the results are announced at the ceremony."

"That would be sensational!" the mayor said. "But what if the original vote's not reversed?"

"Ma'am, according to my intelligence on this issue, I doubt if even one percent'll vote against it."

Mayor Thomas knew in her gut that the President was right; all the signals on the vote seemed heavily in favor of saving the school. The television and radio stations and *The Bulletin* had all conducted their own polls, and at least on paper the President's prediction would turn out right on the money.

"Mr. President," she said, "I do believe we'll be able to get our vote taken before you arrive, and afterwards accommodate your truly generous request to use our city as the site of your meeting with the Chinese Ambassador."

"That's wonderful!" he exclaimed.

She knew this challenge would be the biggest of her career. But if she pulled it off, she was sure the President would see that she was remembered in the future and find ways to throw her some support if her political aspirations continued on course.

"Mr. President, may I ask your opinion on another matter?" she said.

"Please do," he said warmly.

"If the school is saved, we're thinking of converting it into a museum. We thought, with all the attention that's been focused on the Hole, that a building right next door to it might feature information on China, old and new, and on earth sciences. Perhaps each old classroom of the school could become a special learning center. We could present the earth's core in one room, the mantle in another and so on. We could begin a tour there that ended at the Hole itself."

"I love your thinking there," said the President. "In fact, I can picture something like that working very well."

"The publisher of our newspaper, Joel Kincade, believes the museum would become a national attraction overnight. Who knows, we might rival the number of people visiting your White House."

"Really?" said the President. "Well, I could use a few less visitors sometimes, and I'm sure your museum and the Hole would indeed become an attraction. For how long, who knows? Can't tell for sure how these things will go. Could be a passing fancy, could become a permanent American institution. Only time will tell."

"Thank you so much for your confidence and support, Mr. President!"

"Most welcome you are, Ma'am!" said President Lyndon Baines Johnson.

CHAPTER 46

For the first time in weeks, Marty Kent was experiencing mixed emotions. He'd had to deal with so many distractions and answer so many questions. He felt like he'd been pulled in a million directions by a million people from a million different places. So much about this whole thing strained all his imagination and belief, yet it had all come about. And now the President of the United States himself would be making a speech to America from just outside his Hole, *and* a vote that would determine the fate of his home would precede that first big date by just *a single day.*

Though he'd believed deep down that his gift to China could be delivered, it actually still seemed like a dream to him as he peered out his bedroom window at the Hole that started it all. The city had removed the mounds of dirt that had once surrounded the Hole.

All the rough edges at the top of the chasm had been smoothed out as well. The entire neighborhood had been re-landscaped; beautiful potted plants surrounded many of the homes near the Kents', and all the lawns had been mowed that very day. Neighbors had pitched in to spruce up their houses, and day and night, busy city crews labored at adjacent Recreation Park to get the area ready for the Big Day.

Marty now understood the importance of all this attention to detail. He understood what went into making a great impression. His mother had always done just these kinds of things prior to visitors' arrivals at their home, but this big party was off the scales by

Gary Kaschak

comparison. In one week's time, he'd watched an entire city pull together to make Binghamton the belle of the nation's ball.

But the possibility, however remote, of the impending destruction of his home was weighing down some of his thoughts right now. He'd overheard his parents earlier in the day, discussing with a real estate agent the "perfect home for them in neighboring Johnson City, just in case..." Something about the whole thing just didn't seem fair to him, just didn't make sense. The whole world would be tuned-in to *his* world in less than 14 hours. Happy people would be smiling and patting him on the back. He'd be interviewed and photographed and complimented. He'd sign autographs and pose for pictures with total strangers. But when the dust finally cleared and the cameras went home and the world returned to its business, Marty Kent still might lose his beloved home.

He walked to his bed, laid down on his back and placed his hands behind his head. He stared at the ceiling and thought, *Well, so what? Despite that unfairness, it's all somehow been worth it.* It had been, by leaps and bounds, the best summer vacation he'd ever had.

Across his room he'd tacked on the wall the numerous stories and photographs about the Hole. A huge mound of cards and letters people had sent from *everywhere* sat in the far corner of the room. He hadn't yet had time to answer all the mail, but he knew he'd have ample opportunity to do so when things at last calmed down. Answering those cards and letters was important to him, despite the fact that it would be a daunting task. He'd enjoyed all the attention, liked how it felt to be important, so answering that mail would express his gratitude and keep that feeling alive in his heart.

He'd heard all the talk of eminent domain earlier on. He couldn't understand why his home and his school could be knocked down; he couldn't yet understand the reasoning behind it. He'd overheard the adults many times discussing eminent domain, but none of this area of law made sense to him. *But how unfair and unjust the world can be!* He pondered.

A noise from the schoolyard alerted him just then. He rose from his bed and went to the window. The sun was just beginning to set, and Marty's vantage point provided for a perfect view of the school. The hair on the back of his head stood on end as he saw one lone figure toss stones against the school's brick exterior. Few times

282

Marty had seen Scott Gardner all alone. Marty watched as Gardner walked over to the area in which he'd thrown his stones. Scott gathered them together again, then returned to the same place he'd tossed them from and began throwing again—only this time, much more forcefully.

Marty hadn't seen or heard from Scott since Scott's old group of friends came forward to confess their role in covering the Hole. The friends had talked about Scott once or twice in the interim, but not one had stayed in contact with him or been contacted by him.

This solitary fact had certainly made life better for Marty.

And for the first time in his life, Marty now watched his adversary with less fear, and a still less pity. He'd heard his father say, "What goes around comes around" many times in the past, and now Marty figured he knew what his father'd meant. Though Marty didn't see things with complete clarity, he was aware that he and Scott had reversed their perspective roles in life – Marty had turned into a leader and Scott now skulked alone.

Marty had always felt such overpowering fear grip him the moment Scott Gardner appeared, usually out of seeming nowhere. He'd always feared the bully would either pummel or embarrass him; he'd always felt like running the other way and not looking back. But Scott had been as shrewd as he was tough, and Marty had never been able to truly run and hide. But now Marty actually felt compelled to face his adversary, man to man. Not that he'd be looking for a violent confrontation; he still believed Scott Gardner was truly a tough character. He wasn't exactly sure what he was looking for, but when he turned away from the window and raced down the stairs, he knew he'd be meeting his biggest fear face to face, just seconds away.

Marty opened the front door and slowly closed it behind him, so as to not draw any attention to himself. He hopped the four stairs of his front porch, turned right and headed towards Scott, who was still pounding the school's exterior with rocks. Marty swallowed hard, then walked over to where a fence separated the school from the street. He stood on the other side of the fence from Scott Gardner, watching his adversary hurl stones harder and harder, till he saw one stone actually split as it caromed off the wall.

Scott turned to pick up another stone and saw Marty. "What are you looking at, jerk?" he sneered. "Don't you have some new *hole* to dig, to Australia or somewhere else?"

Marty recognized the same tone of voice he'd endured all those years before the Hole to China. He told himself, *Don't let it bother you*, and even looked Scott Gardner straight in the eye.

Scott picked up a large stone and motioned as if to throw it at Marty. But Marty didn't budge or flinch, much less run. He stood his ground before the laughing bully, and he could see in Scott's eyes that the bully had nothing to laugh at now.

Scott roared in anger, then raced towards the fence full tilt, grabbed the chain links and shook the fence like a madman. Still, Marty Kent just watched and let the bully continue making a fool of himself.

Marty said quietly, "I saw you out here. Thought maybe we could talk."

"Talk?" Scott boomed with what he tried to make sound like his old vaunted rage.

"Talk about what? I don't need *you* talking to *me!*"

"I'm tired of always having a problem with you," said Marty. "I'm tired of being pushed around, and I'm tired of seeing you push other kids around. I won't let it happen anymore. But I'd rather forget that any of it ever happened, Scott. I'd rather we would try to be friends."

Marty realized that this stand he was taking could produce a turning point in Scott Gardner's life—depending, of course, on how he responded to it.

"Friends?" Gardner asked, surprised, yet still keeping his cool. "Sure, I'd *love* to be your friend."

Gardner pressed his face as he could to the fence, smiled mock-angelically, and then, smirking like a demon, spat on the ground close to Marty's feet.

Marty looked at the disgusting wet glob near his left foot, but he was neither amused, intimidated nor afraid. But he knew he had his answer: He'd just done his best to make things right between himself and the bully, and that was all he could do. He'd taken the first step towards bringing peace to this relationship, but it was clear it wasn't going to happen this time. He stood still and watched Scott Gardner laugh like a fool, then turn, walk away and disappear into Recreation Park.

CHAPTER 47

The night after his confrontation with Scott Gardner, Marty Kent slept fitfully. He'd seen how two cultures with opposite views on everything could meet civilly, and he thought, Somehow that seemed to come together easily. But right *here, in my own home town, my biggest battle's still raging.* How something so big could happen, yet something so small couldn't puzzled him. He tossed and turned all night, couldn't keep his mind clear. Yet when, in the wee hours of the morning, he finally did fall into a deep sleep, he dreamed of faraway places where people lived in harmony, where there were no wars, even no person-to-person disagreements. He dreamed of the most peaceful place on earth, that place he longed for, the place he'd always thought of as he burrowed into the ground.

He woke with a start and looked at his alarm clock. *6:00 a.m. No point trying to get any more sleep,* he thought. The meeting with the President and Mr. Pang was scheduled for 2:00 p.m., and he still had so much to do. Marty rolled out of bed, quickly dressed, and went downstairs to check out what was happening on the street.

He saw his mother coming towards the stairs. "Marty!" she cried. "I was just coming up to check on you. Did you sleep well, dear?"

"No, I couldn't sleep, Mom," he said. "Guess I'm too excited."

"Well, your father and I couldn't sleep either," his mother said. She came to his side, pulled him into her arms and gave a big hug. "Marty, we're all so proud of you, you know."

Gary Kaschak

Patricia Kent thought back to the beginning of that summer, the day she'd casually joked that maybe her son should go out back and dig a hole. She couldn't believe how the whole thing was ending, after the sweat and tears and effort so many people had put forth. She'd watched as her young son grew from a naive little boy with no goals to a national icon who'd matured before her eyes. Yes, she was proud of him, proud beyond words. *What he did during this memorable summer can never be duplicated by another soul – ever,* she thought.

Eminent domain? she reflected. She knew that what her son had accomplished could never be taken away from him. "Let's go outside," she said. "Everything's getting set up already."

She'd been used to seeing neighbors' cars parked on the street in front of their home; none of the houses in this neighborhood had garages; few of the nearby homes even had any semblance of a driveway. This was city street-parking territory.

But now the street was completely empty of vehicles, except for a large city truck parked at the other end near Laurel Avenue, and the truck's presence there would only be temporary. Dozens of men were unloading hundreds of folding chairs and beginning to line them up in the empty space, starting at the foot of the Kents' home. What she guessed were Secret Service and FBI agents stood on hand, carefully watching and now and then directing the proceedings. At least 30 other men in black suits were stationed around the neighborhood. They were conducting final door-to-door checks to insure the utmost in security.

Names of every single person in the immediate area had been logged and checked against the local census. Automobiles had been relocated to the other side of Recreation Park. The hill leading up to Catholic Central High School was occupied by six federal agents, each having a great vantage point on the neighborhood. They peered through high-powered binoculars, and Marty couldn't help but notice that each of them also shouldered a sighted rifle.

Coordinated by with the Secret Service, literally every police force in the area had been given specific assignments. Binghamton police patrolled Recreation Park and the surrounding streets; Johnson City police would form a barricade outside the vicinity of main event; Maine-Endwell, Union-Endicott and Vestal police had been given

288

other, more cryptic orders by the Secret Service. K-9 units from Norwich and Binghamton police helicopters would stand ready throughout the event, while a dozen ambulances were to be stationed inside Recreation Park.

Marty's head spun, watching all the activity. Things were moving so fast now...

Within an hour, the entire street was set up with countless rows of chairs, and had taken on the look of a high school graduation. As the city workers had vacated the scene, TV and radio crews had arrived to set up their equipment. (They also had been thoroughly screened during the week by both local police and federal agents.) Special "Red and White" cards had been distributed to all fully authorized press; other locals who'd be on hand were given a blue card. Each cards was specifically marked with a name, a special number and a special code for identification—another quick action successfully carried out by the combined authorities.

By noon, many guests had already been cleared, and some had taken their assigned seats, while others milled about under the watchful eye of the heavy security. Some guests, wanting badly to get a firsthand look at the Hole, had strayed close to the Kents' property. But the Kents' home and Horace Mann School were being closely watched, and no one was allowed to come too close to either building. Though Horace Mann had been empty since shortly after the last day of the school year, agents and policemen had now been assigned to stand guard at every window and doorway. At least a dozen more were stationed on the roof, some visible, some invisible to the people gathering below.

The Vestal Police had been assigned to guard the Hole itself; they also sported another six officers in front of the Kents' house and several others at strategic places to guard it.

Marty wondered when the President would be arriving; now he kept looking around, expecting him at any moment. Marty asked his father when President Johnson was scheduled to arrive; Marty's dad said he'd learned that the President would be the last person to arrive on the scene. By 12:45, a huge crowd had assembled; thousands more people scurried around the general area; they hadn't been allowed close to the action, but they hoped to catch glimpses of it from various vantage points. By 1:15, the media had begun live-interviewing local dignitaries and people of interest, including Mayor Thomas, Kelly Trapp and Joel Kincade. They conducted on-the-spot interviews with neighbors, Donald and Patricia Kent. And once they spotted Marty, he naturally became the focal point of their interest.

At 1:15, Marty, his parents and his friends Joel Kincade and Kelly Trapp were called together, then led to a closed-off area in the back schoolyard of Horace Mann. A huge circus-like tent, its canopy covering a good portion of the school's large play area, had been assembled in record time. The entourage was led inside the tent, where TV monitors manned by a dozen or more people wearing headsets were stationed. Marty marveled all the wiring and hardware around him, wondering how it had been put together so quickly.

He and the others were led to the far end of the east corner of the playground; a serious-looking federal agent asked them to wait there. Within a few minutes, a pleasant looking young female agent approached the group and flashed a warm smile. She said, "My name is Amanda Crowell. I'm here to see that you're apprised of the latest developments in today's order of events." She looked at her watch and said, "We better get started; show-time is in just 30 minutes."

She passed around a program-sized pamphlet and asked everyone to follow what she had to say very closely. She spoke with a clipped directness:

"After a government official introduces her, Mayor Thomas will begin the program with some words about *The Hole to China.* She prepared for this last week, and we've screened and mildly edited her speech. Next, she'll introduce the Chinese Ambassador, who'll then make a speech, too, then make his gift presentation to Marty. Then Mayor Thomas will return and introduce President Johnson, who'll act as emcee for the remainder of the proceedings.

We've been fully informed about the gift, so Marty, you'll only need to follow the President's directions from there on. We're keeping the gift's content a secret for just now. When the President concludes his speech, he'll ask all you ladies and gentlemen here follow him to the Hole. You will all take assigned seats on the stage the city's constructed, and the President will tell you what happens next. Any questions?"

Marty raised his hand. "Do I get to say anything?" he asked.

"We've allowed for that possibility, if you're sure you'll feel comfortable speaking" she said. Then she smiled and added, "There'll be a lot of people watching, you know."

"Oh, I know," said Marty. "I wanted to say something when we were in Washington, but I never had the chance. And I sure have something ready to say now."

She looked at Marty's parents; they both nodded approval. She said, "We can fit it in after you receive your gift, I think. Why don't you come with me for a few minutes and give me an idea of what you want to say."

"I won't be talking for very long," said Marty. "Maybe for only a minute."

The pair walked away for a while, and Marty quickly summed up his little speech to Amanda. She placed her hand on his shoulder, nodded and smiled and shared her personal admiration for all he'd done; then Marty returned to join the others in the far corner of the playground.

The little party chatted for a few minutes, mostly about Marty and his discussion with Amanda. Moments later, Amanda quickly strode towards them, motioning for them to come towards her. "We're just about ready," she said. "The Ambassador and the President have arrived. So we need to go outside now."

Amanda and a couple of other agents hustled the group through the tent and led them to the back of the Kents' house. A Secret Service man opened the back door, and they entered the house single file. When the final person had come in, the agent closed the door and remained there, arms folded and a serious look on his face.

Voices sounded from the living room as Amanda led the group there. They turned a corner and watched in awe as both the Chinese Ambassador, Ping Kang, and the American President sat conversing on the Kents' living room chairs. They both appeared relaxed to Marty, and as the two men recognized the entire party was now present, both men stood and introduced themselves to everyone present. Beaming down on Marty, President Johnson took his hand and said, "It's my honor to meet you at last. The whole country is proud of you, son."

Marty felt understandably humbled by the warm praise of the leader of the Free World. *I'm shaking hands with the President—and getting paid a compliment,* he thought. "Thank you, sir, er, Mr. President, sir," he stammered.

"Relax, son," said the President. "Believe me, I'm the one in real awe here."

Amanda, spoke to someone on her headset and then led the contingent to the front door. "Very good," she said into a walkie-talkie. "We're on our way out." She knocked on the door from the inside, three short raps followed by two harder ones. An agent carefully opened the door to the Kents' front porch.

A huge black curtain was drawn completely across from the other side of the street and connected by some sort of pulley system rigged on the front porch. From their vantage point, they could see nothing on the other side of the curtain; they could only hear the noise of hundreds of voices talking on the other side of it. Federal agents accompanied the little group onto the stage, then faded into the background while the honored guests took their assigned seats. Once everyone was situated in proper order, Amanda again spoke into her headset, nodded her head to signify the beginning of the program, pulled the curtain and sat down in a chair off to the side of the stage.

"Ladies and gentlemen, we'll be starting the proceedings in just a few moments," a female voice from the other side said over loudspeakers. "If you'll all please take your seats, we're about to begin."

Most of the gallery had already taken their seats, and less than one minute passed before the distinguished-looking woman who'd just spoken walked forward to the full band of microphones and said: "Ladies and gentlemen, it is my great pleasure to present to you those most responsible for Binghamton's legendary *Hole to China* and this day's festivities!"

On that cue, the curtain drew aside, revealing the small group seated on the stage. As they came into view, they were greeted by a spontaneous, standing ovation. As the applause played out, Marty found the sight and sound of all the people and all the cameras almost overwhelming. The President returned waves from the spectators with the grace and charm of the veteran politician he was. To his left, Mayor Thomas also waved gracefully, looking like she was having great fun. When the standing ovation had lasted for a full minute, led by the President the entire cast of characters on stage joined hands, smiling at the crowd. In another minute, the cheering began to subside, and the people on both sides of the stage took their seats.

"Well, that's certainly a wonderful way to begin," said the woman on the microphone.

Her voice sounded familiar, but Marty couldn't recall her name, nor did he know just why she was affiliated with the ceremony. He only knew that she seemed to be very much at ease on the stage.

She introduced Mayor Thomas, giving the mayor high praise for her role in preparing the entire area in one week. She recognized the mayor as "being one of only a handful of women mayors in the country, and cited several of her outstanding local accomplishments. The mayor was awarded another loud ovation by the throng. She gave a five-minute speech about "inspiration, hope and character." She paid eloquent tribute to Marty and his friends, calling them, "heroes in their own right." She shared about the role Kelly Trapp and Joel Kincade had played in the story, touching upon some of the interesting incidents from a Binghamtonian perspective. She thanked her city workers, the residents, the media, the Chinese Ambassador and, of course, the President, for making this day possible. Her speech, which Marty thought was magnificent, ended with her introduction of Ping Kang, as she commended to the world "this most significant step made by both countries in our relations – significant though small because every long journey must always begin with a first short step."

Ping Kang was greeted by less loud, but still enthusiastic applause; thankfully, Marty thought, there were no hecklers or protestors in sight. Mr. Kang bowed as Mayor Thomas stepped down from the podium to give place to the gentle man from China. Kang adjusted his eyeglasses with one hand and the nearest microphone with the other and began addressing the people:

"To the people of America, to your President, and to young Marty Kent and his friends, I bring greetings from the Chairman of the People's Republic of China."

Kang went on to say how "surprised" he'd been when Marty's gift was delivered to him, and how "immensely touched" he had been to watch the support of the American people build for Marty's generous act. He admitted that before he learned of Marty's dig, he'd been "ignorant" of the American myth of "reaching China by digging a hole," and the audience laughed gently.

Kang explained the delivery of Marty's gifts to his Chairman, and how the idea of "Americans digging a hole to China" inspired his own country to do likewise, "but in the direction of America!"

"And thus it is, young Mr. Kent, that we are honored to present this humble gift to you today, from the Chairman and the people of the People's Republic of China."

Now the moment the nation had been waiting for was upon them. A great hush fell over the crowd as cameras clicked by the dozen. A Chinese affiliate of the Ambassador pulled a child's wagon from the backstage area, containing a small box draped in the Chinese flag, and a second gift not so decorously draped.

Then Ping Kang reached low into the wagon and drew from it a third item, a golden plaque. He held the plaque in both hands, turning it towards the many TV cameras, whose zoom lenses quickly activated for a closer view.

The audience turned towards a large TV monitor that had been installed to the left of the stage. People in the closer rows to the front could see the plaque's excellent craftsmanship and design. It appeared to be about three feet square, with a gold background with bold lettering. The writing was difficult to make out, but the sharp images etched within the plaque showed as plain as day: Two shovels criss-crossed to resemble an open pair of scissors. Above the shovels waved the flags of China and the United States. Centered between the shovels was a large hole, with an inscription just below it.

When Ping Kang was quite sure the cameras had taken ample time to scan the plaque, he placed it gently on a tripod which another stage hand had brought out.

"This plaque says the following," Kang said. "It is titled, *The Hole to China.* The inscription below reads: *When one mind and one pair of hands work together, the improbable can be achieved. When many minds and many hands work together, the impossible can be achieved.*

Amidst another long outburst of applause, Mr. Kang called Marty Kent forward. As the boy made his way to the podium, the cheers rose to near-deafening volume. It took several minutes for things to calm down, but when they finally did, Ping Kang said, "Young Mr.

Kent, this first gift is personal, and comes directly to you from our Chairman. I will present another gift momentarily."

Mr. Kang gestured toward the microphone, and Marty walked to it, while a stagehand adjusted the device to his height. At the mike, Marty peered at the applauding crowd, looked at the wonderful plaque, waited some time for silence and then began:

"I won't talk for long. But I want to say thank you to all the people of Binghamton and the triple-cities, and to all the people of America for this day. Even though I never did actually reach China, in a way I did, 'cause I reached China's heart, if not its soil. This whole experience has been the best thing that ever happened to me. I learned along the way that the world is huge, and that the inside of the earth is huge. I've learned that people don't always get along, and they sometimes just don't know why.

"But the biggest thing I learned is this: All you can do is to *try* to be someone to make a difference, and that it's truly what's inside a person that counts. It's not how they look, it's not how they are at sports, or anything else on the surface. It's about how they are, in caring for themselves, and for others. Thank you again for this beautiful day!"

He stepped down from the stage to the longest standing ovation of the day. Media members signaled him to pick up the plaque, and when he did, the sound of clicking cameras rattled everywhere. Around the country, millions of Americans watched their televisions closely what would prove to be the single-most watched special programming since President Kennedy's funeral.

At last Mayor Thomas came to the microphone and introduced the President.

President Johnson received another standing ovation, of course, though not as long as Marty's. Eventually he held up his right hand to signal for quiet, and shortly afterward, he got it.

"I think we can all agree—this has been quite a day!" began the President. He looked down at the plaque, which Marty had left next to him on the stage. "What a beautiful memento the Chinese people have given Marty. In the best human sense it shows us something invaluable: that even people of opposite views on opposite sides of the world *can* come together under certain special circumstances, in peace and good will. Perhaps this will prove only the beginning of a mutual attempt to overcome the obstacles that have kept our nations mostly opposites on the world stage."

The President spoke for several more minutes, about overcoming long odds, about fairness, equality, discrimination and justice. Marty admired his control, his cool demeanor before millions of onlookers.

Then the President paused in his remarks to call Marty and his friends forward to stand next to him, as he began the final portion of his speech:

"My fellow Americans, it is young men and women like these who make America proud. And now America must take the opportunity to do some giving back."

Many in the audience looked at the President with furrowed brows – what did he mean by "giving back?" Was the President perhaps about to present Marty with a gift of his own? Well, in a roundabout way, that was exactly what the President was about to do.

"Marty," President Johnson said, "we are all well aware of the trials and tribulations you faced this summer. The fact that you galvanized your city, your country and the world while others around you battled to save your home, the homes of others, and this great Horace Mann School—all this is truly an inspiring and remarkable achievement, a glowing testament to the human spirit.

"This stunning building next door, Horace Mann Grade School, has stood the test of time. It's a beautiful building, really, with a quality similar to what you've demonstrated so admirably: *character*—lasting character that in my opinion surely deserves preservation."

A great hush fell over the audience.

The President looked at Marty. "It's common knowledge that your home, and the homes of others here, are scheduled to be demolished in just a few weeks. Yet it doesn't seem fair to me that such a tragic set of circumstances should befall America's newest and youngest hero. It doesn't seem fair that this hole you've dug should be covered to make way for a brand-new school building. It doesn't seem fair that your family, and others in your neighborhood will be forced to be uprooted and placed in places strange to you, with people you don't even know."

He turned to Mayor Thomas and gestured her forward. He then said, "That is why it is my great privilege to announce to you, on behalf of Mayor Thomas and the great city of Binghamton, that the voters have decided—and by a landslide I'm happy to add – to build a new school elsewhere. Horace Mann stands, and your neighborhood stands and your house stands!"

Even though this outcome wasn't coming totally unexpected, Donald and Patricia Kent were still stunned, to say the least. They reached for each other in their seats, while the audience erupted their approval of the voters' decision. Marty's friends embraced him happily, and Mayor Judy Thomas couldn't hide her glee; she both cried and laughed tears of joy.

The President shouted over the crowd's roar, "But that's not all." And when the crowd settled down, he said, "I have recently conducted several conversations with your fine mayor, and not only have Binghamton's voters decided to save the ground the Kents' home is on, but, but America has chosen to preserve the Horace Mann School building – not just as a local landmark, but as a national museum honoring Chinese culture and the earth sciences, especially the inner-earth. It will be a place people from all over the country and all over the world will be welcome to visit. It will become a state of the art, user-participatory facility. Furthermore, the *Hole to China* in the back of the Kents' yard will also be preserved and maintained in perpetuity, as a national treasure."

For a moment the President fell silent, but by then nothing could hold back the people's emotions. Cheers, applause, tears and laughter so filled you would have thought the nation had just been awarded its freedom. Across town, motorists honked their horns, neighbors phoned neighbors, and joy blanketed the entire area.

The President called several times in vain for quiet, and it at last came when most people present had hollered themselves to hoarseness. At last the President was able to be heard over the crowds. "Now," he said, "the Chinese Ambassador will make his second gift presentation to Marty, at the site of the Hole."

Surrounded by feds, the small group walked the short distance to the back yard, where the area around the Hole had been secured by several agents. People left their seats to cram as close as they were allowed to the Hole, and the media was permitted to stake just out in front of the crowds. Dozens of people lined up along the fence separating Horace Mann School from the Kents' home, an excellent vantage point. All in attendance craned to catch at least get a glimpse of the proceedings at the Hole.

Ping Kang stood beside the excavation. The wagon and other gifts that had earlier been wheeled in on stage rested next to him. He adjusted the microphone placed on a small table before him and said: "My friends, I have learned through all this that the task of tunneling a hole from America to China is impossible only in the mind. Therefore I present to the people of America this fresh earth from China, dug by the children of China. We also present to you, Mr. Kent, this shovel, which was used to place the Chinese earth inside this box."

Marty accepted the shovel, grasping it with both hands. At that moment, a special overhead monitor channeling a closed-circuit telecast from China, came alive to show the image of one Chinese boy, surrounded by others, shovel in hand standing next to the Chinese hole.

Then Ping Kang handed the microphone to the President, who whispered to Marty, who then opened the box of earth from China. At once, another closed-circuit monitor showed Marty at the Hole, shovel in hand. The moment the President nodded, Marty stuck his shovel hard into the Chinese dirt, lifted it up and walked to the Hole. At the same time in China, the young boy there did the same, simulcast by satellite. On a final nod from the President, Marty spilled the contents from his shovel into his Hole and stood back, beaming as the earth mixed in with American soil. At the very next moment, on the other side of the world the young Chinese boy scooped up dirt from Marty's box, angled his shovel towards their hole, and watched the earth from America slowly disappear into the depths of the hole below, to a sea of cheers from both sides of the world.

EPILOGUE

From across the great field of green, 22-year-old Marty Kent fixed his eyes on the bleachers above and shielded his face from the glaring rays of the afternoon sun. Several thousand people stood now, cheering for the speaker, President Jimmy Carter, who'd just completed a truly moving speech to the graduates assembled on the football field below.

President Carter hadn't just spouted the usual rhetoric to the *Cornell University* graduating class of 1976. He hadn't tried to stir these new graduates about to be entering the work force to "successfully go after the American dream." Instead, he urged them to begin right away *giving back* to America a part of the knowledge and skills they'd acquired here. "Don't just *blend into* America, ladies and gentlemen – reach out and *shape it.*"

As the people continued applauding the President, the words he'd just listened to took Marty Kent back in time, to that glorious, wonderful summer that had transformed not only the country, but the world, all those around him and himself.

Patricia Jane Allen, Business Administration, was the first to be called. She accepted her diploma and circled back to her seat on the lawn. *Anthony Michael Antonelli, History,* and *Leonard Stewart Arnold, Marketing,* came next, accepted their certificates and paused for pictures by loved ones in the great crowd above.

The flashbacks to that time 10 years ago now hurled to the forefront of Marty's mind.

That 10 years had flown by so quickly seemed impossible to him. A few tears welled up in his eyes as the combined emotions of both the current day and the days that had shaped his life back then melted together.

Marty closed his eyes, allowing the newsreel of his mind's eye to take over, and as it did, the characters and events of that time so long ago played on. As each person came forward in his mind, just as these graduates were now being called forward, he seemed to be able to hit a "stop" button in his memory, to "pause" each person for a closer look, in the exact order he'd come to know them all:

Kelly Trapp, the slender, brunette young reporter who'd befriended him and helped him in so many ways appeared first. Marty had kept very close tabs on her over the years, even after she'd left Binghamton two years following *The Hole to China* story for her dream job at *The Philadelphia Inquirer,* and even after she left the *Inquirer* for a lucrative correspondent's job with *Time* magazine. Kelly had never lost the fight in her, thought Marty. And though she remained, as she'd been back in Binghamton, a bit high strung, she'd mellowed some over time.

She continued to grow, as a person and a professional. Her reporting skills and ability to get inside stories proved second to none. She covered the last days of the Vietnam War; escaping the fall of Saigon in 1975. Her association with China also became her stepping-stone to an even bigger story, accompanying President Nixon as the lone reporter he allowed into China in 1972, the first visit ever to that country by an American President. During that visit, Kelly discovered she'd become fairly well known in China. People honored her wherever she went. She had become an icon to those millions of Chinese who remembered that the door to America had actually been opened years before the arrival of the President.

Bruce David Baldwin, Political Science...

Of course, in China Kelly was able to secure a visit, along with the President, to the hole the Chinese youngsters had dug in 1966.

She later told Marty how impeccably maintained the site was, how it remained under constant guard by the Red Army.

Visitation was allowed by appointment only; the site was more of a secret than the national treasure America's *Hole to China* had become.

Crystal Marie Cline, Accounting...

Kelly may never get married, Marty thought. *Her career is too important to her.*

John David DeSimone, Mathematics...

Joel Kincade, on the other hand, had slowed down somewhat, at least from his duties at *The Bulletin*. Stories written by Kelly Trapp and others during that time ten years ago had caught the national eye. And Kincade hit the talk show circuit, telling his version of the events of that time. Within two years, his book, *The Hole With No Bottom*, was launched and distributed; it ended up heading the *New York Times Best-Seller List* for an amazing *six months*. With its success came more talk shows, more touring, more speaking engagements. Joel Kincade, thought Marty, had truly blazed a new trail and helped maintain the nation's focus on the significance of the Hole.

With the amount of time he now spent traveling, Kincade's duties at *The Bulletin* declined; at last he'd become unable to balance both roles. So he stayed on the paper's staff as consultant and primed his journalism major grandson, Corey Kincade, to climb the ranks within *The Bulletin*. With young Corey in charge, *The Bulletin* was able to maintain the growth spurt they'd experienced in Joel Kincade's time, both with more subscribers and retail advertising revenue than they'd imagined when they began working so hard to recover from near-extinction 10 years earlier.

Jane Evelyn Everett, Computer Science...

Harry Whiting's arrest 10 years ago had been a tragedy young Marty'd had trouble understanding. He just couldn't grasp why any man would want to kill his own mother.

301

Not until his first year at Cornell, when Marty re-read the entire accounts of Whiting's arrest, trial and eventual sentencing, did he fully understand all the circumstances surrounding Whiting's crime.

He was particularly thrilled to re-read Kelly Trapp's stories from that time, now with a more mature perspective. He was a bit sad to learn that Harry Whiting died of a massive heart attack in prison, just six months before his scheduled release. Apparently Whiting had not only rehabilitated himself in prison, he had studied the Bible and understood it so well, he'd become a mentor to other inmates and was looking forward to seeking to join a prison ministry upon his release.

Calvin Lloyd Flynn, Civil Engineering…

Harry's mother, Beatrice, not only outlived her six-month cancer sentence by her doctors, she outlived her son by a year. By that time she'd become somewhat of a medical mystery, to not only the local physicians of Binghamton, but also to scores of cancer institutions and health centers around the country. Doctors were shocked as results of batteries of tests on her lungs showed significant regression in her tumors; and they were equally shocked when the cancer growth stopped altogether. Her early diagnosis had been so dismal, she'd refused even a single dose of chemotherapy, instead opting to participate in a cancer study with a new drug. Doctors around the country were stunned to learn that "experimental drug" she'd been taking was actually a *placebo.*

Karen Ann George, Communications…

Larry Murphy, one of the boys who'd bullied Marty earlier in his life, used his experience with the Hole in many valuable ways. He started serving others first as a 14-year-old summer camp counselor to needy boys. By the end of high school, he was volunteering much of his time to such causes. He'd proven himself through the *Boy Scouts of America* to be a "natural" at living off the land and a natural leader of others as well.

But college wasn't in Larry's plans, Vietnam was. He chose to enlist rather than be drafted, and went on to become one of the Army's youngest Captains. He spent nearly three years fighting in the jungles, before the war wound down and America's young men returned home. Larry had become disgruntled when he returned home, surprised at the cool reaction he and many other soldiers received. Marty had heard that Larry was struggling with the adjustments to living back in the states. Marty had made a few attempts to contact Larry, but had failed each time. He made a mental note just then to do his best to contact Larry soon after graduation.

Paul Douglas Harrington, Sports Medicine...

Scott Gardner and his father both fell on hard times following the events of that year of the Hole. The elder Gardner couldn't quite stay the course to the end of his probation; a bounced check written for less than ten dollars landed him before Judge Cassidy. He somehow managed to pay the fine, did 30 days' jail time. Then on his way home from jail, Mr. Gardner was struck and killed by a drunk driver. The tragedy didn't seem to have much affect on 14-year-old Scott. He'd never had any real relationship with his father in the first place, and his father's death only seemed to speed him faster along the only course he was determined to run. Scott failed the ninth grade for skipping school and hanging around with others like him, getting into trouble. His cigarette smoking turned into a full-fledged, heavy marijuana habit by the end of his second year of ninth grade, at which point he decided to drop out of school altogether.

He hung around the local pool halls and bowling alleys, making a few bucks running errands for the owners. At 16 he'd garnered a part-time job washing dishes, emptying trash, performing any menial task he could find, to survive and buy pot. At 17, with a string of petty arrests on his resume and the addition of a severe drinking problem, he resorted to stealing cars as a way to make a living. Only the fact he was under 18 kept him from the real jails, but he'd ended up living out of a halfway house in upstate New York. Four years had passed, and Marty had heard nothing new regarding Scott Gardner.

Penny Mary Irving, English...

William Running Bear was still in the news. He'd recently represented the Iroquois Nation in Syracuse, New York, battling once

303

again to save several hundred acres of their cherished land from "progress." This turned out to be the longest and toughest battle of his illustrious career; but in the end, he achieved yet another victory. Mayor Thomas had asked him if he'd like to work for the City of Binghamton, but he'd refused; he said he'd rather stay at White Birch Lake and wait for his cases to *come to him.*

For her part, Mayor Thomas, served another term in office, presiding at a time that saw the largest revenue growth in Binghamton's history. Hotels, restaurants, specialty stores and the like literally lined up at the door of the city, wanting in. Of course, all that growth had begun with *The Hole to China* site next door at the Kents' College Street home and the success of *The Horace Mann Museum of Earth Sciences.*

Arnold Armstrong Jefferson, Special Education...

Brenna Nelson and Marty remained best of friends throughout the ten-year period.

They'd attended football and basketball games together, dances and proms. Over the years they'd both grown to realize how the Hole had affected them so profoundly. The budding romance they'd experienced lasted for more than a year, until each discovered they were better suited as friends. Their intellectual development and maturity levels was enough to protect the beautiful personal relationship they shared. They'd become more like brother and sister, sharing in every key moment, every event. But there was no doubt how that summer of 1966 had affected Brenna.

During the early days following the renovation and transformation of Horace Mann School into the museum, Brenna came to like all the attention from outsiders. After all, along with Marty and Kelly, she'd been the focus of the nation back then, but as she grew older and times changed, she slowly fell from the limelight. After the President and Mr. Kang left, she'd at first participated in everything associated with the Hole, helping with tours, having her photograph taken with tourists, sitting for interviews. But as the years went on, she made a decision that her past, tied to the Hole as it had been, would need to become a closed matter; and her future needed to go in a different direction.

She never denied, though, that the events of that time 10 years ago helped shape her thinking forever. But it was time, she reasoned, to think of other things, to break away from *the Hole.* She no longer wanted attention that had been reserved for the young girl she was no more. She, too, had been deeply affected by the bullies of her childhood. She strove hard to analyze Scott Gardner's wayward life, to better understand what drove him and others like him to treat people the way he'd treated Marty. She felt compelled, not to turn away from such people, but to find better answers for them that just *had* to be out there somewhere.

She'd taken some courses at Broome Community College, graduating in 1974 with a basic Liberal Arts degree. She'd thought about moving on to a four-year college, but she'd been experiencing thoughts, *deep* thoughts for years, thoughts that pulled her in another direction. Thoughts she needed to act upon.

At the age of 20, she founded *The Rainbow Room,* through which abandoned houses were purchased with federal funds, then converted into homes for boys like Scott Gardner. This had become a truly successful venture. Her idea to not only renovate to perfection, but to paint every room in her houses with a different color of the rainbow, was a nationally recognized housing-for-the-disadvantaged "hit." And though she for a while shunned the national attention she'd once craved for her involvement with *the Hole*, she came to understood how she could use it to her advantage with this new program, to get support from every known source in government she could.

Debra Margaret Kennedy, Music...

Marty saw the girl seated next to him stand up. He shook his head to wake himself from his "mind-movie" as she glided towards the podium. Yes, he'd lost track of the time, caught up in his nostalgia. He looked out towards the thousands of attendees at this graduation ceremony, trying to catch a glimpse of where his parents and his nine-year-old sister Katie were seated. He was so proud of them, and they of him. Those lost years with his father, the years prior to the hole being dug, seemed far distant now. He wiped a tear from his eye as he thought about and *understood* his father's disappointment over his nipped-in-the-bud athletic achievements. But how wonderfully

305

differently his father had learned to accept Marty, to love him despite all his shortcomings and failures to be all the things his father had so desperately wanted him to be. Marty thought just then of how important father/son relationships could be, recalling Benjamin and Harry Whiting, to Scott Gardner and his dad, and himself and his own father.

And then there'd been, always, Marty's rock-solid mother, who'd maybe done too much for him in those early days, but had been exactly what he'd needed, he thought. She had lovingly provided the foundation of love, care and understanding his naïve mind had needed back then. He smiled to himself. Without her stepping in, making the suggestion to *go out and dig a hole,* none of a host of wonderful things would have happened. And he recalled having been the happiest boy on earth when his sister came into the world – the sister his mother *always wanted.*

Just before his name was called, Marty Kent thought about the difficulties in breaking the cycles of life, the traps that people like Scott Gardner and Harry Whiting fell into, traps that they somehow couldn't escape. He felt humbled, realizing that he would be the *first Kent* to ever graduate from college—for that matter the first who'd ever *attended* college. He was so very proud of what he'd accomplished 10 years earlier, and just as proud at what he'd accomplished now; *But that time, that special time...*he thought. He would always look back on those days as the giant stepping-stones of his life. He knew he had to look straight ahead to the future now, and that was no problem – he was just as eager to explore the world as he'd been at age 12. Now he heard his name called:

*Martin William Kent, Geology...*And he also knew, as he began to rise from his chair and make his own public, yet very private, way to the podium, that whatever happened to him for the rest of his life, it'd have a hard time comparing to that summer when he dug his *Hole to China.*

ABOUT THE AUTHOR

Gary Kaschak has served as a sports writer and/or columnist for The *Vestal News* (upper New York state), The *Green Bay Press Gazette* (Wisconsin) and The *Burlington County Times* (New Jersey). Mr. Kaschak served The *Montrose Independent* (Pennsylvania) as its Sports Editor. He was for some time the Statistician of the Washington Federals (a team in the now-defunct United States Football League [USFL]); and he's served as sports reporter for WKOP radio, out of Binghamton, New York. He's also coached softball and volleyball at the grade-school level.

The *Hole to* China is Mr. Kaschak's second novel; he has also authored *Hands that Break...Hands that Heal,* a well-received teen-sports/inspirational novel published in 2003.

Mr. Kaschak has been married to Maureen for 23 years; they have two children, Kara (18) and Emily (14). The Kaschak family lives in Cedarbrook, New Jersey.